The Physiology of Sexist and Racist Oppression

Studies in Feminist Philosophy is designed to showcase cutting-edge monographs and collections that display the full range of feminist approaches to philosophy, that push feminist thought in important new directions, and that display the outstanding quality of feminist philosophical thought.

STUDIES IN FEMINIST PHILOSOPHY
Cheshire Calhoun, *Series Editor*

Advisory Board

Recently Published in the Series:

*Women's Liberation and the Sublime:
Feminism, Postmodernism, Environment*
Bonnie Mann

Analyzing Oppression
Ann E. Cudd

*Ecological Thinking: The Politics of Epistemic
Location*
Lorraine Code

*Self Transformations: Foucault, Ethics, and
Normalized Bodies*
Cressida J. Heyes

*Family Bonds: Genealogies of Race
and Gender*
Ellen K. Feder

*Moral Understandings: A Feminist Study in
Ethics, Second Edition*
Margaret Urban Walker

The Moral Skeptic
Anita M. Superson

*"You've Changed": Sex Reassignment and
Personal Identity*
Edited by Laurie J. Shrage

*Dancing with Iris: The Philosophy of Iris
Marion Young*
Edited by Ann Ferguson and
Mechthild Nagel

Philosophy of Science after Feminism
Janet A. Kourany

*Shifting Ground: Knowledge and Reality,
Transgression and Trustworthiness*
Naomi Scheman

The Metaphysics of Gender
Charlotte Witt

Unpopular Privacy: What Must We Hide?
Anita L. Allen

*Adaptive Preferences and Women's
Empowerment*
Serene Khader

*Minimizing Marriage: Marriage, Morality,
and the Law*
Elizabeth Brake

*Out from the Shadows: Analytic Feminist
Contributions to Traditional Philosophy*
Edited by Sharon L. Crasnow and
Anita M. Superson

*The Epistemology of Resistance: Gender and
Racial Oppression, Epistemic Injustice, and
Resistant Imaginations*
José Medina

*Simone de Beauvoir and the Politics of
Ambiguity*
Sonia Kruks

*Identities and Freedom: Feminist Theory
Between Power and Connection*
Allison Weir

*Vulnerability: New Essays in Ethics and
Feminist Philosophy*
Edited by Catriona Mackenzie, Wendy
Rogers, and Susan Dodds

*Sovereign Masculinity: Gender Lessons from
the War on Terror*
Bonnie Mann

Autonomy, Oppression, and Gender
Edited by Andrea Veltman and Mark Piper

*Our Faithfulness to the Past: Essays on the
Ethics and Politics of Memory*
Sue Campbell
Edited by Christine M. Koggel and
Rockney Jacobsen

The Physiology of Sexist and Racist Oppression
Shannon Sullivan

The Physiology of Sexist and Racist Oppression

Shannon Sullivan

OXFORD
UNIVERSITY PRESS

OXFORD
UNIVERSITY PRESS

Oxford University Press is a department of the University of
Oxford. It furthers the University's objective of excellence in research,
scholarship, and education by publishing worldwide.

Oxford   New York
Auckland   Cape Town   Dar es Salaam   Hong Kong   Karachi
Kuala Lumpur   Madrid   Melbourne   Mexico City   Nairobi
New Delhi   Shanghai   Taipei   Toronto

With offices in
Argentina   Austria   Brazil   Chile   Czech Republic   France   Greece
Guatemala   Hungary   Italy   Japan   Poland   Portugal   Singapore
South Korea   Switzerland   Thailand   Turkey   Ukraine   Vietnam

Oxford is a registered trademark of Oxford University Press
in the UK and certain other countries.

Published in the United States of America by
Oxford University Press
198 Madison Avenue, New York, NY 10016

© Oxford University Press 2015

Library of Congress Cataloging-in-Publication Data
Sullivan, Shannon, 1967–
The physiology of sexist and racist oppression / Shannon Sullivan.
pages cm. — (Studies in feminist philosophy)
Includes bibliographical references and index.
ISBN 978-0-19-025060-7 (hardcover : alk. paper) — ISBN 978-0-19-025061-4 (pbk. : alk. paper)
1. Human body (Philosophy)   2. Human physiology—Philosophy.   3. Sexism—Philosophy.
4. Racism—Philosophy.   5. Feminist theory.   I. Title.
B105.B64S853 2015
305.8001—dc23
2014046159

1 3 5 7 9 8 6 4 2
Printed in the United States of America
on acid-free paper

For Samantha, Sophia, and Phillip

{ CONTENTS }

{ ACKNOWLEDGMENTS }

I would like to thank a number of people for their help as I wrote this book. Cameron O'Mara and Cori Wong provided valuable research assistance on the gut in the early stages of the project. Members of the Rock Ethics Institute's Critical Philosophy of Race initiative at Penn State, especially Camisha Russell, Paul Taylor, and Nancy Tuana, gave me useful feedback on my initial ideas about epigenetics and race. Erin Tarver helped me polish a version of the material on William James and emotion. Cheshire Calhoun and three anonymous reviewers for Oxford University Press provided a great number of insightful suggestions and comments that improved the final version of the manuscript. Above all, in addition to giving me valuable feedback on specific parts of this book, Phillip McReynolds has supported my work as a whole for many years, even when it seems a little crazy. I can't thank him enough for sticking by me both professionally and personally.

I began this book while at Penn State University and finished it after moving to the University of North Carolina at Charlotte. I thank Dean Susan Welch at Penn State and Dean Nancy Gutierrez at UNC Charlotte for their support of my research.

Portions of this book have appeared elsewhere in different forms, and I am grateful for permission to reprint them here. Sections of "Oppression in the Gut: The Biological Dimensions of Deweyan Habit" (in *A History of Habit: From Aristotle to Bourdieu*, eds. Tom Sparrow and Adam Hutchinson [Lanham, MD: Lexington Press, 2013], 251–270) have been reworked and included in Chapter 2 and, to a lesser extent, the Introduction. "Inheriting Racist Disparities in Health: Epigenetics and the Transgenerational Effects of White Racism" (*Critical Philosophy of Race*, Fall 2013, 1[2]: 190–218) has been revised, expanded, and broken up to become part of Chapter 3 and the Introduction. That article is copyrighted © 2013 by The Pennsylvania State University and is used by permission of The Pennsylvania State University Press. Finally, a modified version of the material in "The Hearts and Guts of White People: Ethics, Ignorance, and the Physiology of White Racism" (*Journal of Religious Ethics*, 2014, 42[4]: 591–611) is included primarily in Chapter 4 but also in the Introduction.

Introduction

PHYSIOLOGICAL HABITS

> Bodies tell stories that people cannot or will not tell, either
> because they are unable, forbidden, or choose not to tell.
>
> —NANCY KRIEGER, *"EMBODIMENT: A CONCEPTUAL
> GLOSSARY FOR EPIDEMIOLOGY"*

Let me begin with an incident that made me think hard about the physiology of racism in particular. A few years ago I taught a large introductory feminist philosophy class in which I was critically discussing stereotypes of African American women and the virtually all-white class was somewhat grudgingly going along. In the course of the analysis, I mentioned racist stereotypes of African American men as frightening sexual predators and the tense, purse-clutching stride that white women sometimes adopt when walking alone at night.[1] As I returned to the main topic for the day, a white female student named Brittney (a pseudonym) quickly raised her hand, stood up, and insisted somewhat confrontationally, "But I *am* scared of black men! If I pass one on the street at night, I can't help it: I tense up and get knots in my stomach." Before I could respond, a visibly perturbed white female teaching assistant for the course leapt up and, in front of the other one hundred students, severely chastised Brittney for being racist, to which Brittney sarcastically replied, "Oh, so only PC things can be said in this class, I can't say how I really feel!" Silenced but unconvinced, Brittney then angrily sat down.

I'll set aside the pedagogical question of how an instructor best should handle classroom situations like the one created by Brittney's comment and my teaching assistant's response to it. What I focus on in this book is the complex tangle of affects, emotions, knowledge, physiology, and privilege illuminated by Brittney's outburst. The experience recounted by Brittney involved bodily manifestations of white privilege in particular, but I have in mind here

---

[1] See, for example, Brent Staples, "Just Walk on By: A Black Man Ponders His Power to Alter Public Space," *Ms.*, September 1986, 54.

male privilege and the domination of women as well. And, of course, the two forms of domination—sexism and racism—aren't mutually exclusive, and they often combine with classed, heterosexist, and other forms of oppression. In the mélange of affective and emotional knowledge and bodily effects of gendered and raced privilege, the role of physiology is especially important for my purposes. Brittney believed that the image of black men as threatening and frightening is real—that is, more than a social bias or cultural stereotype—and she "knew" this because of her physiological, emotional response to them. She really is scared when she encounters black men, as she might have said. She wasn't just making it up to try to discriminate against them, and her body proved it. Since nothing is more real or irrefutable than felt physiological responses—unchosen and unwilled by her, after all—then her body's alarmed response to black men means that they *are* frightening. Philosophy has to reckon with that reality, as Brittney might have continued, and if it can't, then it's a load of politically correct crap that's not worth the bother.

How should feminists and critical philosophers of race respond to claims such as these? While I don't agree with everything Brittney said or implied, I am sympathetic with her position to a significant extent. I think she's right that philosophy must reckon with the lived reality of human physiology and emotions, and this is so even—or maybe especially—in the case of socially-politically charged topics such as sexism and racism. To be fully successful, critical philosophy of race and feminist philosophy, as well as the discipline of philosophy more broadly, need to examine not only the financial, legal, political, and other forms of racist and sexist oppression, but also their physiological operations. In societies in which de jure Jim Crow has been eliminated, white privilege continues to operate as much, if not more so, through human biology than through mental beliefs, hidden and "invisible" because it is a product of gut reactions rather than conscious decision or choice.[2] Sexism against women of all races also can have physiological effects that need to be acknowledged in order to best fight the habits and behavior that cause them. I think here, for example, of the gastrointestinal effects of sexual abuse that I will discuss more fully in Chapter 2. These, too, can be hidden and "invisible," not because the gastrointestinal symptoms go unseen or medically untreated, but because they often aren't connected with social-political problems such as male sexual domination. The physiology of human bodies has a story to tell, as epidemiologist Nancy Krieger claims in the epigraph above, and many times it is a story that a society tries to forbid or doesn't want to hear. Even when individuals and their communities work

---

[2] In contrast with de jure Jim Crow, de facto Jim Crow is alive and well, as Michelle Alexander demonstrates in *The New Jim Crow: Mass Incarceration in the Age of Colorblindness*, revised edition (New York: The New Press, 2012).

hard to forget or erase particular experiences, "the body continues to keep the score."[3] The stories told by human physiology are broad and complex, as much (hi)stories of the world "outside" the skin as they are accounts of the biological and chemical operations "within" it.

I realize that combining the topics of physiology and biology with those of racism and sexism is potentially problematic from the perspective of feminist and critical philosophy of race. The Western world has a long, destructive history of using biology reductively to justify white supremacy, male domination, and related forms of oppression. In the case of white supremacy, Nazi Germany offers a prime example, but it is important to remember that the United States and many other countries were engaged in eugenics in the first half of the twentieth century.[4] And in the nineteenth century, scientific practices such as craniology were created precisely for the purpose of proving the inferiority of non-white races.[5] The nineteenth century also is rife with appeals to women's biology to justify their oppression. For example, women were barred from institutions of higher education because intense studying supposedly would direct energy away from women's uteruses, deforming them with big brains and defeminized bodies.[6] For reasons such as these, until very recently (around the early 2000s), positive explorations of biology and physiology have tended to be avoided by feminists and to be placed completely out of the question for contemporary critical philosophy of race.[7] Even if we utilize contemporary medical knowledge of human physiology—for example, we thankfully no longer think that women's intellectual work shrinks their uteruses—we cannot be certain that we aren't replicating racist and sexist biases embedded in our own time and place.

As valid as these concerns are, however, it would be even more problematic for feminists and critical philosophers of race to refuse to engage with the disciplines of human physiology and biology.[8] To begin, it is not the case that the medical and biological sciences necessarily produce reductive

---

[3] Bessel Van der Kolk, M.D., *The Body Keeps the Score: Brain, Mind and Body in the Healing of Trauma* (New York: Viking, 2014) 46.

[4] Ladelle McWhorter, *Racism and Sexual Oppression in Anglo-America: A Genealogy* (Bloomington: Indiana University Press, 2009).

[5] See Stephen Jay Gould, *The Mismeasure of Man* (New York: W. W. Norton, 1981).

[6] Carla Fehr, "Feminist Philosophy of Biology," *Stanford Encyclopedia of Philosophy*, June 2011, http://plato.stanford.edu/entries/feminist-philosophy-biology/, accessed February 21, 2013.

[7] Claire Blencowe tracks the anti-biologism of 1970s and 1980s feminist discourse in "Biology, Contingency, and the Problem of Racism in Feminist Discourse," *Theory, Culture, and Society*, 2011, 28(3): 3–27. In critical philosophy of race, contemporary appeals to biology tend to be considered exclusively as the methodology of racist pseudoscience, such as that found in Richard Herrenstein and Charles Murray's notorious book *The Bell Curve: Intelligence and Class Structure in American Life* (New York: Free Press, 1996). Elizabeth A. Wilson criticizes feminism's avoidance of biology in *Psychosomatic: Feminism and the Neurological Body* (Durham, NC: Duke University Press, 2004) 3.

[8] See a related argument by Peter K. Hatemi and Rose McDermott, "The Normative Implications of Biological Research," *PS: Political Science and Politics*, 2011, 44: 325–329.

understandings of human existence. Many of the so-called hard sciences increasingly are operating with sophisticated biopsychosocial understandings of how psyche, body, and environments transact to produce human health and disease, sometimes working with more sophisticated understandings than philosophers do, in fact. This isn't true across the board, of course. The field of social epidemiology is noteworthy, for example, for advancing complex accounts of how the "bio," the "psycho," and the "social" in the biopsychosocial are dynamically related and mutually constitutive. Psychology, on the other hand, sometimes does a poorer job of working with transactional accounts of psyche, body, and environment, even in the name of biopsychosocial research. The devil is in the detail of different scientists' work, but the upshot is that there is a growing body of rich, non-reductive scientific research on human bodily life that would benefit feminist philosophy and critical philosophy of race.

It's also not the case that systems of white supremacy and male domination have always heavily relied on biological arguments. Formal apartheid in South Africa (1948–1994), for example, was far more dependent on manufactured beliefs about cultural differences between whites and blacks than on alleged biological hierarchies.[9] In a similar fashion, some contemporary sexist stereotypes in the United States about men and women's different communication styles—for example, women want to talk about problems while men clam up until a solution has been found—rely not on alleged biological differences, but on the supposedly alien social customs of men and women, as if they come from different planets.[10] While it is undeniable that the discipline of biology, along with related fields such as anthropology and evolutionary theory, has a nasty history of promoting white supremacy, white privilege, and male domination, it can be and sometimes has been untangled from them. In cases where white supremacy and male domination rely on supposed cultural or environmental differences, proceeding as if white supremacy and male domination, on the one hand, and biology, on the other, are inseparable means that we might be waging the wrong war.[11] And in cases where biology can help us uncover some of the hidden operations of white privilege and masculinist bias, dismissing biology as reductively racist means that we might be overlooking a powerful ally in the struggle against racism and sexism.

---

[9] Saul Dubow, "South Africa: Paradoxes in the Place of Race," in *The Oxford Handbook of the History of Eugenics*, eds. Alison Bashford and Philippa Levine (New York: Oxford University Press, 2010) 274–288.

[10] John Gray, *Men Are from Mars, Women Are from Venus: The Classic Guide to Understanding the Opposite Sex* (New York: Harper Publishers, 2004).

[11] Thanks to Robert Bernasconi for helping me think about this point, especially in connection with race.

I am concerned that out of an understandable fear of appearing to be sexist or racist, contemporary feminists and critical philosophers of race might avoid examining the role that human biology plays in male privilege and white domination or might restrict the role of the body to the safer political terrain of phenomenology divorced from physiology. The body surely is phenomenological, and understanding the embodied phenomenology of racism and sexism is important to feminist and racial justice struggles.[12] But the body also is biological, neurochemical, and physiological, and social justice movements also need to critically understand those aspects of human embodiment. Leaving out the biological dimension of bodily habits misunderstands them and thus impedes attempts to change them, and this is as true of sexist and racist habits as of less politically charged ones.

The result of refusing to engage the biological and medical sciences is to concede the domain of human physiology to white domination and male privilege, and this is a problematic concession to make. It is to give up on any sort of critical understanding of how a person's physiological responses to the world are constituted, and thus also might be reconstituted for the better. It is, returning to my student Brittney's case, to allow a white woman's tensed, knotted stomach at the sight of a black man to stand as an allegedly apolitical, "natural," and thus unchangeable event.[13] Brittney's emotional and physiological responses to black men were indeed real: she felt them, and they shouldn't be dismissed as if they didn't occur. She was right about that. It's important to be able to acknowledge the reality of her experience in a non-hostile manner, as my teaching assistant was unable or unwilling to do. But Brittney's bodily response was not any kind of proof of a supposedly intrinsic threat posed by black men. Philosophy needs to be able to explain how both of these claims are true, and doing so requires critically approaching, rather than eschewing, physiology and biology.

Where then should one turn for help with this task? The history of philosophy doesn't offer many useful examples of combining critical philosophy of race or feminist philosophy with the hard sciences. Of course, this isn't too surprising since the discipline of philosophy only very recently has paid critical attention to sexism or racism at all. Simone de Beauvoir's *The Second*

---

[12] Linda Martín Alcoff provides an excellent account of the phenomenology of race in "Toward a Phenomenology of Racial Embodiment," *Radical Philosophy*, 1998, 95: 15–26. See also Iris Marion Young's groundbreaking phenomenological analyses of feminine bodies in *On Female Bodily Experience: "Throwing Like a Girl" and Other Essays* (New York: Oxford University Press, 2005).

[13] This concession also enables claims like that of Charles Murray, who rightly (I think) attacks "the reigning intellectual orthodoxy. . . that race is a 'social construct,' a cultural artifact without biological merit" but does so in order to forward the position "that the most natural of all ways to classify humans genetically is by the racial and ethnic groups that humans have identified from time out of mind" (Charles Murray, "Book Review: 'A Troublesome Inheritance' by Nicholas Wade," *The Wall Street Journal*, May 2, 2014, http://online.wsj.com/news/articles/SB100014240527023033800045 79521482247869874, accessed May 14, 2014.

Sex stands out as a somewhat bright spot, devoting its first chapter to careful consideration of what biology tells us about the alleged differences between the sexes. This is a complicated and important chapter in Beauvoir's book since it argues that sexism—and even the necessity of two sexes—isn't mandated by nature. At the same time, however, it uses biological givens associated with sexual reproduction to link the existentially important categories of immanence and transcendence with females and males, respectively.[14] Aside from the specter of male privilege in Beauvoir's account of biological reproduction and gestation, my main concern with *The Second Sex* is that its overall trajectory appears to be away from biology, as well as away from psychoanalysis and historical materialism (in Chapters 2 and 3 of the book). This trajectory tends to position feminist phenomenology and existentialism in opposition to the alleged determinism of the biological, psychological, and economic sciences. On Beauvoir's view, all three of these latter fields diminish the role of human freedom by ultimately making human existence the product of structural forces rather than of individual choice. The message from Beauvoir—perhaps echoing Maurice Merleau-Ponty's earlier warning to phenomenologists that "scientific points of view . . . are always naïve and at the same time dishonest"—seems to be that feminists would do well to stay away from the hard sciences.[15]

Fortunately, not all feminists have done so. In the past thirty-five years or so, the field of philosophy of biology has blossomed, including feminist versions of it. Situated primarily in analytic philosophy, mainstream philosophy of biology occasionally takes up ethical matters, asking for example about the morality of cloning or the role of "selfish genes" in evolutionary development but rarely, if ever, about sexism or especially racism.[16] It is feminist philosophy of biology that has pressed critical issues regarding gender and

---

[14] Simone de Beauvoir, *The Second Sex*, trans. Constance Borde and Shelia Malovany-Chevallier (New York: Vintage Books, 2011) 21–48.

[15] Maurice Merleau-Ponty, *Phenomenology of Perception*, trans. Colin Smith (London: The Humanities Press, 1962), ix. For this reason, Merleau-Ponty urges "a foreswearing of science" (*Phenomenology of Perception*, viii). This distrustful attitude toward science continues in Merleau-Ponty's later work, as in his "Nature" lectures which (m)align physiochemistry with the ontic, everyday, and empirical, in contrast to the ontological and the "*Urstiftung* of 'foundations'" connected with Being (quoted in Cameron O'Mara, *Feminist Reflections on the Nature/Culture Distinction in Merleau-Pontyan Philosophy*, [University Park: Penn State University, 2013 (dissertation)], 251). Written twenty years after *The Second Sex*, Beauvoir's *The Coming of Age* offers a better approach toward the hard sciences. As Beauvoir declares in the book's preface, "nowadays we know that it is pointless to study the physiological and the psychological aspects [of human existence] separately, for each governs the other" (Beauvoir, *The Coming of Age*, trans. Patrick O'Brian [New York: G. P. Putnam's Sons, 1972], 9).

[16] For more on philosophy of biology, see Paul Griffiths, "Philosophy of Biology," *Stanford Encyclopedia of Philosophy*, July 2008, http://plato.stanford.edu/entries/biology-philosophy/, accessed February 19, 2013; Michael Ruse, ed., *Philosophy of Biology*, second edition (Amherst, NY: Prometheus Books, 2007); and the journal *Biology & Philosophy*, also edited by Michael Ruse.

(to a lesser extent) race. The important work of feminists such as Ruth Bleier, Anne Fausto-Sterling, Evelyn Fox Keller, Donna Haraway, and Sarah Hrdy has criticized the sexist nature of many core concepts in biology, including male competitiveness in sexual selection, rape as an evolutionary strategy, and sex differences in brain anatomy.[17]

Even more recently, a cluster of feminist approaches to embodiment that tend to be friendly to the hard sciences has emerged under the umbrella of "material feminisms."[18] Not to be confused with the materialist feminism that grew out of Marxist feminism in the late 1970s,[19] material feminisms focuses on the fleshy materiality of the human body and the natural environments that it inhabits. Here again, Donna Haraway's influential work in primatology on the co-constitution of the human, the non-human, and the technological stands out, as does Karen Barad's research in quantum physics developing the concept of agential realism.[20] Other feminists working in Science, Technology and Society (STS)-related fields, such as Rebecca Jordan-Young and Sarah Richardson, recently have challenged biologically reductive accounts of sex differences and developed theoretically sophisticated and thoroughly empirically grounded accounts of how the biological and the social are entangled.[21] Anne Fausto-Sterling's work on bones, to which I will return below, offers a particularly insightful model of how to account for race and sex in biosocial terms.[22] Given the diversity of this work, it's important to note the deliberate use of the plural "feminisms" in "material feminisms." There are many different possible approaches to understanding the materiality of lived embodiment, and its variety is one of the emerging area's strengths. Not all of those

---

[17] Carla Fehr, "Feminist Philosophy of Biology," *Stanford Encyclopedia of Philosophy*, http://plato.stanford.edu/entries/feminist-philosophy-biology/, accessed February 19, 2013.

[18] See, e.g., Stacy Alaimo and Susan Hekman, eds., *Material Feminisms* (Bloomington: Indiana University Press, 2008).

[19] See, for example, Christine Delphy, "A Materialist Feminism Is Possible," *Feminist Review*, 1980, 4: 79–105, http://www.palgrave-journals.com/fr/journal/v4/n1/full/fr19808a.html, accessed June 24, 2013; Monique Wittig, *The Straight Mind and Other Essays* (Boston, MA: Beacon Press, 1992); and Rosemary Hennessy and Chrys Ingraham, eds., *Materialist Feminism: A Reader in Class, Difference, and Women's Lives* (New York: Routledge, 1997).

[20] Donna Haraway, *Simians, Cyborgs and Women: The Reinvention of Nature* (New York: Routledge, 1991); Karen Barad, "Meeting the Universe Halfway: Realism and Social Constructivism Without Contradiction," in *Feminism, Science, and the Philosophy of Science*, eds. Lynn Hankinson Nelson and Jack Nelson (Norwell, MA: Kluwer Academic Publishers, 1997).

[21] See, for example, Rebecca M. Jordan-Young, *Brainstorm: The Flaws in the Science of Sex Differences* (Cambridge, MA: Harvard University Press, 2010); Sarah S. Richardson, *Sex Itself: The Search for Male and Female in the Human Genome* (Chicago: The University of Chicago Press, 2013); and Kristen W. Springer, Jeanne Mager Stellman, and Rebecca M. Jordan-Young, "Beyond a Catalogue of Differences: A Theoretical Frame and Good Practice Guidelines for Researching Sex/Gender in Human Health," *Social Science & Medicine*, 2012, 74(11): 1817–1824.

[22] Anne Fausto-Sterling, "The Bare Bones of Sex: Part 1—Sex and Gender," *Signs*, 2005, 30(2): 1491–1527, and Fausto-Sterling, "The Bare Bones of Race," *Social Science & Medicine*, 2008, 38(5): 657–694.

approaches explicitly draw on the hard sciences. But material feminisms tend to welcome philosophical engagements with the sciences that go beyond mere criticism for their sexism and racism (and other forms of oppression), and for that reason I would like to partially situate this book under its umbrella.

I say only partially because of an unfortunate tendency for some material feminists to position the field in opposition to "postmodern" feminism, depicting continental feminist philosophy as overly focused on the discursive at the expense of the bodily.[23] Judith Butler's (in)famous work on gender performativity often is presented as a prime example of this alleged failing, but the problem supposedly is widespread given that "postmodern feminism has retreated from the material."[24] I'm not convinced that Butler's philosophy suffers from a radical split between the linguistic and the bodily, but in any case, let me be clear that the focus on physiology in this book does not pit it against postmodern, poststructuralist, or other forms of continental philosophy. In fact, psychoanalytic theory in particular will be very important to the analysis of the physiology of racism and sexism that follows. This is because a psychoanalytic notion of the unconscious is crucial for producing an account of the hormones, tissues, chemicals, and biological processes of the lived body that is non-reductive, psychologically rich, and fully material.

As the recent work of Elizabeth Wilson and Catherine Malabou has demonstrated, feminist philosophy (and critical philosophy of race, I would add) can benefit tremendously from linking psychoanalysis with the hard sciences, including biology and neurology.[25] Wilson's engaging examination of the neurobiological details of various bodily maladies brings out the psychic complexity of the human body's muscles, organs, nerves, and blood vessels. Her work demonstrates how defense mechanisms can be more muscular than cerebral and, correspondingly, why the nervous system as a whole—not just the brain—is crucial to understanding the operations and motivations of the unconscious.[26] Wilson is willing to risk biological reductionism in order to reveal "in biology a complexity usually attributed only to nonbiological

---

[23] Alaimo and Hekman, "Introduction: Emerging Models of Materiality in Feminist Theory," in Alaimo and Hekman, eds., *Material Feminisms*, 1–3.

[24] Alaimo and Hekman, "Introduction," 3. Karen Barad and especially Anne Fausto-Sterling offer helpful material feminist alternatives to this view of "postmodern" feminism and of Butler's work in particular. See Barad, "Posthumanist Performativity: Toward an Understanding of How Matter Comes to Matter," *Signs: Journal of Women in Culture and Society*, 23(3): 801–831, and Fausto-Sterling, "The Problem with Sex/Gender and Nature/Nurture," in *Debating Biology: Sociological Reflections on Health, Medicine and Society*, eds. S. J. Williams, L. Birke, and G. A. Bendelow (London: Routledge, 2003), especially page 126.

[25] Catherine Malabou, *The New Wounded: From Neurosis to Brain Damage*, trans. Steven Miller (Bronx, NY: Fordham University Press, 2012); Wilson, *Psychosomatic* (2004). For more on the relatively new field of neuropsychoanalysis, see Mark Solms and Oliver H. Turnbull, "What Is Neuropsychoanalysis?" *Neuropsychoanalysis*, 2011, 13(2): 133–145.

[26] Wilson, *Psychosomatics*, 10.

domains," and that risk pays off handsomely for feminist understandings of embodiment.[27] It enables feminists to understand human physiology as a crucial part of human psychic and social life.

While Malabou focuses exclusively on the brain, the encounter she stages between psychoanalysis and neurology provides important lessons about the material unconscious for feminist philosophy and critical philosophy of race. Examining the similarities between organic trauma (for example, Alzheimer's disease or a physical blow to the head) and sociopolitical trauma (for example, war or relational abuse), Malabou argues that the brain damage produced by both of them is simultaneously neuronal and psychic. Unconscious war injuries such as those evident in post-traumatic stress disorder cannot be understood as some kind of psychic disturbance divorced from physiological injury to the brain. This powerful argument leads Malabou to consider a potential problem with considering the unconscious to be fully material: How does one do so without producing a reductive understanding of the unconscious as merely non-conscious? How are the body's physiological operations not just something of which a person happens to be consciously unaware, but also—at least occasionally—a site for dynamic and forceful resistances and defense mechanisms?

Malabou's response highlights the importance of affect to the unconscious, and thus also to human physiology. "There is no doubt," she admits, "if we simply characterize the cerebral unconscious as the nonconscious place from which homeostatic processes are managed, we do risk falling in this trap an adhering to a very insufficient, precritical, definition of the unconscious."[28] We avoid this trap by recognizing that the brain is affective: it cares about itself as it modulates, informs, and otherwise transacts with the world around it. "Cerebral auto-affection," as Malabou calls it, "makes possible the attachment of life to itself which becomes the basis of all ulterior erotic investments."[29] When those living connections, relationships, and investments are troubled or troubling—whether because of an organic or a sociopolitical trauma—then unconscious problems, symptoms, and resistances tend to result.

Malabou's notion of material (cerebral) auto-affection enables me to distinguish affect—the broad, invested attunement with/in the world of a live organism—from specific emotions, such as anger, fear, joy, sadness, and so on.[30] Emotion marks the crystallization or intensification of affect, a state or

---

[27] Wilson, *Psychosomatics*, 13. It is because of this complexity that I say that Wilson risks, rather than engages in, biological reductionism. In my view, Wilson mischaracterizes her own work when she says that it shows "the uses of biological reductionism. . . for feminist accounts of the body" (13).

[28] Malabou, *The New Wounded*, 41.

[29] Malabou, *The New Wounded*, 41.

[30] I treated affect and emotion as synonyms in *Good White People: The Problem with Middle-Class White Anti-Racism* (Albany: State University of New York Press, 2014), although in retrospect I would distinguish them there, too.

experience (not necessarily consciously felt) in which affect becomes something more specific than an existential orientation or leaning. Emotions are always affective on my terms, but not all affect is emotional (although it can become so: there is no sharp line dividing affect and emotion). My understanding of affect and emotion thus is different from and, in my view, preferable to the one typically found in most contemporary humanities literature, which considers "affect" to be precognitive physiological states and changes and "emotion" to be the accompanying cognitive and socially mediated feeling of, for example, fear.[31] That account problematically treats emotion as non-bodily, divorces the physiological from the social, and replicates many of the problems found in contemporary cognitivism, which I will discuss in Chapter 1.

I will return to these issues and to Malabou's and Wilson's work in the remainder of this book, extending Malabou's notion of the auto-affective cerebral unconscious to the entire body and following Wilson's example of positive uses of biology to analyze the physiological operations of racism and sexism. As I do so, I will use the language of "unconscious habit" rather than "the unconscious." This is because the latter can misleadingly suggest a discrete entity or pre-existing force that is either inside one's head or, on a marginally better embodied account, is located somewhere inside one's body, such as the brain. Construing the body as a container for something fundamentally non-bodily, this view of the unconscious misunderstands its relationship with both human biology and the broader socio-material world. "The unconscious" is not so much a thing as it is a way of doing things, and it only comes into being through engagement with other people, institutions, cultures, and so on. The term "unconscious" characterizes ways in which human beings bodily and dynamically transact with the world, and thus using "unconscious" as an adjective or adverb better describes those transactional habits.[32]

Not all habits are unconscious, of course. Some are merely non-conscious, such as the habit of always putting on one's right shoe first or of always driving a particular way to the grocery store. But in a world characterized by sexism and racism, many a person's habits tend to be shaped by and in response to male privilege and white domination, and this shaping often takes place unconsciously. Those bodily habits are not merely unreflective or non-conscious; they don't just happen to go unnoticed at a particular moment. They instead actively obstruct attempts to bring them to conscious

---

[31] Felicity Callard and Constantinea Palpoulias, "Affect and Embodiment," in *Memory: Histories, Theories, Debates*, eds. Susannah Radstone and Bill Schwarz (Bronx, NY: Fordham University Press, 2010) 247.

[32] Shannon Sullivan, *Revealing Whiteness: The Unconscious Habits of Racial Privilege* (Bloomington: Indiana University Press, 2006) 62.

awareness and deviously thwart efforts to transform or eliminate them. As unconscious, these are habits that tend to conceal themselves from the person who is constituted by them, even as they can be readily detected or glaringly obvious to others.[33]

Let me say more about the relationship between habit and physiological functions since physiology often is downplayed or omitted when philosophers discuss habit. This omission occurs even when habit is appreciated as a bodily phenomenon. For example, the well-known "I can" of Merleau-Ponty's habitual body emphasizes the lived experience of acting in the world, rather than the body's physiological functions.[34] While I wholeheartedly agree that lived experience is important to understanding habit, the body's phenomenological gestures, styles, and movements unfortunately tend to be all that Merleau-Ponty's account of habit examines. Physiological details are not particularly relevant to his phenomenological analyses, at least not to those of habit itself. In slight contrast, American pragmatist John Dewey uses physiological functions of digestion and respiration as points of comparison with habit.[35] From Dewey, we can learn about habit by recalling how digestion and respiration work since, for him, habit and physiological functions are alike one another in significant ways. The comparison of habit with digestion and respiration in Dewey's work tends to be merely that, however: a comparison. Dewey avoids the stronger claim that digestion, respiration, or other internal physiological functions are themselves instances of habit. For Dewey, physiological examples help illuminate the salient features of habit, but they are only analogies or metaphors that could be replaced by a host of other examples.[36]

The relationship between habit and physiology is much more than metaphorical, however. On my view, physiological functions *are* habits, not just similar to them, and a person can have a distinctive character based on the kind of physiological habits that help compose her. The central point of comparison is that both habit and physiological function are transactional: they are constituted in and through a dynamic relationship with their environment. Taking a wide assortment of quick examples, riding a bicycle, walking in high heeled shoes, or interrupting people while they talk all illustrate how habits are constituted in and through a dynamic relationship with the

---

[33] For more on unconscious habits, see Sullivan, *Revealing Whiteness*, especially Part One.

[34] Merleau-Ponty, *Phenomenology of Perception*, 137.

[35] John Dewey, *Human Nature and Conduct*, vol. 14 of *The Middle Works: 1899–1924*, ed. Jo Ann Boydston (Carbondale: Southern Illinois University Press, 1988) 15.

[36] In the first chapter of *Human Nature and Conduct*, Dewey quickly switches from physiological examples to comparisons of habit with the arts. Yet Dewey should be credited for being more open to the hard sciences than Merleau-Ponty, as when Dewey claims that "to understand the existence of organized ways or habits we surely need to go to physics, chemistry and physiology rather than to [a narrow, individualized] psychology" (Dewey, *Human Nature and Conduct*, 45). For additional philosophical accounts of habit, see Tom Sparrow and Adam Hutchinson, eds., *A History of Habit: From Aristotle to Bourdieu* (Lanham, MD: Lexington Press, 2013).

world "outside" them: bicycles, sidewalk pavement, shoes, societal expectations of femininity, and other people. Walking in high heeled shoes, to stick
with one example, isn't an activity that is contained within a person's feet and
legs. It is located, so to speak, between feet, legs, shoes, floors, and gendered
expectations. In fact, we could go so far as to describe walking in high heeled
shoes as an activity done by a gendered and male privileged world by means
of a woman's comportment of her feet and legs. The point of this unusual
way of describing walking is not to claim that the organism is passive while
the environment is active. The point instead is to counter assumptions that
the environment plays little role in establishing who and how a person is. As
Dewey would put it, the habit of walking in high heels is a "wa[y] of using and
incorporating the environment in which the latter has its say as surely as the
former."[37]

Likewise, physiological functions are transactional. Breathing, for example, cannot take place by means of lungs alone; it requires air (or oxygen,
more precisely). Likewise, digestion occurs only when the stomach and intestines have food to process and absorb. Respiration and digestion are made up
of a cooperative, active relationship between organism and environment. The
"between" here is important: even though the lungs are crucial to respiration, respiration cannot be located inside the human body considered sharply
distinct from the air that is "outside" it. Nor is digestion complete within the
human body, as if the stomach and intestines owned the process apart from
the food on which it works. Rather than describe respiration and digestion
as activities done by the human body by means of air and food, we just as
accurately could depict them as "things done *by* the environment by means of
organic structures."[38] Again, the point is not that the organism is passive, but
that it does not unilaterally control the activities in which it is engaged. Both
organism and environment are actively involved in physiological functioning.

In the case of both physiological functions and habit, their transactional
relationship with the world means not only that the environment helps constitute the function or habit, but also the function or habit helps constitute,
and possibly change, the world. The relationship between both physiological
function and habit and their environments is non-viciously circular. As the
environment helps form the physiological functions and habits a person has,
her physiological functions and habits enable her to take up and respond to
the world in particular ways, which then alter her environment and thus indirectly affect both her and other people's physiological functions and habits.
In the case of digestion, the introduction of food to the stomach and intestines allows the body to digest it, which enables a person to respond to the
world with the output of waste matter, which alters the environment for good

---

[37] Dewey, *Human Nature and Conduct*, 15.
[38] Dewey, *Human Nature and Conduct*, 15, emphasis in original.

(nutrient-rich fertilizer) or ill (toxic sewage) in ways that feed back into her and other people's food sources and prospects for future digestion. Likewise, as a gendered world shapes a woman's (and a man's) habits of walking and occupying space, those habits both enable and constrain the way that she might respond to the world, perhaps maintaining gendered expectations regarding shoes and locomotion and perhaps challenging or transforming them. Either way, her response helps (re)constitute the environment that then feeds back into expectations for both her and other women's (and men's) footwear habits.

The cyclical relationship between physiological function and habit and their environments demonstrates their plasticity, which means that function and habit are simultaneously durable and corrigible. Plasticity does not mean that something is extremely flexible or supple or that it can easily or quickly be changed into a new shape. As William James clarifies, plasticity "means the possession of a structure weak enough to yield to an influence, but strong enough not to yield all at once."[39] Because they are plastic, physiological functions and habits help constitute the self, and their constitution makes the self something that endures over time as the particular, recognizable self that it is. In the case of habit, one way to put this point is to say that habits are ontological, providing a person with her character. Character is the interpenetrated collection of habits that gives a person coherence and prevents her from being, as Dewey says, "a juxtaposition of disconnected reactions to separated situations."[40] At the same time, however, the ontological status of habit does not mean that it is static or fixed. Habits are always, in principle, capable of change, even if in practice they sometimes become rigid and inflexible. Since habits are formed in transaction with different environments and since those environments inevitably overlap, habits, and thus human ontology, are always potentially modifiable. A live organism only stays alive by means of an active relationship with its environment: when environments change or conflict with each other, then the habits—the selves—built in transaction with them are disrupted and must change too.

While we usually don't speak of physiological functions as having a character, they also are simultaneously durable and corrigible. Digestion, for example, is a way of responding to food that allows the organism to endure over its life span as the particular being that it is. The reliable consistency and ongoing durability of processes of digestion help maintain an organism as *this* particular organism and not decaying organic matter returning to the soil. At the same time, if they are to keep an organism alive, processes of digestion

---

[39] William James, *The Principles of Psychology*, Volume Two (New York: Dover Publications, 1950) 105. See also chapter one of Catherine Malabou, *What Should We Do with Our Brain?* trans. Sebastian Rand (Bronx, NY: Fordham University Press, 2008).

[40] Dewey, *Human Nature and Conduct*, 29.

must be somewhat flexible and capable of change. When the environment changes—for example, when spoiled food is ingested—the stomach and intestines usually do not, and should not, engage in their typical process of digestion, for to do so would be to absorb poisonous matter. In that case, the gut responds to its environment in a different manner: through diarrhea or vomiting.

To conceive of physiological functions as having a character is to conceive them as ontological. By means of their habitual transactions with the world—which includes the social, political, and historical, as well as the material world—physiological functions help constitute the particular beings that each of us are. It also is to conceive of physiological functions as epistemic. The knowledge that an organism has—about the world, about itself, about others—has a bodily basis. Human beings, for example, come to know things through our physiological, affective transactions with the world, just as dogs, cats, and trees do. In contrast, inanimate objects, such as tables and chairs, do not have an affective relationship with the world, with themselves, or with other beings, nor do they possess knowledge. This understanding of bodily knowledge does not mean that the body is always right or that an organism is always consciously aware of the knowledge that it has. In fact, much of a human being's bodily knowledge is non-conscious and/or unconscious. (So, too, for cats, dogs, and other non-human animals. As for trees, it appears that all of their knowledge is non-conscious.) Physiological habits nonetheless have significant epistemic value and are an important source of an organism's knowing-how and knowing-that as it engages with/in the world.[41]

This way of thinking about physiology, environment, ontology, and knowledge calls for a reconsideration of the conflict typically presumed to exist between Darwinian and Lamarckian understandings of physiological change, one that is important to my use of habit in this book. Charles Darwin is the winner in the customary story, the one who understood that acquired characteristics cannot be passed down from generation to generation. Jean-Baptiste Lamarck is the loser, the fool whose "misfortune [is] that, at least in the English-speaking world, his name has become a label for an error."[42] While there are numerous facets to Lamarckian biology, what he is remembered (maligned) for most is his position that "all the acquisitions or losses wrought by nature on individual . . . are preserved by reproduction to the next individuals which arise."[43] This claim is relatively uncontroversial when it is relegated to the fields of psychology, sociology, and economics.[44]

---

[41] For more on the epistemic aspects of bodily habits, see Shannon Sullivan, *Living Across and Through Skins: Transactional Bodies, Pragmatism and Feminism* (Bloomington: Indiana University Press, 2001).

[42] Richard Dawkins quoted in Elizabeth Wilson, *Psychosomatic: Feminism and the Neurological Body* (Durham, NC: Duke University Press, 2004) 66.

[43] Lamarck quoted in Wilson, *Psychosomatic*, 66.

[44] Wilson, *Psychosomatic*, 67–68.

And perhaps it is forgivable even in the field of biology prior to the advent of modern genetics. But once the barrier between "the transferral [*sic*] of information from the somatic tissue to the DNA of the reproductive cells" was established in the late nineteenth century—an inviolable boundary known as Weismann's barrier—then "the central dogma of molecular biology" that invalidated Lamarckism was firmly in place.[45] Lamarck's ideas became passé, an embarrassing relic of pre-genetic history, and notions of non-genetic biological inheritance were relegated to the dustbin.

Yet, as Elizabeth Wilson persuasively has argued, "Darwin was as much a Lamarckian as he was a proponent of natural selection."[46] While he rejected certain aspects of Lamarckism, such as the belief that all organisms evolved into higher, more progressive forms, Darwin agreed with Lamarck about the permeable, dynamic relationship between biology and environment.[47] We can see this especially in the role that habit plays in Darwin's understanding of reflexive movements and nervous system activity. Darwin claims, for example, that the automatic reflex of an aggressive dog to crouch and lower its head was, in dogs' phylogenetic past, a voluntary act undertaken when they were hunting their prey. Through acquired habit, this posture became reflexive and inheritable, that is, innate. As Darwin explains, "Some actions which were at first performed consciously, have become through habit and association converted into reflex actions, and are now so firmly fixed and inherited, that they are performed, even when not of the least use."[48] Habit is the physiological site in which the acquired and the innate mingle, where the influence of the environment, including other organic beings and people, durably constitutes an organism's biological constitution via its reflexes.

The same can be said for many reflexes of the nervous system. Take the example of automatic blinking at loud noises, similar to the startle reflex with which babies are born. Darwin explains this innate reflex as a once-malleable habit that gained fixity and durability over the years of phylogenetic history: "There has been more than enough [time] for these habits to have become innate or converted into reflex actions; for they are common to most of all of the common quadrupeds, and must therefore have been first acquired at a very remote period."[49] Voluntary actions, acquired habits, and automatic reflexes lay on a continuum, according to Darwin, and habit serves as the hinge between the voluntary and the involuntary, the acquired and the innate, and the present and the past.

---

[45] Bowler, quoted in Wilson, *Psychosomatic*, 67.
[46] Wilson, *Psychosomatic*, 65.
[47] Wilson, *Psychosomatic*, 66.
[48] Darwin, quoted in Wilson, *Psychosomatic*, 71.
[49] Darwin, quoted in Wilson, *Psychosomatic*, 72.

Habit also serves as a Lamarckian hinge between biology and society for Darwin. Consider blushing, which is an intersubjective, psychophysiological event governed by the autonomic (sympathetic) nervous system. The contemporary use of "sympathetic" (as well as "parasympathetic") for the two parts of the central nervous system is significant, as Wilson explains, because the term historically is rooted in an appreciation of the rapport that can occur between body parts and organs even if they are not proximal or physically connected to each other.[50] Sympathy was a clinical term for describing affinities between different diseases since "distant organs were thought to respond sympathetically to another organ's anguish."[51]

A contemporary example of physiological sympathy might be the statistical tendency for colon cancer to spread to the lungs if the malignant cells have metastacized all the way through the intestinal wall.[52] We could say that the colon and lungs have some sort of sympathy with each other, even though they do not lie next to each other and even though we do not fully understand their relationship. It's not clear why the colon "chooses" the lungs in particular and not, for example, the stomach or the bladder, which lie in closer proximity to the colon. Perhaps the lungs are especially attuned to the colon in ways that we do not understand. Another example appears to be the placenta and the mouth. Recent research in maternal fetal medicine has demonstrated not only that the placenta is not a sterile organ, as is widely believed, but also that the bacteria in it are not the same as the ones in the vagina, as was hypothesized by the investigating scientists. Instead, "on comparing the placenta microbiome with other body sites, the [research] team found that it was most similar to the [pregnant woman's] oral microbiome rather than sites nearby, such as the vaginal or intestinal microbiomes."[53] Like the colon and lungs, the mouth and the placenta of a pregnant woman tend to have a distinctive rapport with each other that we are only beginning to understand.

In the case of blushing, the autonomic (sympathetic) nervous system causes blood to flow to the capillaries of the face, neck, or chest, sometimes in patterns that are distinct to a person. When this happens, the act almost always is involuntary.[54] Blushing generally cannot be willed, and it tends to

---

[50] Wilson, *Psychosomatic*, 73.

[51] Wilson, *Psychosomatic*, 73.

[52] National Cancer Institute at the National Institute of Health, "Metastatic Cancer," March 2013, http://www.cancer.gov/cancertopics/factsheet/Sites-Types/metastatic, accessed May 16, 2013.

[53] Honor Whiteman, "Placenta 'Not a Sterile Environment,' Study Suggests," *Medical News Today*, May 22, 2014, http://www.medicalnewstoday.com/articles/277206.php, accessed May 29, 2014. See also Kjersti Aagaard, Jun Ma, Kathleen M. Antony, Radhiku Ganu, Joseph Petrosino, and James Versalovic, "The Placenta Harbors a Unique Microbiome," *Science Translation Medicine*, 2014, 6(237): 237ra65.

[54] Some very skilled actors and people trained in certain medication and martial arts techniques do seem able to blush and even change the temperature and color of their hands at will. Thanks to an anonymous reviewer for pointing this out.

be doubly out of a person's conscious control in that it requires the presence or thought of another person's attention. A completely isolated individual, if such a thing ever existed, could not blush. As Darwin explains, "we cannot cause a blush ... by any physical means—that is by an other action of the body. It is the mind which must be affected ... [by] thinking of what others think of us."[55] Here we can see the sympathy not just of a person's body parts with each other—brain with facial muscles and blood vessels—but also with the emotionally charged presence (sometimes imagined) of another person. Blushing is a physiological habit, a way of transacting with the world that illustrates how other beings are entangled in the psychosomatic functioning of a person's body.[56]

The habitual patterns that this sympathetic relationship takes sometimes run in families, a point that is pertinent to this book. Darwin comments on a family of two parents and ten children that blushed to an extraordinary degree and in a distinctive way: big red splashes first appeared on the chest and then spread to the face and neck. When the doctor asked the mother if the daughter he was examining always blushed in this manner, she said, "Yes, she takes after me," and then she proceeded to confirm her response by blushing exactly as her daughter had done.[57] Blushing very well may have a genetic component, which would help explain why mother and daughter blushed in the same way. But its genetic component, if one exists, cannot be understood in a narrow fashion since it is intimately connected to the psychosocial, including in this case (sexualized) emotions of modesty or shame and the attentive gaze of another person (especially of the opposite sex). Blushing is an instance of physiological habit that vividly demonstrates the inadequacy of biology-culture dualisms. As Elizabeth Grosz has argued, Darwin's approach to biology and time complements feminist and critical race thinking by disturbing dualistic differences and rethinking "life and matter in terms of their temporal and durational entwinements."[58]

I'll return to the topic of sympathy and address the historical, familial, and other entwinements of the psychological, social, and physiological in the chapters that follow. My primary goal in doing so will be to understand the physiological effects of racism and sexism: how racism and sexism can help constitute the body's muscle fibers, chemical production, digestive processes, genomic markers, and more. I say "constitute" rather than "construct" since the latter tends to suggest a form of social construction that either ignores the role of biology or considers bodies to be passive recipients of social and

---

[55] Darwin quoted in Wilson, *Psychosomatic*, 75.

[56] Wilson, *Psychosomatic*, 76.

[57] Wilson, *Psychosomatic*, 76–77.

[58] Elizabeth Grosz, *Becoming Undone: Darwinian Reflections on Life, Politics, and Art* (Durham, NC: Duke University Press, 2011) 5.

cultural forces. By "constitution" I intend a dynamic, transactional relationship between the social and the biological in which the two are inextricable.[59] In my discussion, I use "white privilege" to refer to the seemingly invisible, often unconscious forms of racism that pervade the United States after the end of de jure Jim Crow, and "white domination" and "racism" as general terms covering both overt white supremacy and covert white privilege. I use phrases such as "male privilege," "masculinist bias," and "male domination" interchangeably to describe sexism targeting women and other feminized people. The physiological effects of racism and sexism are different for members of dominant and subordinate groups. The effects of racism are not the same for white people and people of color, for example. But both groups are affected physiologically by social-political practices of white domination. In a racist and sexist world, racism and sexism get inside the physiological bodies of all of us in some fashion or other, no matter what our gender or race.

To best see how this occurs, a particular understanding of the physiological body is needed. Developing that understanding of the body will be a second goal of this book. This is a body whose unconscious habits are biological. They are located in the physiological materiality of not only (or perhaps even primarily) the brain, but in the hips, pelvic floor, stomach, heart, and other bodily tissues and organs. The notion of biologically unconscious habits is not in contrast with allegedly non-biological ones. The position of this book is that "the unconscious" is fully biological and physiological. Unconscious habits don't "reside" anywhere else. This position doesn't reduce the psychological (typically understood as mind) to the physiological (typically understood as body, in opposition to mind). It instead recognizes the psychological complexity of our biological, physiological bodies and, in so doing, transforms the meaning of "psychological." Rather than being narrowly related to the mental and its cognitive (read: non-bodily) functions, "psychological" on this account means something closer to its Greek root *psyche*, or soul, which is an organism's vitality or that which animates her. This definition also brings out the affective dimension of the psychological. A person's affective animation is as much physical as it is mental, or rather it entangles the physical and the mental such that opposing one to the other no longer makes any sense.

That complexity exists because the physiological body is both affective and emotional and because both affects and emotions are physiological. Chapter 1, "The Hips: On the Physiology of Affect and Emotion," argues that given affect and emotion's importance both to the operation of unconscious habit and to a non-reductive, psychologically complex account of human

---

[59] "Entanglement" sometimes is used in recent feminist STS literature to capture a similar idea. See, for example, Kristen W. Springer, Jeanne Mager Stellman, and Rebecca M. Jordan-Young, "Beyond a Catalogue of Differences: A Theoretical Frame and Good Practice Guidelines for Researching Sex/Gender in Human Health," *Social Science & Medicine*, June 2012, 74(11): 1818.

physiology, feminist philosophy and critical philosophy of race need an account of affect and emotion as thoroughly somatic, not something "mental" or extra-biological layered on top of the body. They also need an account of human physiology that appreciates how emotion and affect are interpersonal, social, and can be transactionally transmitted between people. Developing that account, Chapter 1 takes the hips and pelvis as a case study, using an example of tight pelvic and hamstring muscles to argue for the transactional physiology of affect and emotion. Setting the stage for subsequent chapters, "The Hips" presents an account of the affective body as the psychosomatic substrate from which biologically unconscious habits develop.

The stomach and intestines have been described by biologists and neuro-gastroenterologists as the place where the inside of the human body meets the outside world.[60] It perhaps is no surprise, then, that the gut is a prime site for the development of biologically unconscious habits related to social privilege and oppression. For this reason, Chapter 2, "The Gut and Pelvic Floor: On Cloacal Thinking," examines the human enteric nervous system to discern some of the physiological effects of sexism and male privilege. For example, women who have been sexually abused disproportionately suffer from gastro-intestinal maladies, such as irritable bowl syndrome (IBS) and Crohn's disease. It's not a figure of speech to say that their bodies have difficulty digesting a world that abuses them in the way it often does. To understand their digestive problems, however, we cannot narrowly focus on the gut. We must appreciate the affective relationship of the entire digestive track with both itself and the pelvic floor. Examining the body's digestive tube from the throat to the cloaca—the phylogenetic common origin of the pelvic floor's separate urinary, genital, and anal tracks—Chapter 2 develops what colorectal surgeon Ghislain Devroede has called *la pensée cloacale*, or cloacal thinking.[61] Cloacal thinking treats the gut and pelvic floor as psychosomatically integrated. It blurs without erasing boundaries between the function and substance of the digestive track's "parts," refusing to consider them as isolated from either each other or from the "outside" world.

The gut's transactional relationship with the world can result in more than the individual incorporation of social-political phenomena such as sexism and male privilege. As Chapter 2 also explains, the transactional process of incorporation can be transgenerational. The gut's particular relationship

---

[60] John B. Furness and Nadine Clerc, "Responses of Afferent Neurons to the Contents of the Digestive Tract, and Their Relation to Endocrine and Immune Responses," in volume 122 of *Progress in Brain Research*, eds. E. A. Mayer and C. B. Saper (Elsevier Science, 2000) 159, emphasis added; Michael D. Gershon, *The Second Brain: A Groundbreaking New Understanding of Nervous Disorders of the Stomach and Intestines* (New York: Harper Paperbacks, 1999) 84.

[61] Ghislain Devroede, *Ce que les maux de ventre dissent de notre passé* (Paris: Payot & Rivages, 2002) 109; Ghislain Devroede, "La pensée cloacale," http://www.crifip.com/articles/la-pensee-cloacale. html, accessed May 21, 2013.

with the world can result in a person's physiologically passing the harmful effects of sexism to her offspring. We will see, for example, that it can result in a woman's transmitting the psychosomatic effects of sexual abuse to her fetus in a physiological but non-genetic fashion, via the inheritance of the mother's malfunctioning anal muscles. As this book will demonstrate, the psychophysiological effects of sexism and sexual abuse are not necessarily confined to the person who directly experiences them.

Neither are the effects of racism and white privilege. Chapter 3, "The Epigenome: On the Transgenerational Effects of Racism," examines non-genetic, psychophysiological inheritance across generational lines in the context of white domination. Focusing on the effects of racism in black bodies, this chapter draws on the field of epigenetics to show how people of color can biologically inherit the deleterious effects of racism. Examining disparities in preterm birth rates between African American and white women, Chapter 3 details how transgenerational *racial* disparities are in fact *racist* disparities that can be manifest physiologically, helping constitute the chemicals, hormones, cells, and fibers of the human body. Epigenetics helps demonstrate how racism can have durable effects on the biological constitution of human beings that are not limited to the specific person who is the target of racism, but instead extend to that person's children and grandchildren. In this way, the field of epigenetics can help philosophers and others understand the transgenerational biological impact of social forces such as racism.

White domination doesn't merely impact the physiology of people of color. It also helps constitute the bodies of white people, as Chapter 4, "The Stomach and the Heart: On the Physiology of White Ignorance," demonstrates. This demonstration is complicated, however, by the fact that medical and health science literature has only recently begun to acknowledge the existence of racism, and then only as a health problem for people of color. Racism would seem to have nothing to do with white people themselves. While they frequently are the subjects of scientific studies, there's a glaring absence of discussion in scientific literature of white people as physiological beneficiaries of racism. Reading this literature with an eye for the operations of white ignorance, however, we can detect the physiological effects of racism in white bodies. Chapter 4 focuses on white people's stomachs and hearts in particular. Returning to the example of my student Brittney, the chapter locates unconscious habits of white privilege in the clenching muscles of white people's stomachs. It also argues that white people's relatively good cardio health should be viewed as a physiological effect of white privilege, rather than as a neutral or normal health condition. In the case of both white stomachs and white hearts, a racialized knowledge grounded in white ignorance helps structure contemporary white physiology.

The conclusion of the book, "Social-Political Change and Physiological Transformation," explores how the unjust physiological effects of racism and sexism might be countered as part of feminist and critical race movements for social justice. Social-political change can result in physiological transformation, and this change can take place in a number of ways. Most important are institutional changes. Equitable health policies, different forms of training and education in medicine, and other legal, economic, and geographical changes to institutional practices can ameliorate the harm of racist and sexist oppression. In addition, however, physiological changes can take place on a personal, individual level, and those transformations can range from greater to lesser involvement of conscious awareness of physiological states. In particular, I am interested in transformative methods on the individual level that work directly with biologically unconscious habits rather than detouring through conscious thought. Developing the notion of a physiological therapy that doesn't prioritize bringing unconscious habits to conscious awareness, the final chapter proposes a double-barreled approach of working for institutional change and transforming biologically unconscious habits as a response to the physiological effects of racism and sexism.

Two things are deliberately left missing from this book. First, there is no separate chapter on the brain, and this is because the brain is not solely or even primarily where individual forms of racism and sexism reside. The lived, personal effects of racism and sexism can be found anywhere in the human body: in hearts, stomachs, intestines, chemical and hormonal attachments, as well as in the brain. Of course, their effects also are institutional, and institutional forms of racism and sexism have a great impact on individual, personal ones. But the macro does not erase the micro; the power of institutional racism and sexism does not eliminate the reality of racism and sexism in people's personal lives. That reality is not exclusively, or perhaps even primarily, cerebral. The entire body has an affective relationship with the world as an organism modulates, informs, and otherwise transacts with its various environments. Not just cerebral auto-affection, but also stomach auto-affection, heart auto-affection, hip auto-affection, hamstring auto-affection, anus auto-affection, and other forms of bodily feeling and affection are part of a person's attachment to life, both her or his own and that of other people. The gut, heart, pelvis, and other body "parts" are not just physiological, but also psychological organs. When their affective relationships with the world are traumatized by sexism and/or racism, the result tends to be painful symptoms manifested in biologically unconscious habits.

Second, in an important respect, what also are missing from this book are sex, gender, and race, in distinction from sexism and racism. This is not a book about whether sex, gender, and race are more biological than they are cultural, or whether they are more physiologically real than other salient characteristics of contemporary human life, such as class, ability, nationality, and so on. Especially in the field of critical philosophy of race, which has tended to focus on debates about the reality of race, it is time to move past stalemates generated by misguided dichotomies between the biological and the cultural. Rather than get trapped in those debates, this book concentrates on the physiological effects of sexism and racism, on both men and women and both white people and people of color. Sociopolitical phenomena, such as racism and sexism and their effects, can be physiological. They are not represented or reflected in physiology, not even "simultaneously" as if a kind of parallelism were at work between the non-bodily (mind and/or society) and the body. Culturally informed beliefs and memories *are* physiological just as they *are* socio-psychological.

I think that disdain for the biological, and thus implicit support for a biology-culture dualism, can crop up in feminist philosophy and critical philosophy of race because of an understandably fierce desire to change an unjust world. But it is not the case, as sometimes is assumed, that culture is malleable and biology is irrevocably fixed. For one thing, culture and other "non-biological" aspects of the human world can become quite sedimented such that they are very difficult to change. And on the flipside, understanding human biology as habitual means recognizing that changes to an individual's biological character can and do occur through its relationship with its environment. The plasticity of human life doesn't necessarily make change easy. Change often is difficult to achieve, no matter which aspect of human existence—cultural or biological, to oversimplify—is in question. But the hard problems of changing human behavior and beliefs are not reserved for the biological aspects of human life. They are shared across the board of human existence, even as different tactics for change might be in order depending on whether the more cultural or more biological aspects of human existence are at stake. Because bodily habits are transactionally constituted by the world around them, work to eliminate societal problems, such as sexism and racism, needs to address all aspects of that transaction, including the biological.

In critical philosophy of race in particular, we fall into a vicious trap when we assume or endorse a dichotomy between "'race as biological' (now out of favor) and 'race as *merely* a social construction.'"[62] As anthropologist Troy Duster has argued, this false dilemma profoundly misunderstands the meaning and effects of social constructionism.[63] As we will see, a number of sociologists, psychologists, anthropologists, and social epidemiologists have documented in vivid empirical detail how the social and political world is literally incorporated into the muscles, hormones, fluids, tissues, and chemicals of human bodies.[64]

---

[62] Troy Duster, "Buried Alive: The Concept of Race in Science," in *Genetic Nature/ Culture: Anthropology and Science beyond the Two-Culture Divide*, eds. Alan H. Goodman, Deborah Heath, and M. Susan Lindee (Berkeley: University of California Press, 2003) 272, emphasis in original).

[63] Duster, "Buried Alive," 263.

[64] On the philosophy side, see also Jonathan Michael Kaplan, "When Socially Determined Categories Make Biological Realities: Understanding Black/White Health Disparities in the U.S.," *The Monist*, 2010, 93(2): 281–297.

Not only does so-called social construction not mean that what is constructed is unreal, but it also does not mean that what is constructed is non-biological. My hunch is that the language of "social construction" too easily lends itself to this trap, and thus it should be avoided. Far superior is social epidemiologist Nancy Krieger's development of "embodiment" as an ecosocial concept designating active organisms that physiologically incorporate their world through activity it.[65] As I understand it, Krieger's notion of embodiment is very similar to the concept of transaction. If the language of social construction is retained, however—as it generally seems to be in the empirical sciences—then we must be willing to speak of biology as social constructed. Not merely the discipline, but biological and physiological matter itself: cortisol levels, allostatic loads, nerve growth factors, muscle fibers, bone tissue, epigenetic markers, and so on. The inequalities of the social world are no different than, for example, the food we eat and the air we breath: they "become literally embodied into physio-anatomic characteristics that influence health" and other salient aspects of human existence.[66]

As Anne Fausto-Sterling has shown, racial, class, and sex/gender differences can materialize in the very bones of human beings. Challenging nature versus nurture debates about bone development, health, and disease, Fausto-Sterling reveals how "our bodies physically imbibe culture" and that over the course of life, different types of "experience[s] shape the very bones that support us."[67] These experiences can include physical trauma, the type of labor performed over a lifetime, how much sunlight one was exposed to, what kinds of sports one participated in, how much stress one has been subject to, and more.[68] The role of sunlight (ultraviolet light) in bone health and disease is particularly interesting since it is necessary to convert inactive vitamin D to an active form, and vitamin D increasingly is being recognized as crucial to bone mineral density and strength (as well as to cell growth, the protection of brain cells, and the prevention of autoimmune diseases).[69] Class, gender, race, ethnicity, skin color, religious doctrines (especially as they affect clothing choices), age, and geography are all complexly tied to the question of who is allowed and/or required to be outside and thus to obtain sufficient UV exposure for good bone and overall health. Bones often materialize in different ways for different groups of people, and those material realities can help open or close different social and cultural possibilities for those people.

---

[65] Nancy Krieger, "Embodiment: A Conceptual Glossary for Epidemiology," *Journal of Epidemiology & Community Health*, 2005, 59: 350–355.

[66] Nancy Krieger and George Davey Smith, "'Bodies Count,' and Body Counts: Social Epidemiology and Embodying Inequality," *Epidemiologic Reviews*, 2004, 26(1): 92.

[67] Anne Fausto-Sterling, "The Bare Bones of Sex: Part 1—Sex and Gender," *Signs*, 2005, 30(2): 1495.

[68] Fausto-Sterling, "The Bare Bones of Sex," 1491; Fausto-Sterling, "The Bare Bones of Race," 678.

[69] Fausto-Sterling, "The Bare Bones of Race," 673, 672: Fausto-Sterling, "The Bare Bones of Sex," 1508.

"We are always 100 percent nature and 100 percent nurture," as Fausto-Sterling convincingly demonstrates, with nature and nurture each helping make up how the other functions and develops.[70]

In a similar fashion, cultural anthropologist Leith Mullings has argued, "while race may not be biological, racism has biological consequences."[71] Her analysis of the social context of reproduction in Harlem reveals the physiological effects on African American women of what Mullings calls the Sojourner Syndrome. Named after Sojourner Truth, the Sojourner Syndrome is a more gendered, and thus a more intersectional, approach to "John Henryism," in which African Americans expend a great deal of effort and take on extraordinary responsibilities in order to survive in the midst of racial oppression.[72] African American women confront a different type of racial oppression than African American men do since African American women do not benefit from male privilege. They also are "exclude[ed] from the protections of private patriarchy offered to white women by the concepts of womanhood, motherhood, and femininity."[73] Furthermore, their identities as black women can contribute to the instability of their class status, for example, through gendered and raced wage and employment discrimination; simultaneously, "race dilutes the protections of class" for those black women who are middle class.[74] The end result often is a survival strategy resembling the larger-than-life coping efforts of Sojourner Truth, which can have certain financial, educational, and social benefits, but which also can come at a high price for black women's psychosomatic health.[75] As the Harlem Birth Right project has investigated, the health of black women in the United States on average is worse than that of white women at every economic level.[76] Understanding and combating this disparity requires grappling with the intersectional ways that oppression can become physiologically embodied.[77]

---

[70] Fausto-Sterling, "The Bare Bones of Sex," 1510. See also Anne Fausto-Sterling, *Sex/Gender: Biology in a Social World* (New York: Routledge, 2012), and Evelyn Fox Keller, *The Mirage of a Space Between Nature and Nurture* (Durham, NC: Duke University Press, 2010).

[71] Leith Mullings, "Resistance and Resilience: The Sojourner Syndrome and the Social Context of Reproduction in Central Harlem," in *Gender, Race, Class & Health: Intersectional Approaches*, eds. Amy J. Schulz and Leith Mullings (San Francisco: Jossey-Bass, 2006) 364.

[72] Mullings, "Resistance and Resilience," 362.

[73] Mullings, "Resistance and Resilience," 362.

[74] Mullings, "Resistance and Resilience," 363.

[75] Mullings, "Resistance and Resilience," 364.

[76] Mullings, "Resistance and Resilience," 367.

[77] See also the important work of David R. Williams, including David R. Williams, Yan Yu, James S. Jackson, and Norman B. Anderson, "Racial Differences in Physical and Mental Health," *Journal of Health Psychology*, 1997, 2(3): 325–351; David R. Williams, "Race, Socioeconomic Status, and Health: The Added Effects of Racism and Discrimination," *Annals of the New York Academy of Sciences*, 1999, 896: 173–188; Pamela Braboy Jackson and David R. Williams, "The Intersections of Race, Gender, and SES: Health Paradoxes," in *Gender, Race, Class and Health: Intersectional Approaches*, eds. Amy J. Schulz and Leith Mullings (San Francisco: Jossey-Bass, 2004) 131–162; and Michelle Sternthal, Michelle J. Natalie Slopen, and David R. Williams, "Racial Disparities in

The social-versus-biological trap rejected by these scholars is neither neutral nor innocent. As Krieger argues, it manifests an ideological position, popular with conservative foundations in the United States, that tends to be unsupportive of social justice movements.[78] By casting social justice concerns (such as the health effects of racial discrimination) as politically correct but unscientific and the pursuit of biological facts (especially regarding genes) as rigorous even if "bravely" politically incorrect science, the false dilemma between the social and the biological serves the interests of white supremacy and white privilege.[79] In the name of defending a neutral, apolitical version of science, the dilemma deceptively attempts to paint social justice concerns as ideologically biased and thus as something for "real" science to stay well clear of. This not only furthers a racialized epistemology of ignorance that makes it difficult to understand the white-dominated world in which we live, but it also leaves in place staggering health disparities across racial groups and does nothing to reduce the shockingly high levels of morbidity and mortality for African American people in particular.

Which seems to be the point of the trap, one can say without too much cynicism. Critical philosophers of race thus need to avoid it, and that means shelving the well-worn mantra in philosophy (and elsewhere) that race is not biological. In that respect, then, this book *does* concern the reality of race as constituted by the effects of racism. Critical philosophers of race no longer can simply criticize the concept of "race as bad biology," as anthropologist Clarence Gravlee succinctly puts it.[80] We should acknowledge that race *is* biological—not in the pre-critical sense of a static, essential category but in the critical, dynamic way in which "*race becomes biology*" through the embodiment of racial inequalities.[81] As we will see, racial differences are physiologically, biologically real in that racism has fundamentally impacted the physical health and functioning of African American and other people of color. It also has fundamentally impacted—that is, unfairly benefited—the physical health and functioning of white people. This acknowledgment is not a capitulation to racism, but instead an important part of the struggle against it. Critical philosophy of race should be also a critical physiology of race.

Health—How Much Does Stress Matter?" *Du Bois Review: Social Science Research on Race*, 2011, 8(1): 95–113.

[78] Krieger, "Stormy Weather," 2155.

[79] Krieger, "Stormy Weather," 2155.

[80] Clarence C. Gravlee, "How Race Becomes Biology: Embodiment of Social Inequality," *American Journal of Physical Anthropology*, 2009, 139: 48.

[81] Gravlee, "How Race Becomes Biology," 54, emphasis in original; see also Dorothy Roberts, *Fatal Invention: How Science, Politics, and Big Business Re-create Race in the Twenty-First Century* (New York: The New Press, 2012) 129–130. Gravlee's lack of attention to epigenetic processes has the effect of overemphasizing genetic ones, however, as when he claims, "the embodiment of social inequality passes through biological systems regulated by genes" (54).

For similar reasons, feminist philosophy also should be a critical physiology of sex/gender. Following recent feminist work in biomedicine and related STS fields,[82] I use the intertwined term "sex/gender" since physiology underlies both, not just sex (typically understood to be biological) in contrast to gender (typically understood to be cultural). I also say "sex/gender" to avoid the elision or trivialization of sex that sometimes happens when gender is understood as creating the category of sex. Gendered (and often sexist) expectations certainly help construct biological sex, but that doesn't make the biological basis of sex any less real, nor should it be taken to mean that gendered differences have no basis in physiology. Even in its sophisticated forms, which reject the idea that a cultural gender overlays a foundation of biological sex, distinctions between sex and gender too often continue to operate with the same old biology-culture dualism, now flipped on its head. "What is sorely needed if gender scholars are to analyze sex productively," as Asia Friedman has argued,

> is an alternate conceptual paradigm for understanding the anatomical and social/cultural components of what we currently call sex and gender. . . . It is not enough to simply broaden the circle of scholarly focus so that we do not limit our analysis to the gender half of the sex/gender dichotomy, but examine the sex half as well while retaining its definition as a fixed natural binary. It is also not enough to simply (re)collapse the categories sex and gender, but this time making everything gender rather than sex, which risks dematerializing both sex and gender.[83]

Jettisoning biology-culture dualisms instead must involve critically rethinking the physiological dimensions of sex/gender.

Doing so is crucial to the psychosomatic health of women of all races. Just as the biology-culture trap leaves significant racial health disparities in place, it also does little to relieve the psychosomatic suffering of women who, for example, disproportionately suffer from various pelvic floor dysfunctions, gastrointestinal illnesses, and autoimmune problems. Sex/gender is biological, not in a pre-critical sense of an unchanging bodily given but in the critical, dynamic way that sexed/gendered differences can become biological through the embodiment of the effects of sexist (and often abusive) practices. This view of sex/gender as biological does not operate through the prioritization of reproduction, as the category of sex often is used or assumed

---

[82] Anelis Kaiser, Sven Haller, Sigrid Schmitz, and Cordula Nitsch, "On Sex/Gender Related Similarities and Differences in fMRI Language Research," *Brain Research Reviews*, October 2009, 61(2): 49–59. See also Springer et al., "Beyond a catalogue of differences," 1818, and Fausto-Sterling, "The Bare Bones of Sex," 1516.

[83] Asia Friedman, "Unintended Consequences of the Feminist Sex/Gender Distinction," *Genders*, 2006, 43 http://www.genders.org/g43/g43_friedman.html, accessed June 12, 2013.

to do.[84] Neither, as I envision it, does a critical approach to the physiology of sex/gender necessarily result in merely two sex/genders. A multiplicity of biological sex/genders are possible, including intersexed and transgendered ones. In a sexist, male-privileged world, what makes sex/gender biologically real is neither reproduction nor a sex binary, but the physiological incorporation of sexist oppression, which often is also heterosexist. Improving the lives of women and other subpersons who are seen as "legitimate" targets of sexual assault means reckoning with the biological reality of the sexist effects of male domination.

I believe that there is a great deal that feminist philosophy and critical philosophy of race can say that simultaneously respects the gut experiences of my student Brittney as physiologically real and understands those experiences as the effects of a racist and sexist world. Her bodily experience is the beginning of a story that philosophers need to be able to tell, not the end. There also is a great deal that human physiology has to say about biologically unconscious habits of racist and sexist oppression, stories that aren't always told verbally or consciously because people are reluctant, unable, or forbidden to tell them. This book makes a small contribution to the conversation in hopes that dialogue will grow between feminist and critical philosophy of race, on the one hand, and the biological and medical sciences, on the other. Sexism and racism have put down some of their toughest roots in the physiological habits of human bodies, and so it is there that feminist philosophy and critical philosophy of race also must work.

---

[84] My position thus differs from Linda Martín Alcoff's realist position on sex difference, which holds, "*Women and men are differentiated by virtue of their different relationship of possibility to biological reproduction, with biological reproduction referring to conceiving, giving birth, and breast-feeding, involving one's body*" (Alcoff, *Visible Identities* [New York: Oxford University Press, 2006], 172, italics in original).

1

The Hips

ON THE PHYSIOLOGY OF AFFECT AND EMOTION

The traffic between the biological and the social is two-way; the
social or psychosocial actually gets into the flesh and is apparent
in our affective and hormonal dispositions.

—TERESA BRENNAN, *THE TRANSMISSION OF AFFECT*

The bodily sounding-board is at work . . . far more
than we usually suppose.

—WILLIAM JAMES, *THE PRINCIPLES OF PSYCHOLOGY*

Michael Lee, now a master yoga therapist, recounts a powerful experience when
he was first practicing yoga. He was in triangle pose, a relatively simple posture,
suitable for beginners; it is very challenging, however, if a person has tight hips
and hamstrings. As Lee explains, after he was in the pose for a few minutes,

> One of my friends was using a wall to support me in the triangle pose on
> my right side when my body began to quiver uncontrollably. I witnessed
> an intense red-blue, burning sensation in my right hip and believed I had
> pressed into the posture as deeply as I could, feeling pain that wasn't really
> pain. My mind was shouting, "Get out of here! Stop now! Get on with it!". . .
> The escalating sensations in my right hip were becoming almost unbear-
> able when my attention shifted from what was happening in my body to
> what was taking place in my attitude. I was becoming more and more agi-
> tated and wanted to release out of the posture. . . . The hot, fire-red burn-
> ing seemed to pour out of my hip like a volcanic eruption. My whole body
> vibrated and I felt warm tears streaming down my face without my know-
> ing why. My body began to feel very small as I re-experienced myself as an
> eight-year-old boy on a school playground about to be beaten up by a group
> of older boys. The terror of that frightened child permeated every cell of my
> being as I continued to release emotionally. . . .[1]

---

[1] Quoted in Amy Weintraub, *Yoga for Depression: A Compassionate Guide to Relieve Suffering Through Yoga* (New York: Broadway Books, 2004) 213.

Lee's experience of strong emotions being released from bodily muscles and fibers apparently is not unusual. While I don't know of any empirical studies documenting how often this type of situation occurs, it shows up so frequently in online and other discussions of practicing and teaching yoga that it cannot be dismissed as idiosyncratic. Many yoga practitioners speak of experiencing and witnessing other people's sudden and unexplained crying when they are in particular yoga postures.[2] In a related fashion, some physical therapists who practice massage therapy also have witnessed sudden and unexplained crying on the part of their patients when a particular muscle or joint of the body is massaged.[3] By "unexplained," I mean that no physical injury occurred while the body was being stretched or kneaded that would explain the person's crying. As Lee's experience demonstrates, the crying in question here does not occur because, for example, a tendon suddenly tore or a muscle was worked too hard. The tears in these situations are emotional and apparently are unrelated to the bodily experience that a person currently is undergoing. Lee's traumatic childhood experience would seem to have nothing to do with performing a hip stretch in yoga class decades later.

The two events are connected, however, and understanding their connection requires understanding the affective and emotional dimensions of human physiology. As this chapter will argue, affect and emotion play a significant role in human experience and human beings' bodily retention, or memory of their experiences, including but not limited to traumatic events. We might not always consciously remember our experiences, but they and the knowledge they provide of the world often endure in our physiological constitution. Some bodily experiences are merely non-conscious, while others are unconscious, depending on whether active psychosomatic mechanisms are at work to keep them out of conscious awareness. Whether non-conscious, unconscious, or conscious, however, all bodily experiences are instances of the body's affective (and thus epistemic) relationship to itself and its various environments. To understand Lee's experience, we need first to understand how emotion and affect are physiological and, reciprocally, how human physiology is fully affective and often also emotional. This, in turn, will allow us to appreciate the physiology of unconscious affects and emotions. Not just the

---

[2] In addition to multiple examples found in Weintraub's *Yoga for Depression* (pages 201–225 in particular), see Cressida J. Heyes, *Self Transformations: Foucault, Ethics, and Normalized Bodies* (New York: Oxford University Press, 2007) 129; Donna Raskin, "Emotions in Motion," n.d. http://www.yogajournal.com/practice/1215, accessed June 20, 2013; Vicki Santillano, "How Yoga Unlocks Emotions: Camel Pose, Then Crying?" n.d. http://www.divinecaroline.com/beauty/how-yoga-unlocks-emotions-camel-pose-then-crying, accessed June 20, 2013; Lauren, "Open Hips, Out Come the Emotions," 2012, http://bluelotusyogamaine.blogspot.fr/2012/08/open-hips-out-come-emotions.html, accessed June 20, 2013. Gaby Winguist, yoga instructor, also reports this phenomenon (personal correspondence).

[3] Physical and osteo-therapist Jennifer Bullock (personal correspondence).

hips, but the entire human body is constituted of affective habits and thus is capable of developing unconscious habits as well. Lee's experience provides a particularly vivid illustration of how this can happen. After examining the general physiology of affect and emotion, I'll return to unconscious affective and emotional habits and Lee's hips in particular.

Feminist philosophy of emotion has been crucial to establishing the philosophical importance of emotion, challenging both the sharp opposition of emotion and reason and the idea that emotions are meaningless and/or trivial.[4] It successfully has argued for the epistemic importance of emotions, considering them to be important sources of knowledge about the world. Different groups of people tend to be allowed and/or forbidden to experience different emotions—anger in particular. Who is permitted to feel angry? When? Where? With whom? And about what? As feminists have demonstrated, the answers to these questions can tell us a great deal about gendered, raced, and other hierarchies pervading a culture or society.

Elizabeth Spelman explains how early positivist accounts of emotion considered emotions to be "dumb" in that they supposedly are irrational or a-rational outbursts that have nothing meaningful to say, and this made it somewhat "dumb," or stupid, for philosophers or anyone else to pay them much attention.[5] Along with other feminists such as Marilyn Frye and Alison Jaggar, Spelman turns to cognitivist theories of emotion to develop a feminist-friendly alternative to "the Dumb View."[6] Cognitivist theories hold that emotions have cognitive content: they manifest beliefs or judgments. Emotions also are intentional: they are about some object or situation, and thus they are one way in which human beings project themselves into the world. On a cognitivist view, we also could say that emotions make a claim to knowledge. The claim might turn out to be wrong, but it is not a meaningless

---

[4] See, for example, Marilyn Frye's chapter "A Note on Anger," in Frye, *The Politics of Reality: Essays in Feminist Theory* (Freedom, CA: Crossing Press, 1983); Alison M. Jaggar, "Love and Knowledge: Emotion in Feminist Epistemology," in *Gender/Body/Knowledge: Feminist Reconstructions of Being and Knowing*, eds. Alison M. Jaggar and Susan R. Bordo (New Brunswick, NJ: Rutgers University Press, 1989) 145–171; and Elizabeth Spelman, "Anger and Insubordination," in *Women, Knowledge, and Reality: Explorations in Feminist Philosophy*, first edition, eds. Ann Garry and Marilyn Pearsall (Boston: Unwin Hyman, 1989) 263–274.

[5] Spelman, "Anger and Insubordination," 265. See also Jaggar, "Love and Knowledge," 148–149. Perhaps because they were thought to be dumb (in both senses of the term), emotions continued to play a role in animal research in the early twentieth century, after they were dismissed in the realm of human psychology (see Anne C. Rose, "Animal Tales: Observations of the Emotions in American Experimental Psychology, 1890–1940," *Journal of the History of the Behavioral Sciences* 2012, wileyonlinelibrary.com, DOI: 10.1002/jhbs.21562).

[6] See note 4 above. To be clear, I am not claiming that all feminists working on emotion appeal to cognitivism. For other approaches, see, e.g., Sara Ahmed, *The Cultural Politics of Emotion* (New York: Routledge, 2004), and Teresa Brennan, *The Transmission of Affect* (Ithaca, NY: Cornell University Press, 2004), discussed later in this chapter.

outburst. When a person is angry, for example, she is angry about something that has happened in the world. She is judging, or making a knowledge claim, that something wrong has occurred. On a cognitivist account, her claim demands uptake, even if one ultimately disagrees with the judgment it makes. The claim and thus the emotion demand that they be taken seriously as a plausible way of understanding the world. This also is to say that the person feeling the emotion implicitly asserts that she is a credible person whose worldview should be taken seriously.

In the fields of critical race theory and critical philosophy of race, bell hooks is well known for powerfully analyzing the complicated relationships between emotion, knowledge, and racism. As she does so, she contributes to a feminist tradition of emphasizing the epistemological significance of emotion and feelings. hooks explains that "black folks have, from slavery on, shared in conversations with one another 'special' knowledge of whiteness gleaned from close scrutiny of white people."[7] This knowledge was special in that it was not written down in the (white) annals of history, but its ability to help black people survive in a white supremacist society was treasured nonetheless. Black domestic servants, which meant black women in particular, played an especially important role as "informants," bringing "knowledge back to segregated communities—details, facts, observations, and psychoanalytic readings of the white Other."[8]

What that knowledge revealed was terror. In the black imagination, whiteness often was (and is) "associated with the terrible, the terrifying, the terrorizing."[9] Whether the Ku Klux Klan in white hoods or the white salesman who crossed the track to peddle Bibles or insurance, white people wielded a frightening power to harm black people physically, economically, socially, and spiritually. As hooks recounts,

> I learned as a child that to be "safe" it was important to recognize the power of whiteness, even to fear it, and to avoid encounter. There was nothing terrifying about the sharing of this knowledge as a survival strategy; the terror was made real only when I journeyed from the black side of town to a predominantly white area near my grandmother's house. . . . [I] would have to pass that terrifying whiteness—those white faces on the porches staring us down with hate. Even when empty or vacant those porches seemed to say *danger*, you do not belong here, you are not safe.[10]

White terror encourages black people to stay "in their place," to not protest against white supremacy, and, above all, to not feel (or at least to not express)

---

[7] hooks, *Killing Rage: Ending Racism* (New York: Henry Holt, 1996) 31.
[8] hooks, *Killing Rage*, 31.
[9] hooks, *Killing Rage*, 39.
[10] hooks, *Killing Rage*, 45–46.

anger toward white people and white institutions. It forces black people "to choke down [their] rage" and slanders black anger at white domination as trivial and/or pathological.[11] But rage can be a powerfully constructive force and, on hooks's view, it even is "a necessary aspect of resistance struggle."[12] Rather than deny or repress their rage, black people need to reckon with the knowledge that it contains: knowledge about the severity and persistence of white domination even after the end of de jure Jim Crow, as well as knowledge about the grief, pain, and other psychological wounds caused by white domination that have been displaced into their rage.[13]

Rage isn't the only emotion hooks summons in the face of white domination. She also writes movingly of yearning for something that she fears black communities have lost and, in particular, for renewed spirits and strategies to fight against white domination and black hopelessness.[14] Perhaps in response to that yearning, hooks turns to the emotion of love. The "love ethic" that she develops doesn't focus on romantic or sexual love, but rather "love as the will to nurture our own and another's spiritual growth."[15] For hooks, love is a "profoundly political" emotion, one that can provide a "platform on which to renew progressive anti-racist struggle . . . by restor[ing] the true meaning of freedom, hope, and possibility in all our lives."[16] Love contains a kind of wisdom that can help rebuild black and other communities that have been damaged by racism.

It's not hard to understand why cognitive theories of emotion would appeal to feminists, as well as to critical philosophers of race. Emotions long have been associated with oppressed peoples, such as women and people of color, and the dismissal of oppressed peoples has been tightly bound up with the dismissal of emotion. To argue that emotions are cognitively and epistemologically significant is to insist, for example, that the realms of the feminine and of blackness are important and should not be denigrated. It also is to take a crucial step in the dismantling of sharp dichotomies between reason and emotion. We could say that as a vehicle for gaining knowledge and making claims about the world, emotion is very similar to reason. Emotions often follow a particular logic, just as rationality can have different emotional overtones. Rather than opposed, emotion and reason can be considered complementary modes of transacting with/in the world. They are related, compatible ways of gaining knowledge and, more generally, undergoing experience.

---

[11] hooks, *Killing Rage*, 13, 26.
[12] hooks, *Killing Rage*, 16.
[13] hooks, *Killing Rage*, 27.
[14] bell hooks, *Yearning: Race, Gender, and Cultural Politics* (Boston, MA: South End Press, 1999).
[15] bell hooks, *All About Love: New Visions* (New York: HarperCollins Publishers, 2000) xix, 6.
[16] bell hooks, *Salvation: Black People and Love* (New York: HarperCollins Publishers, 2001) 16, xxiv.

Without disagreeing that cognitive approaches to emotions are superior to "the Dumb View," I want to develop a richer account of the embodied physiology of emotion (and affect) than cognitivism tends to allow. In particular, I am concerned that cognitive approaches to emotion continue to operate with a mind-body dualism that implicitly undercuts any authority granted to emotion. Cognitive accounts tend to explain emotions as having an affective (or "feeling," on my terms) component and a cognitive component. The so-called affective component feels (for example, stomach qualms and clammy hands) and the cognitive component identifies what the feeling is (for example, anxiety).[17] The cognitive component tends to take center stage, however, shoving the "affective" side of emotion to the margins and failing to explain how the feeling and cognitive components of emotion are related. Contemporary cognitivism insists that emotions and feelings are not the same thing, even if feeling can be a contingent component of emotion.[18] As Jaggar argues, the net result is highly problematic: "insofar as [cognitive accounts of emotion] prioritize the intellectual over the feeling aspects, they reinforce the traditional western preference for mind over body."[19] On a cognitivist account, bodily feelings are still dumb, and a non-bodily intellect has all the smarts.

While the epistemological significance of emotion has been well established by Spelman, Jaggar, hooks, and other feminists, a full appreciation of the physicality of emotion has not been. In particular, feminists and critical philosophers of race need to be cautious that a bias against bodily feelings does not sneak back into their accounts of emotion via cognitivism. There are small signs of this, for example, even in Jaggar's excellent work on outlaw emotions, which "excludes as genuine emotions both automatic physical responses and nonintentional sensations, such as hunger pangs."[20] But if feminists and critical philosophers of race fully reckon with the embodiment of emotion, they can and should consider automatic physical responses and sensations, including hunger pangs, to be possibly legitimate instances of affect, and perhaps even emotion. (I will return later to the specific example of hunger pangs.) Feminists and critical philosophers of race would benefit from a more robust account of the role that physiology plays in emotional and affective transactions with the world than cognitivism can provide. We need an alternative to both cognitivism and positivism that gives center-stage to bodily feelings, emotions, affects, and physical responses to the world, without construing the body as dumb. To develop such an alternative, I propose to identify affect with physiological processes and to underscore the

---

[17] Jaggar, "Love and Knowledge," 149.

[18] Jesse Prinz, "Are Emotions Feelings?" *Journal of Consciousness Studies* 2005, 12(8–10): 9. This is why, as Prinz notes, when it comes to emotion, "the debate between [defenders of cognitive theories] and the Jamesians is old and enduring" (21).

[19] Jaggar, "Love and Knowledge," 150.

[20] Jaggar, "Love and Knowledge," 148.

physiological basis of emotion, guided by the philosophical psychology of William James.

In *The Principles of Psychology*, James notoriously claimed that the popular notion that emotions cause bodily changes gets things backwards. According to him, the order is precisely the reverse: bodily changes cause emotions. His theory is that "the bodily changes follow directly the perception of the exciting fact," which means that nothing disembodied or "mental" intervenes between a stimulating object or situation in the world and a person's bodily response to it.[21] Thus, to use James's example, we tremble upon seeing a bear while hiking in the forest and then feel afraid. We don't first feel something mental called fear and then begin to tremble. A person's stomach flutters and her intestines cramp and so she feels anxious prior to taking an important exam. She doesn't first experience mental anxiety about the exam and then get butterflies in her stomach. Put as succinctly as possible, James claims that we are sad because we cry; we are not crying because we are sad.

James acknowledges that his theory will seem counterintuitive to many people, especially when stated so crudely.[22] Let's return to the example of crying. Tears come out the eyes of my young daughter all the time, and sometimes (I discover after some difficulty) they are not tears of sadness, as I had assumed, but tears of anger (likely because of something her older sister said). What sense can one make of the claim that my daughter's anger came *after* her tears? Doesn't the emotion of anger prompt her physiological response of crying? Why else would she be crying? Moreover, sometimes her tears are tears of sadness after all. If crying causes the emotion, how do we explain why crying sometimes causes sadness and other times causes anger? The different emotions that can be felt when crying would seem to prove that the physiological event cannot be the cause of the emotion.

James provides compelling replies to all of these objections and more, but before I dive into their detail, I must underscore what James calls "the vital point" of his theory. It is this: *"If we fancy some strong emotion, and then try to abstract from our consciousness of it all the feelings of its bodily symptoms, we find we have nothing left behind,* no 'mind-stuff' out of which the emotion can be constituted, and that a cold and neutral state of intellectual perception is

---

[21] William James, *The Principles of Psychology*, Volume Two (New York: Dover Publications, 1950) 449.

[22] Joseph T. Palencik documents some of the hostility to James's theory of emotion when it was first published, in Palencik, "William James and the Psychology of Emotion: From 1884 to the Present," *Transactions of the Charles S. Peirce Society* 2007, 43(4): 769–786. See also discussions of James's theory of emotion in John Kaag, "Getting under My Skin: William James on the Emotions, Sociality and Transcendence," *Zygon* 2009, 44(2): 433–450; James O. Pawelski, *The Dynamic Individualism of William James* (Albany: State University of New York Press, 2007) 46–49; and Bruce Wilshire, *William James and Phenomenology: A Study of the Principles of Psychology* (Bloomington: Indiana University Press, 1968).

all that remains."[23] The crux of James's theory in fact does not concern causation at all. It is that emotion is necessarily, inevitably, and entirely a bodily phenomenon. (This view need not omit the crucial role of socialized meaning and experience, to which I will return.) Emotions are not mental—understood in opposition to the body—as James's delightful dismissal of "mind-stuff" insists, and they cannot be disassociated from their physiological sensations.

Insisting on the bodily nature of emotions does not devalue or debase them. James is adamant on this point, which is just as vital as his rejection of emotional "mind-stuff." He argues that emotions "carry their own inner measure of worth with them; and it is just as logical to use the present [i.e., James's] theory of emotions for proving that sensational processes need not be vile and material, as to use their vileness and materiality as a proof that such a theory cannot be true."[24] As Jeremy Carrette has explained, on James's view "physiology was about opening the world, not closing or reducing its possibilities."[25] At its heart, James's theory of emotion challenges hierarchies of mind over body that plague many accounts of emotion and, indeed, the field of philosophy as a whole. James's insistence on the bodily nature of emotions does not debase or trivialize them because the body is neither base nor trivial.[26] As bodily phenomena, emotions come equipped with an inner measure of worth. They can gauge the value and status of objects in the world in their own right. As I will emphasize below (but perhaps James did not sufficiently), they are co-constituted by socialized beliefs and frameworks that a person has learned throughout her life. Fully physiological, emotions are not at all dumb. They can be very smart.

This vital point demonstrates why James's self-described crude explanations of emotion evoking causation are misleading. James himself occasionally uses such language, as when he claims that "the general causes of the emotions are indubitably physiological" and "each emotion is the resultant of a sum of elements [organic changes], and each element is caused by a physiological process."[27] But a dualistic, linearly causal reading of James should be resisted.[28] The main point of his theory is not to establish which

---

[23] James, *The Principles of Psychology*, 451, emphasis in original.

[24] James, *The Principles of Psychology*, 453.

[25] Jeremy Carrette, *William James's Hidden Religious Imagination: A Universe of Relations* (New York: Routledge, 2013) 115.

[26] As J. M. Barbalet documents, contemporary philosophers have been concerned that James trivializes emotion (rather than debases it, as went the nineteenth-century concern) as an "'epiphenomenon'" or as "'froth on the top of the real business of behavior'" (Barbalet, "William James' Theory of Emotions: Filling in the Picture," *Journal for the Theory of Social Behaviour* 1999, 29(3): 252–253).

[27] James, *The Principles of Psychology*, 449, 453.

[28] My concern here is similar to that of Barbalet, who charges that reductionist readings of the complexity of James's work on emotion are commonplace in the psychology of emotions ("William James' Theory of Emotions," 262). See also Kaag, "Getting under My Skin," 437, on James's disagreement with traditional concepts of emotion as "linear and unilaterally causal."

comes first, the bodily sensation or the emotion. It is to insist that nothing non-bodily, no "mind stuff," comes between them.[29] The language of causation invokes a kind of misplaced dualism in which there are felt bodily sensations, on the one hand, and there are emotions, on the other, and the task is to determine which precedes the other. In contrast, James's theory of emotion is more accurately considered a form of monism: bodily changes (all of which are felt on James's account) and emotions just *are* two ways of describing, or we could even say experiencing, the same event or situation.[30] James supports this view when he claims, in contrast to the view that emotion is a "mental affection," that "*our feeling of the same* [bodily] *changes as they occur* IS *the emotion.*"[31] James capitalizes the "is" to underscore the identity of felt bodily changes and emotion. There is no issue of temporal order between them. Again James asserts, "the emotion here [in the case of "morbid fear"] is nothing but the feeling of a bodily state, and it has a purely bodily cause."[32] Interestingly, James here uses causal language immediately after insisting on the identity of emotion and a felt bodily state, indicating that there is no tension between these two views on his account. (I'll return to this point shortly.) The question of emotion's cause is not whether emotions or bodily changes come first in time, but whether emotion is a bodily or mental phenomenon. And James's answer to that latter question is consistent and clear: something happens in the world that catches our attention, and we directly undergo bodily changes in response that, because felt, are emotions. Period. There is no disembodied mental perception of the event needed to generate an emotion that then triggers a bodily response to the event.

My reading of James's account of emotion differs from Jesse Prinz's influential Jamesian perceptual theory of emotions, and this difference helps explain why I dwell on the issue of causation, even though it is not vital to James's theory of emotion.[33] For reasons similar to mine, Prinz also turns to James's psychology to counter cognitive accounts of emotion. Prinz argues that emotions are involuntary embodied appraisals of the world that give organisms an evolutionary survival advantage.[34] This is why we can say with

---

[29] Barbalet captures the point well when he argues "James is not concerned... with the causal effect of emotion on behavior but with the question of whether emotion is embodied or not" ("William James' Theory of Emotions," 254).

[30] I thus disagree with John Deigh that James's conception of emotions renders them epiphenomenal (Deigh, "Emotions: The Legacy of James and Freud," *International Journal of Psychoanalytics* 2001, 82: 1252). I also think Deigh misunderstands James when he claims that on James's account, emotions are never meaningful and never explain anything because they are "merely" bodily processes.

[31] James, *The Principles of Psychology*, 449, italics in original.

[32] James, *The Principles of Psychology*, 459.

[33] See Jesse Prinz, *Gut Reactions: A Perceptual Theory of Emotion* (New York: Oxford University Press, 2004).

[34] Prinz, *Gut Reactions*, 51, 59–60, 102, 240, 243.

Prinz that emotions are gut reactions. On Prinz's account, however, emotional appraisals are mental representations of the world (or, more precisely, of the organism-environment relation).[35] "Emotions are mental states," as he explains, that "can be inextricably bound up with states that are involved in the detection of bodily changes."[36] Emotions allow us to "perceive," which is to say "register" or "detect," bodily changes that are triggered by events in the world, which hopefully leads to appropriate behavioral changes.[37] Events in the world cause bodily changes, which in turn cause emotions. Thus while bodily changes play an important role in Prinz's theory, he clearly states that they are not essential to it. As he cautions at the close of his perceptual theory of emotion,

> [m]any researchers try to pack both too much and too little into emotions. They pack in too much by assuming that bodily changes, propositional attitudes, action dispositions, and feelings are essential parts or preconditions for emotions. I have argued that all of these things are only contingently related to emotions. They are the causes and effects of emotions. Those causes and effects are certainly worthy of study, but they should not be mistaken for the emotions themselves.[38]

For Prinz, the crucial component of cognition is control: cognitive states and processes are those that the organism, rather than the environment, controls.[39] This is why emotions are not cognitive on his account. They are, however, mental entities that are distinguishable from bodily changes. Even though it is bound up with bodily states and processes, emotion for Prinz is a mental representation of the body, and thus his theory appears to operate with a problematically dualistic account of body and mind.

Again, James's own use of causal language can make it difficult to resist a dualistic understanding of his ideas about emotion. Prinz focuses on the passages in James's *Principles* in which James describes emotions as effects of bodily changes. In contrast, I want to emphasize the passages in which James asserts the identity of felt bodily changes and emotions. What should one do, then, with these apparently conflicting and certainly confusing claims made by James? One option, sometimes popular with readers of James, is to bite the bullet and conclude with exasperation that James just flat-out contradicts himself. We could wish his explanations were clearer, but they are not. For all the benefits of his creative thinking and colorful writing, James was not a systematic thinker and thus his explanations sometimes are confused.

---

[35] Prinz, *Gut Reactions*, 52, 55, 58.
[36] Prinz, *Gut Reactions*, 52.
[37] Prinz, *Gut Reactions*, 58.
[38] Prinz, *Gut Reactions*, 244.
[39] Prinz, *Gut Reactions*, 45.

This approach is not entirely misguided, but there is another option that can reconcile the seemingly contradictory claims made by James about emotion and bodily changes. We should pause to check the assumption that those claims necessarily conflict with each other. This will enable a more generous reading of James that doesn't dismiss him as muddle-headed. James's claims that emotion is an *effect* of a bodily cause and that emotion *is* a bodily state when felt can be read as complementary if causation is not assumed to be linear. Aristotle perhaps was the first philosopher to teach us about the multiple and complex ways that causation can occur.[40] What we today usually think of as causation is only one possible type, namely something close to what Aristotle called efficient causation, in which event A temporally precedes event B and thus makes event B happen. But another type of causation relevant to how we read James's work is what Aristotle called material causation, in which the matter of a thing makes it be what it is. Thus the wood that a table is made of is the table's material cause (while the carpenter who builds the table is its efficient cause). The crucial point here is that temporality and linear causation are irrelevant to material causation. What is relevant is the "stuff" that constitutes something. If we understand James's causal claims about emotion as describing something like its material rather than its efficient cause, his seemingly contradictory claims are not contradictory at all. Bodily changes don't exist first and then come to be represented or registered by (mental) emotions. Bodily changes instead are the stuff out of which emotion is constituted. Their relationship is neither temporal nor linear. Emotions just are bodily changes when those changes are constituted by evaluative judgments (or appraisals, in Prinz's terms) of the transactional relationship that an organism has with its various environments.

This reading of James through an Aristotelian lens admittedly is not based on evidence that James was thinking of Aristotle when he wrote the *Principles*. (I note, however, that the pragmatist account of habit that James, with Peirce and Dewey, helped develop, has its roots in Aristotle's account of virtue discussed in the *Nicomachean Ethics*, which involves the education and management of emotional habits.[41]) Rather than ask about James's intentions when writing the *Principles*, I want to argue in pragmatist fashion for the fruitfulness of reading James's causal language in a complex, non-linear way. This reading is more consistent with James's overall corpus than a linear reading since it complements his (and pragmatism's more generally) attempts to eschew rigid dichotomies. It also saves us from writing off the apparent contradictions in James's emotion chapter as the faults of a confused or imprecise thinker. These "contradictions" can be read instead

---

[40] Aristotle, *The Metaphysics*, trans. Hugh Tredennick (Cambridge, MA: Harvard University Press, 1989).

[41] Aristotle, *Nicomachean Ethics*, trans. Terence Irwin (Indianapolis, IN: Hackett Publishing, 1985).

as a radical attempt to think emotion as bodily in ways that challenge mind-body dualisms. This understanding of James's causal claims best complements the pragmatist—and often non-linear—spirit of James's work across his career.

Let's now return to the organism's relationship with the world and to the "exciting objects," as James calls them, that generate the bodily changes that are emotions. On James' account, the exciting object can be ideal, imagined, and/or anticipated. It need not have occurred, or occurred yet, or it could be an event that is similar to something that happened in the past. For example, even before a person receives a painful shot in the arm, she can feel fearful about the event, recalling the pain she felt the last time she got a shot. The not-yet-happened quality of the upcoming shot does not change the physiological basis of emotional responses to it, however. One can anticipate, or even imagine a situation, and that imagined event can trigger bodily reactions (such as a clenched gut and tense shoulders at the thought of going to the doctor) that are felt as emotions (in this case, of anxiety and fear).

Although James does not elaborate the following point, his discussion of exciting objects is the place in his account to underscore how people's experiences and expectations help give meaning to—we could say, materialize in—the physiology of their emotional responses to the world. The needle that the nurse brings up to your arm, as well as your fearful reaction to it, are part of a social world that is entangled with past experiences (and not merely your own) that give the event of receiving a shot its epistemic-emotional meaning. When James claims that "bodily changes follow directly the perception of the exciting fact," we don't need to insert the social world as an intervening third term because it is experientially baked into our bodily understandings of and knowledge about the world.[42] It is why "we" know to be scared of a bear encountered in the forest, but that "we" is a particular "we" with a cultural and perhaps personal bank of experiences and relationships with the world that codes bears as frightening. Not everyone would have that knowledge or experience fear. For example, something like respect for the power and strength of bears might be an alternative form of emotional knowledge that would evoke a different response to stumbling upon one. It's not that one of these forms of knowledge necessarily is right while the other is wrong. And no form of knowledge, bodily or otherwise, is infallible. The point instead is that human bodies are socialized in different ways for emotions, and we don't need to look for something "mental" apart from human bodies and the world in which they transact to find the social and cultural sources of their meaning. James's fully naturalistic account of emotion does not flatten the

---

[42] William James, *The Principles of Psychology*, Volume Two (New York: Dover Publications, Inc., 1950) 449. For more on the sociality of James's theory of emotion, see Kaag, "Getting Under My Skin."

social and political terrain into something "vile and [reductively] material," as James reassured his nineteenth century audience. The social meaning and judgments embodied in our emotions are precisely part of the "inner measure of worth" that emotions frequently carry.

James also speaks of anticipating not just events, but also emotions themselves. He gives the example of a person (apparently James himself) who once fainted at the sight of blood and then later felt anxious watching the preparations for a bloody surgical operation. It might seem in this case that the emotion (of anxiety) precedes bodily symptoms of a future fainting spell (plummeting blood pressure, dizziness, etc.), but James argues that the situation instead is one of anticipating bodily symptoms by recalling them from the past, which helps bring on feelings of anxiety in the present. The person who once fainted and now stares at the surgical knives "anticipates certain feelings [for example, of dizziness] and the anticipation precipitates their arrival."[43] Anxiety can beget anxiety, in other words, but this doesn't make it (or any other emotion) a piece of disembodied mental stuff. Even in their ideality—their anticipation and recollection—emotions can't be separated from actual physiological changes because they just are the feeling of those changes.

Properly speaking, then, my daughter's anger at her older sister didn't come *after* she began crying, but this is not to say that her anger preceded her tears. Both causal accounts of the situation are misleading, although I think James would say the first one is superior to the second if we insist on using "crude," causal language. On James' fully considered account, my daughter's anger *is* her felt bodily response of crying (at the "exciting object" of her sister's snub). Her tears and her anger are part of an organic whole, an embodied organism's transaction with the world, not separate phenomenon that we have to puzzle to put back together in the correct sequence. But what then about tears of sadness? If felt bodily changes and emotions just are the same thing, how do we explain different emotions, such as anger and sadness, as felt experiences of the same bodily phenomenon, such as crying?

James's answer would be that it is not the same bodily phenomenon. Of course, on a gross level, it is the same: whether they are tears of anger or sadness, my daughter is crying. But why do we tend to assume that all crying is the same? If the felt emotions of crying are different—anger versus sadness, and there are many others, such as frustration and even joy, that we could add to the list—then why not hypothesize that the bodily changes being experienced are subtly, or even not-so-subtly, different too? Invoking his earlier accounts of movement and instinct in *Principles,* James takes the bull by the horns and argues

---

[43] James, *The Principles of Psychology*, 458.

the changes [in the body excited by objects] are so indefinitely numerous
and subtle that the entire organism may be called a sounding-board. . . .
The various permutations and combinations of which these organic activities are susceptible make it abstractly possible that no shade of emotion,
however slight, should be without a bodily reverberation as unique, when
taken its totality, as is the [emotion] itself.[44]

This helps explain why it is so difficult to imitate or reproduce an emotion
on demand, apart from a genuine instance of its exciting object. There are
many physiological changes and responses to the world that compose any
particular emotion, and in addition to their large number and complex inter-
relations, most of those changes are not under our conscious control. "We
may catch the trick with the voluntary muscles," as James explains, "but fail
with the skin, glands, heart, and other viscera."[45] As James claims, our entire
physiological being is like a sophisticated sounding board that quivers and
vibrates in response to the world in innumerable ways.[46] The shades of difference in an organism's reverberations are what give rise to a vast number of
emotional possibilities, each with their own unique physiological stamp.

Again, at a gross level, this uniqueness might not be obvious. I sometimes
can tell the difference between my daughter's tears of sadness and her tears of
anger, but most of the time they are indistinguishable to my eye and ear. But
if we obtained just slightly more sophisticated physiological data, we might
find that there are differences in, for example, her heart rate, her blood pressure, or her adrenaline output when she cries tears of anger versus those of
sadness. Those complex bundles of related but slightly different physiological phenomena would be different sorts of tears. And on James's account,
those chemically different tears also would be felt differently by my daughter.
(I'll return shortly to this issue as I part ways with James's claim that bodily
changes necessarily are felt.)

As Jesse Prinz notes, the claim that emotions are physiologically distinct
continues to be controversial today. "Nevertheless," he rightly asserts, "existing [empirical] evidence is suggestive" and supports James' so-called abstract
possibility.[47] For starters, tears contain a variety of substances, such as proteins, enzymes, lipids, metabolites, and electrolytes, and the specific chemical
makeup of non-emotional tears (for example, reflexive tearing to clear debris
from the eye) is different from emotional tears.[48] This last fact helps explain

---

[44] James, *The Principles of Psychology*, 450.

[45] James, *The Principles of Psychology*, 450.

[46] James, *The Principles of Psychology*, 471.

[47] Prinz, *Gut Reactions*, 72.

[48] Shani Gelstein, Yaara Yeshurun, Liron Rozenkrantz, Sagit Shushan, Idan Frumin, Yehudah
Roth, and Noam Sobel, "Human Tears Contain a Chemosignal," www.sciencexpress.org, January 6,
2011, 1. Also published in *Science*, January 14, 2011: 226–230.

why a person doesn't typically feel sad or angry when she cries to flush an eyelash out of her eye. This isn't proof of the physiological difference between sad and angry tears, but it does demonstrate that not all tears are chemically the same and their difference is related to a person's emotions.

Even more helpful for James's case is a study reported by Prinz that at least some emotions can be distinguished by their physiological states.[49] Psychologists recently measured the heart rate, finger temperature, and electrical conductivity of the skin associated with six different emotions: happiness, anger, fear, sadness, disgust, and surprise. What they found was not that each emotion was marked by a unique physiological change, but rather that they could be distinguished by the *pattern* of their various changes. Based on heart rate and skin conductance, so-called positive emotions such as happiness were distinguishable from so-called negative emotions such as anger and fear. Moreover, there were differences in pattern between the negative emotions: for example, anger produced higher finger temperatures than fear did, while anger, fear and sadness all produced a higher heart rate than disgust did. James's abstract possibility thus needs to be clarified: if "bodily reverberation" means a single physiological change, then the case that each emotion is physiologically distinct is difficult to make. But if "bodily reverberation" includes a distinctive pattern or coalition of physiological states, then James's position becomes much stronger. Some emotions have distinctive patterns of physiological changes, and as Prinz notes, if future research included a greater number of physiological responses, then further and more fine-tuned distinctions between different emotions could emerge.[50]

It thus is not that James was wrong and emotions must precede felt bodily changes, such as crying. It rather is that James appears to have been right in ways that were far ahead of his time: different physiological combinations can and often do feel emotionally different to an organism. In the case of tears, a chemical combination of these proteins and those hormones, for example, is emotionally-physiologically felt by the organism as different (say, sadness and a higher heart rate, to oversimplify) from the combination of these other proteins and those other hormones (say, anger and warmer fingertips, again to oversimplify). And indeed, the feeling of different chemical combinations in tears isn't necessarily restricted to the organism who is crying. It also can be physiologically experienced by other people. (I will return to this issue below.)

I have been careful to this point to describe emotion as the feeling of physiological changes, consistent with James' claim that all emotions are (consciously) felt. James makes this claim as strongly as possible, with his characteristic italics and capitalization: "*every one of the bodily changes,*

---

[49] Prinz, *Gut Reactions*, 73.

[50] Prinz, *Gut Reactions*, 73.

whatsoever it be, is FELT, *acutely or obscurely, the moment it occurs. . . .* [E]very change that occurs must be felt."[51] But I want now to complicate James' identification of emotion with feeling. In one respect, as we have seen, this identification is entirely welcome because it insists that emotion is fundamentally physiological. But in another respect, the identification of emotion and feeling is problematic because it oversimplifies emotions by neglecting ones that are not felt. We need to distinguish two types of unfelt emotions: non-conscious emotions, which occur without our noticing them but that can fairly easily be brought to conscious attention; and unconscious emotions, which tend to be tangled up in processes of repression, actively resisting conscious awareness, because they are too personally painful or socially unacceptable to consciously acknowledge. Both non-conscious and unconscious emotions are physiological, but if feeling always and necessarily involves conscious awareness, then neither is necessarily felt.

James acknowledges that people often don't pay attention to the subtleties of their various bodily feelings, but he argues that if a person slows down enough to give them some attention, she will be surprised at how much emotional information about herself she can receive. As James says,

> It would be perhaps too much for to expect [a person] to arrest the tide of any strong gust of passion for the sake of any such curious analysis as this; but he [or she] can observe more tranquil states . . . [and] it is surprising what little [bodily] items give accent to these complexes of sensibility. When worried by any slight trouble, one may find that the focus of one's bodily consciousness is the contraction, often quite inconsiderable, of the eyes and brows . . . and so on for as many more instances as might be named.[52]

According to James, we might not be able to consciously control all of our bodily changes and states, but we can profitably attune ourselves to them and the way that "our whole cubic capacity is sensibly alive."[53]

No doubt James is right that much can be learned from greater conscious awareness of one's bodily changes. His work on emotion has been hailed as foreshadowing contemporary techniques of homeostatic regulation, such as biofeedback, in which a person uses on-the-spot physiological information (such as heart rate) to modify both her emotional and biological states.[54] But James is wrong to equate emotion with conscious feelings. There is both anecdotal and experimental evidence for non-conscious emotions. Prinz gives the example of being awakened in the night by the sound of shattering glass.[55] You

---

[51] James, *The Principles of Psychology*, 451, emphasis in original.
[52] James, *The Principles of Psychology*, 451.
[53] James, *The Principles of Psychology*, 451.
[54] Kaag, "Getting Under My Skin," 438–439.
[55] Prinz, "Are Emotions Feelings?" 17.

listen hard to hear where it came from while reaching under your bed for a baseball bat . . . and then you hear your cat meow and realize that she knocked a water glass off the table. Then, and only then, do you realize that your heart is racing and your body was tense but now is beginning to relax. You were afraid, but in the midst of your adrenaline-surged focus on the cause of the breaking glass, you didn't notice what you were feeling. You only became aware of your feeling of fear after the exciting event (as James would call it) passed.

James might reply that this merely is an example of one of those strong gusts of passions that a person can't be expected to arrest in order to focus on her bodily sensations. In principle, however, it could be done and the emotions could be felt at the time they were experienced. I think James is right, but I do not think he so easily can account for experimental evidence that emotions can impact a person's behavior without her realizing what she is feeling. In a recent social psychology study, for example, subjects were presented with pictures of faces that were neutral, angry, or happy, but the pictures were presented too rapidly for the subjects to be consciously aware of what they had seen.[56] When they subsequently were given a fruity drink and asked about the drink and their feelings, subjects who had seen the angry face and those who had seen the happy face reported being in the same mood as each other. They were statistically indistinguishable in terms of their consciously felt moods. The subjects who had seen angry faces, however, drank less of the beverage and ranked it as less appetizing than the subjects who had seen happy faces. The behavior and judgment of the subjects seems to have been impacted by their own emotional states, positive in one case and negative in another, but in both cases completely unawares. Studies such as these strongly suggest that unfelt emotions can be part of a person's self, impacting her life without her being aware of it.

Prinz uses the term "unconscious" to describe unfelt emotions, but he does not intend the term in its psychoanalytic sense, nor does he address instances of repressed emotion. Some unfelt emotions actively resist a person's conscious attempts to identify and change or eliminate them, however, and those emotions alone warrant the description "unconscious." Take the example of one of Sigmund Freud's earliest patients, Fraulein Elizabeth Von R., who was erotically attracted to her brother-in-law.[57] Out of love for her sister and a strong sense of conventional morality, Elizabeth did not act on her desire. Moreover, she was not even able to consciously acknowledge it (even though Freud—and perhaps others—became aware of it). Her erotic feelings did not disappear, however; they manifested themselves in physical pain in her

---

[56] This study is summarized in Prinz, "Are Emotions Feelings?" 17.

[57] Josef Breuer and Sigmund Freud, *Studies on Hysteria*, ed. and trans. James Strachey (New York: Basic Books, 1957) 135–181.

thigh that was medically inexplicable. It was as if being consciously aware of her painful thigh was much easier than being consciously aware of her forbidden emotions, and so Elizabeth chose the former over the latter. As Freud explains, if Elizabeth had become conscious of her erotic love for her brother-in-law,

> she would also inevitably become conscious of the contradiction between those feelings and her moral ideas and would have experienced mental torment. . . . She had no recollection of any such sufferings; she had avoided them. It followed that her feelings themselves did not become clear to her. . . . Her love for her brother-in-law was present in her consciousness like a foreign body, without having entered into relationship with the rest of her ideational life.[58]

As Elizabeth's case suggests, the isolation of unconscious emotions from conscious awareness isn't an accident or oversight, as if they had been overlooked but easily could be felt if a person's just turned her attention to them. Unconscious emotions can remain completely foreign to a person's conscious life, as Elizabeth's forbidden love apparently did. This is not a principled claim that unconscious emotions can never be felt. After all, the goal of psychoanalytic theory and practice (Freud's version, in any case) is to bring unconscious emotions and beliefs to conscious awareness so that the pain and disruption they are causing can be ameliorated. But in practice, unconscious emotions can be thoroughly inaccessible to conscious awareness in ways that non-conscious emotions are not.

I want to underscore that the difference between non-conscious and unconscious emotions turns on the question of accessibility to conscious awareness, not on the question of which are "really" or more fully emotional. Unconscious habits, such as those connected with Elizabeth's love, often are more closely identified with emotions, likely because of the strong, forbidden experiences with which they are associated. Non-conscious habits, such as (for the sake of argument) the way a person puts on her shoes or drives a car, sometimes are treated as if they are unrelated to issues of emotion. They are assumed to be unanimated by any particular affective or emotional investment in the world. Freud's early work on affect (by which he meant something that includes "emotion") perhaps is at the root of this problem, characterizing catharsis and abreaction as the discharge of unconscious affect, as if the repressed body contained too much emotion and thus the body freed from repression would be rendered relatively unemotional.[59]

In contrast, on the account I am developing here, all physiological movements and states are potentially emotional because, following Malabou, they

---

[58] Breuer and Freud, *Studies on Hysteria*, 165.
[59] Sigmund Freud, *Studies on Hysteria*, 8–11.

all are instances of a bodily organism's affective relationship with itself and the world. Let me say more about my use of "affective" to refer to a living being's interested comportment to the world. Affect often is diffuse and difficult to identify with precision, unlike emotion, which is a more discrete, concentrated type of affective investment. Affect could be thought of caring in that an organic body cares about itself as it engages and forms attachments and aversions with/in the world. As John Dewey has argued along similar lines, the "difference between living and non-living things is that the activities of the former are characterized by needs, by efforts which are active demands to satisfy needs, and by satisfactions."[60] When an organic body no longer has those interested, affective relationships, it dies. It no longer transacts with the world in such a way as to maintain its physiological organization as *this* being and not another.

In contrast, inorganic beings don't care: they don't manifest an interest in guiding their relationships with the world. Take a piece of iron as an example. As Dewey explains, "iron as such exhibits characteristics of bias or selective emphasis [i.e., it rusts when it comes in contact with H^2O but not with CO^2], but it shows no bias in favor of remaining simple iron; it had just as soon, so to speak, become iron-oxide. It shows no tendency in its interaction with water to modify the interaction so that consequences will perpetuate the characteristics of pure iron. If it did, it would have the marks of a living being."[61] To be alive is to be in favor of some things and opposed to others. It is, in other words, to be affective. Being affective, moreover, does not require repression even as affectivity is a condition for the possibility of repression. Even homeostasis, which is the basic physiological process by which an organism maintains its autonomic, neuroendocrine, and other bodily functions, can be considered an affective process involving sensations and motivations with autonomic and behavioral effects.[62] We should not reductively flatten even these most basic physiological processes into quasi-mechanical actions that are solely for the purpose of survival. They too are animated by an interested, motivated relationship with the world, which perhaps is most obvious when we think of pain as a member of the family of homeostatic emotions.[63] The human body is fully affective not just

---

[60] John Dewey, *Experience and Nature*, vol. 1 of *The Later Works, 1925–1953*, ed. Jo Ann Boydston (Carbondale, IL: Southern Illinois University Press, 1988) 194.

[61] Dewey, *Experience and Nature*, 195.

[62] A.D. (Bud) Craig, "A new view of pain as homeostatic emotion," *Trends in Neurosciences*, June 2003, 26(6): 303–307. Catherine Malabou also argues "homeostasis is an affective economy" (Malabou, *The New Wounded: From Neurosis to Brain Damage*, trans. Steven Miller [Bronx, NY: Fordham University Press, 2012] 37). See also Dewey, *Experience and Nature*, 194, on "satisfaction" as reestablishing an organism's pattern of equilibrium that "need" had put into tension or disequilibrium.

[63] Craig, "A new view of pain as homeostatic emotion," 303.

when it develops unconscious habits, but also when it is constituted by less spectacular, non-conscious ones.

With this emendation of James, we can say that neither affect nor emotion should be identified with feeling, but this not because unfelt emotions and unfelt affects are some kind of non-bodily mind stuff. And it also is not, contra cognitivism, because the feeling component of emotions and affects is cognitively insignificant. On my terms, both affect and emotion can be either felt or unfelt, although affect is even more likely than emotion to be unfelt. James was right both to elevate the status of bodily feelings and to argue that all emotions are bodily, but not to insist all bodily states are consciously felt. Some bodily states are non-conscious, and some even actively resist conscious awareness and thus are unconscious. All bodily states are affective, however, and they all at least potentially have epistemological value. This is because whether consciously felt or not, they all say something about a person's relationship to and engagement with the world. As for emotion, while not all bodily states are emotions, all emotions are bodily. The upshot here is that the body is never dumb, and to identify emotion and affect with physiological changes and conditions does not trivialize or demean them. In many ways, this is the most significant contribution that James can make to a feminist and critical philosophy of race on the subject of emotion and affect: he shows us how to embrace physiological processes as an important source of affective and emotional knowledge.

But does James's embrace of physiology in his account of emotion cause a different type of problem for feminist and critical philosophy of race, namely that of smuggling in an atomistic view of the individual? This would be an individual—albeit embodied in James' case—that supposedly is sealed off from the world around it, as if one could understand first the affective and emotional physiology of the individual and then secondarily ask how the individual's emotions and affective relationships with the world either impacted or were changed by it. John Dewey had precisely this concern, objecting in part to James' first major book on the grounds that "the point of view [in *The Principles of Psychology*] remained that of a realm of consciousness set off by itself."[64] In contrast to Dewey, James famously focused on the value and uniqueness of the individual throughout his career. And there are passages in James' chapter in *Principles* on emotion in particular that sound as if the individual and her emotions are contained fundamentally within the self. When contrasting emotion with the instincts, for example, James claims that even though they shade into each other, "emotions . . . fall short of instincts in that the emotional reaction usually terminates in the subject's own body, whilst

---

[64] John Dewey, "From Absolutism to Experimentalism," in volume 5 of *John Dewey: The Later Works, 1925–1953*, ed. Jo Ann Boydston (Carbondale, IL: Southern Illinois University Press, 1988) 157.

the instinctive reaction is apt to go farther and enter into practical relations with the exciting object."[65] And when James discusses the "moral education" of how to eliminate unwanted and/or undesirable emotions, his instructions to the reader tend to be asocial and non-transactional, remaining firmly in the realm of willing oneself to change one's bodily comportment. As he recommends, "we must assiduously, and in the first instance cold-bloodedly, go through the *outward movements* of those contrary dispositions which we prefer to cultivate. . . . Smooth the brow, brighten the eye, contract the dorsal rather than the ventral aspect of the frame, and speak in a major key, pass the genial compliment, and your heart must be frigid indeed if it do not gradually thaw!"[66]

James most likely is an individualist, but I won't try to establish here whether or not his individualism is atomistic.[67] What I wish to point out instead is that his individualism—whatever its nature—and his emphasis upon physiology are not the same thing. They can be peeled apart, and one can give physiology pride of place in an account of emotion and affect (and ontology more generally) without supporting atomistic individualism. While I don't believe that a transactional account of the physiology of emotion and affect necessarily conflicts with James' *Principles*, the transactional aspects of both physiology and emotion/affect need strengthening in his work if it is to be helpful to feminist and critical philosophy of race. A fully adequate account of emotion and affect must appreciate and elaborate the constitutive emotional and affective economy that circulates inter- and transpersonally.

In order to explain that economy, let me return to the section of James' recommendation regarding moral education in which he urges a depressed person not only to contract or relax certain muscles, but also to "pass the genial compliment." Here, if only briefly, James appreciates that emotions are not sealed up within an individual, but can arise from engagement with the social environment. This doesn't mean that James is qualifying or backing away from a physiological understanding of emotion. It means instead that the physiological and the social are co-constituted in complex and dynamic ways. James suggests that saying something kind to a friend changes your relationship with the social world in ways that can change your bodily

---

[65] James, *The Principles of Psychology*, 442.

[66] James, *The Principles of Psychology*, 463. Compare Bessel Van der Kolk's discussion of the Polyvagal Theory, which is "based on the subtle interplay between the visceral experiences of our own bodies and the voices and faces of the people around us. It explain[s] why a kind face or soothing tone of voice can dramatically alter the way we feel" (Van der Kolk, *The Body Keeps the Score: Brain, Mind, and Body in the Healing of Trauma* [New York: Viking, 2014] 78).

[67] For more on James' individualism, see Pawelski, *The Dynamic Individualism of William James*. Jeremy Carrette has argued that James's individualism is social, rather than private, in Carrette, *William James's Hidden Religious Imagination*, 134–155. See also Kaag, "Getting Under My Skin" on James, emotion and sociality.

condition and thus also your emotional state. How then might this complex relationship work?

James is fairly silent in response to this question, but he can point us in one helpful direction. As he argued for the bodily nature of emotion, James was more correct than he realized when he claimed, "if I were to become corporeally anaesthetic, I should be excluded from the life of the affections."[68] James means that if a person didn't experience bodily changes and feelings—as if she were disembodied—then that person wouldn't be able to experience emotion. But the life of emotion that this mythically disembodied person would miss out on is far greater than merely one's own. It also would be the life of emotions more generally, including the ability to read other people's emotions.

We can find support for this claim in a recent controlled study of the effects of Botox, which greatly reduces the ability of facial muscles to move (hence eliminating wrinkles).[69] People in the study who used Botox suffered an impaired ability to recognize other people's facial emotions, as compared to another group who underwent a cosmetic procedure (using a dermal filler) that didn't affect muscular movement. On the flipside, in the second part of the study people who had a resistant gel applied to their facial skin (similar to a facial mask) experienced an amplified ability to read and understand the facial emotions of other people. The latter group was able to move their facial muscles, but to do so they had to contract their muscles in an exaggerated way to combat the resistance of the dried gel. What is especially significant about this study is that the methods it used to restrict muscular movement did not alter the participants' central nervous system. For example, they did not involve simultaneous tasks that occupied a person's attention, which might mean that a person's increased cognitive load would explain why she had trouble reading another person's face. It was the physical movement of muscles, or lack thereof, that correlated with a person's increased or reduced ability to understand other people's facial emotions.

The methods used in this study underscore the claim that emotion is bodily motion, and they also help explain why paying someone a compliment with a genial expression on one's face might alleviate depression: the world becomes less alienating and more of a place of communication and community with others. Move your facial muscles—the more vigorously the better—and not only will you amplify your own emotional life, but you also will be better able to understand the emotional world around you. Freeze or eliminate your facial muscular contractions, and not only will you dampen

---

[68] James, *Principles of Psychology*, 452–453.
[69] David T. Neal and Tanya L. Chartrand, "Embodied Emotion Perception: Amplifying and Dampening Facial Feedback Modulates Emotional Perception Accuracy," *Social Psychological and Personality Science*, November 2011, 2(6): 673–678.

many of your own emotions, but you also will isolate yourself from others by losing the ability to relate to them.

Teresa Brennan's notion of the transmission of affect offers a complementary avenue for understanding the affective and emotional economies that circulate between people. As Brennan comments on James' account of emotion, she pushes it beyond its narrow focus on the physiological without undermining the role of the body in emotional experience. In her words (using "affect" for James's "emotion"),

> the affect might, indeed, be the passive perception of a bodily motion (as William James surmised), but this need not mean the motion caused the affect, or the affect the motion. In some cases both affect and motion (hormones in these cases [that Brennan discussed earlier]) are responding to a third factor altogether: the social environment, whose air can be thick with anxiety-provoking pheromones (or "human chemosignals," to use the preferred term).[70]

Like James, Brennan insists that the important issue on the table is not whether bodily changes cause emotions or vice versa. But improving upon James, Brennan explicitly redirects the issue to more than just the physiological nature of emotions. Agreeing that emotions and affects are bodily, she focuses on the way that they are generated by a social environment, just as a person's physiological (and thus emotional/affective) state helps generate a particular social, psychological atmosphere. The traffic between the physiological and the social runs two ways, as Brennan asserts in the epigram above, which means that the social gets into the flesh of our bodies and that our flesh helps constitute the atmosphere of the social world.

The transactional nature of the social and biological also means that one person's physiology can get into the physiology of another person via emotional and affective pathways. Brennan calls this the transmission of affect: "the emotions or affects of one person, and the enhancing or depressing energies these affects entail, can enter into another [person]."[71] For example, a friend's sadness can make you sad too, just as her joy can make you very happy. The transmission of emotions doesn't necessarily produce the same emotion in the one who receives it, however. A person's joy can make you feel resentful of her happiness and good fortune. Or a family member's anger can make you depressed and withdrawn. The key point in all these examples is that affective and emotional transmission is not the transmission of mental attitudes or "mind stuff." We might say that it is the transmission of "body

---

[70] Brennan, *The Transmission of Affect*, 77.

[71] Brennan, *Transmission of Affect*, 3. See also Nicholas A. Christakis and James H. Fowler, *Connected: The Surprising Power of Our Social Networks and How They Shape Our Lives* (New York: Little, Brown and Company, 2009).

stuff": one person's bodily state is transmitted to another person's flesh, altering most directly the receiving person's physiology (and then indirectly the original person's physiology as well, through the resulting bodily changes in the receiving person that are then part of the social environment that feeds back into the original person).

But what exactly is this body stuff that's being transmitted? What is the physiological mechanism by which one person's flesh could affectively enter and alter another person's flesh in their mundane, everyday interactions? One possible answer is found in the phenomenon of entrainment. Often referred to as chemical or electrical, entrainment occurs when "one person's or one group's nervous and hormonal systems are brought into alignment with another's."[72] Nervous entrainment tends to operate via sight, touch, and hearing, as well as bodily movements, especially those that are rhythmic.[73] Line dancing offers an excellent example of nervous entrainment, as does a crowd's doing the wave in a large sports stadium. These phenomena illustrate how nervous entrainment can be compatible with conscious purpose and guidance.[74] The alignment of one's bodily gestures and muscular contractions with those of other people can be a product of deliberate, thoughtful attempts to achieve synchronization.

Hormonal/chemical entrainment, in contrast, almost always happens non- or unconsciously, and according to Brennan, it is one of the primary vehicles for affective and emotional transmission, via the sense of smell and pheromones in particular.[75] Pheromones are "compounds that regulate a specific neuroendocrine mechanism in other people without being consciously detected as odours [*sic*]."[76] A popular example of hormonal/chemical entrainment via pheromones within human circles is the alignment of menstrual cycles in a group of girls or women when they live together.[77] While the methodology of the initial research that made this claim has been criticized strongly, its larger point concerning the existence of hormonal entrainment has been supported in subsequent empirical studies. Evidence exists, for example, that odorless compounds taken from the armpits of women in the late phase of their menstrual cycles speeds up the production of certain hormones and shortened the menstrual cycles of other women who sniffed them, while samples taken from the same women during ovulation delay the production of those hormones in other women and thus lengthened their menstrual cycle.[78]

---

[72] Brennan, *The Transmission of Affect*, 9.

[73] Brennan, *Transmission of Affect*, 70. See also Van der Kolk, *The Body Keeps the Score*, 58–59, 213.

[74] Brennan, *Transmission of Affect*, 70.

[75] Brennan, *Transmission of Affect*, 9–11.

[76] Kathleen Stern and Martha K. McClintock, "Regulation of ovulation by human pheromones," *Nature*, March 1998, 392: 177.

[77] Martha K. McClintock, "Menstrual Synchrony and Suppression," *Nature*, 1971, 229: 244–245.

[78] Stern and McClintock, "Regulation of ovulation by human pheromones," 177.

Another, less controversial example of pheromonal influence between human beings is provided by mother-newborn interactions. Since the early 2000s, "it [has become] increasingly clear that pheromone-like chemicals probably play a role in offspring identification and mother recognition" via chemicals excreted around the mother's nipple-aureola area during and shortly after giving birth.[79] Newborn babies will wriggle toward their mother's breast to attempt to nurse, and scientists hypothesize that women's different olfactory patterns help newborns distinguish their mother from other people.[80]

Sight and hearing also can contribute to chemical entrainment, but the drawback to focusing on them is that they tend to be treated as senses possessed by atomistically separate individuals. Not so in the case of smell and pheromones. As Brennan explains, "repeatedly, we will find that sight is the preferred mechanism in explaining any form of transmission (when evidence for transmission is noted), because this sense appears to leave the boundaries of discrete individuals relatively intact. Smell and various forms of neuronal communication are not such respecters of persons."[81] Hormones, pheromones, and other sorts of chemosignals are material parts of a person that can waft through the air into the flesh of another person. This happens most powerfully via the nose and related neurons involved in smelling and odorless forms of olfactory perception.

The different chemosignals found in tears further support Brennan's claims about entrainment. It's not just the case that tears of sadness, for example, have a chemical make-up distinct from that of non-emotional tears. Their distinct chemical make-up also can physiologically and emotionally impact other people in distinctive ways. In a recent study of human tears, neurobiologists demonstrated that women's emotional tears of sadness reduced testosterone levels in men.[82] They also reduced the men's sexual arousal, both self-rated and physiologically measured. The tears were collected from women who watched sad movies in isolation, and then the tears were presented to men in a separate setting. The men alternatively sniffed, on separate days, unmarked vials of either tears or standard saline, and then were asked to rate the level of sadness and degree of attractiveness of on-screen images of women's faces that were intentionally selected by the researchers to be emotionally ambiguous. The set-up of this study allowed the researchers to narrow the explanatory cause of the men's evaluations of the women's faces

---

[79] Stefano Vaglio, "Chemical Communication and Mother-Infant Recognition," *Communicative and Integrative Biology*, May–June 2009, 2(3): 279–281, http://www.ncbi.nlm.nih.gov/pmc/articles/PMC2717541/, accessed June 17, 2013.

[80] Vaglio, "Chemical Communication and Mother-Infant Recognition," http://www.ncbi.nlm.nih.gov/pmc/articles/PMC2717541/, accessed June 17, 2013.

[81] Brennan, *Transmission of Affect*, 10.

[82] Gelstein et al., "Human Tears Contain a Chemosignal," 1.

to the chemical composition of sad tears versus, for example, their emotional reaction upon seeing and hearing a woman crying.

The emotional tears impacted the men's testosterone and sexual arousal levels even though they could not be distinguished from plain saline in terms of their odor. The overall smell, including perceived the perceived intensity, pleasantness, and familiarity, of the women's tears was indistinguishable from that of saline.[83] Neither the saline nor the emotional tears smelled like much of anything. Strictly speaking, then, we might say that the transmission of emotion documented by the emotional tears study was not an instance of smelling, but an instance of the transmission of pheromones. The men non-consciously detected the sadness of the women who cried and that "odor" altered their physio-affective condition.

And what about the women, we might well ask? For example, what about the impact of women's tears of sadness on other women—in general, and also on their levels of sexual arousal? Or the impact of men's tears on women—again, in general and also in terms of women's libido? Reading this study with a feminist lens, these questions and a number of others follow. In particular, we could ask about the scientists' choice to study women's tears in narrow relation to men's sexual arousal (or lack thereof), as if women's sadness was significant only if and when it impacted men in unwanted ways. Because the study is silent on these issues, it has the unsettling effect of implying that sad women are to blame if men experience a low sex drive and that women should appear happy and avoid crying so that men can remain vigorously masculine. Read with a critical eye, however, the study nonetheless is valuable for its demonstration of the physiological-emotional circuits that can connect people. It's not overly simple to summarize the study by saying that the flesh of sad women got into and deflated the flesh of a group of men via the chemicals "contained" in the women's tears—using scare-quotes, of course, because the point is that the chemicals and women's emotions weren't contained at all. They traveled across and through people, not collapsing their emotional identities but certainly enacting the permeability of the boundaries between them. The men in the study had physio-affective reactions that were different than those of the women—in that sense the men had their "own" affect and emotions. But in another crucial sense, one that draws sharp lines between things to distinguish them, the men's affects and emotions were not entirely their own. This is because they were regulated in part by the emotions of the women.

Let me now return to Jaggar's exclusion of hunger pangs and other automatic physical responses and (seemingly) unintentional sensations from the realm of emotion and affect to argue that even in this most challenging case,

---

[83] Gelstein et al., "Human Tears Contain a Chemosignal," 1, 2.

we can find not only affect and emotion, but also their possible transmission between people. Perhaps most simply, hunger pangs can be defined as a bodily change that signals a need for nutrition. In this sense, hunger is one of the body's several homeostatic emotions.[84] But hunger just as briefly, if not simply, could be defined as a bodily change that signals a desire for food. Being hungry does not necessarily mean that one's body lacks calories, and people can be hungry for a variety of reasons, as the term "desire" hints. Consider a homesick college student who walks past a bakery and instantly experiences hunger pangs when she smells dinner rolls just like her mother or father bakes at home. Her hunger is an automatic physical sensation, a physiological response to the world that she did not consciously will. She did not "intend" her hunger in that sense, but her hunger nonetheless is intentional because it picks out a particular part of the world as meaningful to her life. (I suspect that many physiological sensations that seem not to be about anything—that is, "dumb"—turn out to be quite intentional, or "smart," on a non- or unconscious level.) Above all, with James, I would say that her hunger is at minimum an affect, and possibly also an emotion. I also would caution that the term "homeostatic" not be read reductively. The physiological pang experienced by the student in this example is not "merely" a physical pain. It also is a complex emotional-affective mixture of longing, sadness, and the need to reestablish psychosomatic balance and attachment with the world.

Lack of hunger also can tell us a great deal about automatic physical sensations as affective, and perhaps also as emotional in some cases. Oftentimes, people who are severely depressed do not experience hunger and have a very difficult time drumming up the desire to eat. Their lack of hunger is not simply a physiological event. It also is a social-psychological experience in which a person lacks meaningful connections to and with the world. As Elizabeth Wilson has argued, "the struggle to eat ... when depressed is a struggle to mediate difficult, attenuated, or lost relations to others and the outside world."[85] A lack of hunger can be a statement that a depressed person does not want to take in the world, and this gut-level refusal is not a metaphor but a literal socio-affective-physiological experience. In return, for a depressed person to recover a physical sense of hunger often is for her to regain an affective-emotional life that includes engagement and caring, both for herself and for others.

Understanding hunger simultaneously as an automatic physical response and an affect and/or emotion, we can see why it might make sense to talk about its possible transmission between people. One person's hunger pang might not

---

[84] As are temperature, itch, thirst, and even pain. Craig, "A New View of Pain as Homeostatic Emotion," 303.

[85] Elizabeth A. Wilson, *Psychosomatic: Feminism and the Neurological Body* (Durham, NC: Duke University Press, 2004) 45.

make another person feel the same physical sensation in her stomach, but it could have a significant effect on her mood and outlook on life. My hunger could be a physical manifestation of anxiety and stress, for example, and eating a way for me to distract myself from my worries rather than for me to obtain needed nourishment. In that case, I could infect those around me with my hunger—that is, with my psychosomatic state of stress—as I anxiously gulp down a beignet to alleviate my hunger pangs. And once I have transmitted my stress to other people, they too might begin to feel a subtly clenched pain in their stomachs—perhaps not identifying it as hunger (or maybe they too will begin to have pastry craving pangs), but physiologically changed nonetheless by my original bodily sensations.

On the account of affect and emotion developed to this point, we can say that affect and emotion are fully physiological; that human physiological states and conditions necessarily (because living) are fully affective and have the potential also to become emotional; that affect and emotion are transactional and interpersonal, at the same that they remain highly personal; that distinctions can and should be made physiologically between conscious, nonconscious, and unconscious affects and emotions; that feeling can be distinguished from both affect and emotion without resorting to cognitivism; and that feeling can be distinguished from both affect and emotion without making affect and emotion some sort of extra-bodily mind-stuff *and* without making affect and emotion epistemologically dumb. How might this account help us understand Michael Lee's hips and other cases of unexplained crying that occur when the body's muscles and fibers are moved?

The childhood fear generated by Lee's traumatic experience might have been, and likely was consciously felt at the time that Lee was beat up. Based on Lee's narrative, it then seems to have passed out of consciousness, becoming something that he didn't feel or think much about as an adult. It did not disappear, however, nor was it a matter of happenstance that he didn't notice its ongoing presence in his life. Using the language often employed by yoga practitioners and teachers, we might say that his fear was stored unconsciously in his body, more precisely in the tendons and muscles of his hips. (I will complicate this description below.) His increasingly tight pelvis and hamstrings worked to keep him from feeling the frightening experience he underwent as an eight-year-old boy. His hips, in other words, were the site of his unconscious resistance to conscious knowledge of how the childhood trauma persisted in his life and shaped his self. They provided a kind of muscular armor that shielded him from terror, but at the price of bodily flexibility—which is to say, at the price also of affective and emotional flexibility.[86] Conscious emotional pain was traded for conscious

---

[86] I take the term "muscular armor" from Wilhelm Reich, *Character Analysis*, third edition, trans. Vincent R. Carfagno (New York: Farrar, Straus and Giroux, 1972). See, in particular, chapter XIII,

physical pain through a process of repression and the creation of an unconscious habit. The physiological deal was made outside of conscious awareness so that Lee would notice only his tight hips.

It might be tempting to call Lee's hips "hysterical" because of the way that they embody emotional trauma, but my rendition of Lee's yoga experience differs from what Freud's notion of hysteria would provide on a couple of crucial points. While there are multiple types of hysteria analyzed in Freud's work—for example, anxiety hysteria, hysteroepilepsy, hypnoid hysteria, and retention hysteria—it is conversion hysteria that primarily has captured feminists' attention and that will be my focus here.[87] Despite the term's origins in the Greek word for "uterus"—and hence hysteria's sexist association with women in particular—hysteria is not restricted to women, nor is it necessarily characterized by a panicked loss of control as the colloquial use of the word suggests. Conversion hysteria occurs when a person's experience of a psychologically traumatic event is transformed—converted—into physical pain. Freud claims that because sexual conflicts and traumas produce "the most important and the most productive of pathological results," hysteria's association with the uterus is "nearer the truth" than other views that dismiss sexuality as unimportant to neuropathology.[88] Yet Freud also acknowledges that "the non-sexual affects of fright, anxiety, and anger [can] lead to the development of hysterical phenomena" and that "hysteria due to fright" counts as "traumatic hysteria proper."[89] Thus without necessarily prioritizing sexuality in the etiology of hysterical suffering, we can appreciate that in conversion hysteria, a person's desire or her experience of a troubling socio-psychological event tries to evade conscious attention by taking physio-biological form.

How does this conversion take place? Freud's answer is that emotions fuel it. Commenting on his patient Fraulein Rosalia H.'s twitching fingers, which hid/expressed her irritation at being suspected of complicity with her uncle's incestuous desires, Freud explains that "the energy for the conversion had been supplied, on the one hand, by freshly experienced affect [sic] [after Rosalia's aunt saw her playing the piano for her uncle] and, on the other, by recollected affect [after spurning her uncle's sexual advances years earlier]."[90] The initial sexual assault was not enough to make Rosalia's fingers twitch. It took a second upsetting event, related to the first, to generate enough emotion to trigger the hysterical conversion. The issue is purely quantitative, according

---

"Psychic Conflict and Vegetative Conflict," 285–354, and chapter XIV, "The Expressive Language of the Living," 355–389. While I don't wish to endorse all of Reich's ideas, I share his view that psychoanalysis should take biology seriously.

[87] Wilson, *Psychosomatic*, 4.

[88] Breuer and Freud, *Studies on Hysteria*, 247.

[89] Breuer and Freud, *Studies on Hysteria*, 246, 247.

[90] Breuer and Freud, *Studies on Hysteria*, 173.

to Freud: "the question [is] ... how much affective tension of this kind an organism can tolerate. Even a hysteric can retain a certain amount of affect that has not been dealt with; [however] if, owing to the occurrence of similar provoking causes, that amount is increased by summation to a point beyond the subject's tolerance, the impetus to conversion is given."[91] The seemingly uneventful event of being seen by her aunt playing the piano for her uncle was enough to tip Rosalia into hysteria, unable to control her resentful fingers which wished to flick away her aunt's unjust suspicions of her.

We can see here why, on Freud's own terms, his famous claim that "hysterics suffer mainly from reminiscences" is somewhat misleading.[92] It's not just that hysterics remember an event that was traumatic. Many people do so and they don't necessarily develop hysterical symptoms. The difference is that hysterics still have a high level of non-discharged emotion attached to their memories, sustaining them (both the hysterics and their memories) as traumatic/traumatized. When memories fade and lose their traumatic edge, it is because they have lost most or all of their emotional charge. The most important way in which this happens, Freud explains, is through "an energetic reaction to the event that provokes an affect [*sic*]. By 'reaction' we here understand the whole class of voluntary and involuntary reflexes—from tears to acts of revenge—in which, as experience shows us, the affects are discharged."[93] Reactions that successfully do this are what Freud calls "abreactions": they provide a channel for the release of emotion, which de-traumatizes the memory by robbing it of its energetic component.[94] The memory might linger, but without sufficient emotional fuel, it can't do much. It can't disrupt a person's psychosomatic health by generating hysterical symptoms.

On Freud's account, affect (emotion) is a problem, which helps explain why the psychoanalytic cure of catharsis involves discharging emotions. He tends to describe emotions as something burdensome to get rid of, something that makes a person ill. Or perhaps more accurately, while emotion is thoroughly central to Freud's studies of hysteria, it is only negative emotions that make an appearance in them: "negative" in that they threaten good health. The question of positive emotions that might promote good health and thus that should be cultivated rather than discarded never comes up in Freud's account of hysteria. Of course, Freud's work focuses on ill people who are suffering from various kinds of mental and physical pain, and thus is it might be understandable that negative emotions are his main focus. Nevertheless one effect of his work on hysteria is the narrowing of the broad category of affect and range of emotion to the limited category of negative emotions. This

---

[91] Breuer and Freud, *Studies on Hysteria*, 174.

[92] Breuer and Freud, *Studies on Hysteria*, 7.

[93] Breuer and Freud, *Studies on Hysteria*, 8.

[94] Freud introduces the term "abreaction" on Breuer and Freud, *Studies on Hysteria*, 8.

narrowing is problematic because it interferes with an appreciation of the live body as always and fully affective.

Let's return to the question of how exactly the conversion of emotion takes place. Doing so will help reveal the problematic mind-body split at the heart of conversion hysteria. How does a strong experience of fright, shame, and resentment, to take up Rosalia's case again, turn into uncontrollably twitchy fingers? Freud admits that he is stumped by this question, exclaiming, "I cannot, I must confess, give any hint of how a conversion of this kind is brought about. It is obviously not carried out in the same way as an intentional and voluntary action."[95] He then presses further, offering a tentative answer:

> [W]hat *is* it that turns into physical pain here? A cautious reply would be: something that might have become, and should have become *mental* pain. If we venture a little further and try to represent the ideational mechanism in a kind of algebraical [*sic*] picture, we may attribute a certain quota of affect to the ideational complex of these erotic feelings which remained unconscious, and say that this quantity (the quota of affect) is what was converted.[96]

Affect, or emotion, here is malleable and free ranging. It has the ability to transform itself into either mental or physical pain, operating as a kind of bridge that connects the mind and the body. Crossing this bridge does not occur intentionally or voluntarily; a person cannot consciously choose whether she will experience a traumatic event as physical or as mental pain. There is something about the "energy" of emotion that does this for us. (Thinking of emotion as energy here brings out its connection to libido for Freud: "libido is an expression taken from the theory of the emotions" and is defined by Freud as "the energy . . . of those instincts which have to do with all that may be comprised under the word 'love.'"[97]) The ability of emotion to exist both in the world of the mind and in the world of the body is what enables transformative exchanges between the psychic and the somatic.

Elsewhere, however, Freud associates affect (emotion) more closely with the mental, for example, when he distinguishes between "physical pain and psychic affect."[98] This helps explain Freud's ambiguous use of the verb "should" above, when he says that the "affect" that turns into physical pain "might have become, and *should* have become *mental* pain."[99] On the one hand, we could understand Freud to mean that affect (emotion) should have become mental pain because that would make it easier to detect and cure. This would be the

---

[95] Breuer and Freud, *Studies on Hysteria*, 166.

[96] Breuer and Freud, *Studies on Hysteria*, 166, emphasis in original.

[97] Sigmund Freud, *Group Psychology and the Analysis of the Ego*, ed. and trans. James Strachey (New York: W.W. Norton, 1959) 29.

[98] Breuer and Freud, *Studies on Hysteria*, 175.

[99] Breuer and Freud, *Studies on Hysteria*, 166, emphasis added to "should."

"should" of a doctor wishing to heal his patient. On the other hand, however, if affect (emotion) is primarily psychic, then Freud could have meant that the emotion associated with a traumatic event should have become mental pain because that it is its natural expression. The malleability of emotion means that it can contort and transform itself into something alien to itself, such as physical pain, but the physiological body is not its natural home. In its original and most straightforward form, emotion is "ideational." The defense provided by conversion hysteria thus robs affect from the ideas to which it properly belongs.[100] This is the "should" of a mind-body dualism that dismisses the physiological body as relatively unimportant to hysteria.

This claim might seem puzzling given that conversion hysteria is precisely transformation of the psychic into the somatic. As Elizabeth Wilson has argued, however, the hysterical body is clearly separate from the physiological body for Freud.[101] The somatic symptoms of hysteria, such as Rosalia's twitching fingers, do not have anything to do with, for example, the fingers' many bones, tendons, muscles, and blood vessels. Divorcing the hysterical and physiological body in this way allows Freud to solve (or rather, avoid) the difficult problem of how to explain somatic hysterical symptoms, such as Dora's infamous paralyzed vocal cords, that are not accompanied by any biological injury. How can Dora have perfectly physically healthy vocal cords and be incapable of speaking? Likewise, how can Rosalia be incapable of controlling her flicking fingers if their nerves are not physiologically damaged? Freud's answer, in an essay published the same year as *Studies*, is that the "injury" to the body must occur elsewhere than organically: "*the lesion in hysterical paralyses must be completely independent of the anatomy* [biological structure] *of the nervous system*, since in its paralyses and other manifestations hysteria behaves as though anatomy did not exist or as though it had no knowledge of it."[102] The body of Freudian hysteria is the everyday, lived body, not the scientific, biological body and—what is crucial—the former has no meaningful relationship or connection with the latter.

Affect, or emotion, thus might have a somatic element to it on Freud's account, but it nonetheless is independent of the physiological body. If emotions are not quite mind stuff because of their ability to convert from the mental to the physical, they clearly are not fully body stuff either. Above all, emotions are never to be equated with physiological conditions, movements, and changes for Freud. There admittedly was a point in Freud's early thought when he regarded the energy of what he calls affect to be physiological. In

---

[100] Breuer and Freud, *Studies on Hysteria*, 280.
[101] Elizabeth Wilson, "Gut Feminism," *Differences: A Journal of Feminist Cultural Studies*, 2004, 15(3): 67.
[102] Quoted in Wilson, "Gut Feminism," 67, emphasis in original.

various essays written from 1888 to 1895, Freud refers to energy as "excita-tion," referring for example to "displacements of excitability in the nervous system."[103] But by 1895, when *Studies* was published, Freud was well on his way to abandoning physiological explanations for hysteria and other psycho-pathological problems. Even though he hoped the biological sciences some-day would catch up with psychoanalysis and the two could be rejoined,[104] Freud eventually repudiated "all attempts at equating nerve-tracts of neurons with paths of mental association."[105] A crossroads between physiology and psychology quickly emerged in Freud's thinking, and Freud chose the latter path. Nervousness changed its meaning in his work from "of the nerves" to "neurotic," and the mind stuff of a separate psychic (libidinal) energy became the focus of his research.[106] Freud imposed a psychic topology on the body, and even though a relay between the two realms existed, psychic energy pos-sessed its own domain apart from the organic body.[107]

This is why we should refuse to call Lee's hips hysterical. On the account of emotion and affect I wish to endorse, emotion and affect are not a bridge between the mental and the physical, nor does conversion of affective and emotional energy from the psychological to the physiological take place. We should resist claims that emotions like Lee's are "trapped" in the body and that the physical pain of tight hips "mirrors in the physical body what is blocked in the emotional body."[108] Even though these well-intended descriptions are meant to emphasize the bodily dimensions of emotion that yoga engages, they ultimately have the opposite effect, making emotional and affective energy seem alien to physiology. The splitting of the body into the emotional/affective body versus the physical body smuggles a covert mind-body dualism back into embodiment, reminiscent of Freud's separation of the hysterical body and the organic body. The two may both be called "body," but the split authorizes understanding the body apart from its physiological structure and functioning.

The separation of the emotional/affective from the physical body also problematically renders unconscious habits alien to physiology. Like affect (emotion) on Freud's account, unconscious habits may be malleable and have the ability to bridge the psychic and the physical, but the fact that

---

[103] James Strachey, "Notes from the Editor," in Josef Breuer and Sigmund Freud, *Studies on Hysteria*, ed. and trans. James Strachey (New York: Basic Books, 1957) 334.

[104] Mark Solms and Oliver H. Turnbull, "What is Neuropsychoanalysis?" *Neuropsychoanalysis* 2011, 13(2): 134. See also Freud's 1920 claim in *Beyond the Pleasure Principle* that "biology is truly a land of unlimited possibilities. We may expect it to give us the most surprising information and we cannot guess what answers it will return in a few dozen years to the questions we have put to it" (quoted in Solms and Turnbull, "What is Neuropsychoanalysis?" 134).

[105] Strachey, "Notes from the Editor," 336.

[106] Malabou, *The New Wounded*, 8.

[107] Malabou, *The New Wounded*, 25–32.

[108] Weintraub, *Yoga for Depression*, 213.

unconscious desires are "converted" into the physical symptoms of hysteria reveals the fundamentally non-biological character of the unconscious for Freud. When, in contrast, we avoid mind-body dualism, identify affect with bodily changes, and recognize emotions as fully bodily, a much different understanding of unconscious habit emerges. I will call it biologically unconscious habit, following Wilson's notion of the biological unconscious.[109] As discussed in this book's introduction, I prefer the term "unconscious habit" to "the unconscious" since the latter tends to imply a distinct psychological entity separate from both body and society. But whether referred to as "the biological unconscious" or "biologically unconscious habits," the point is that all unconscious activity is fundamentally biological.[110] In other words, biologically unconscious habits are not a subset of a larger group of unconscious habits, some of which are narrowly "mental" or non-biological. (Likewise, on Wilson's account, the unconscious is not divided up into a biological and a non-biological portion.) If unconscious habits are fundamentally biological, then the body is not their instrument, nor is it quite accurate to say that the body is their ally.[111] Even though the language of friendship avoids instrumentalism, it nonetheless maintains too much distance between biology and unconscious habits. Understood as biological, unconscious habits are constitutive of and thus inseparable from physiological conditions and organic changes.[112]

Anecdotal evidence intriguingly suggests that biologically unconscious habits can be particularly active in the hips and upper hamstrings. As the motto of one yoga studio puts it, "Free your hips and your mind will follow."[113] Yoga Zone instructor Alan Finger elaborates a similar point as he guides beginners through a pose called Lying Leg Extension: "Now this is an incredible posture for releasing stress from behind the legs, where [a] tremendous amount of unconscious stress locks its stuff. You don't know what it is, it just happens to lock in their [sic] little shops fears, anxieties, etcetera."[114] On a recent blog discussing the relationship between yoga and emotional

---

[109] Wilson, "Gut Feminism," 77. Wilson develops the notion of a biological unconscious in conversation with Sándor Ferenczi's psychoanalytic work on materialization.

[110] This is not a claim that everything biological is non-conscious or unconscious. That claim would tend to support a dualism of consciousness and mind on the one side, and the non-conscious/unconscious and the body on the other. On my view, human biology generates both conscious and non- or unconscious habits, which is to say that all forms of our mental life are inherently biological.

[111] Wilson refers to the body as the "symbiotic ally" of the unconscious on Wilson, "Gut Feminism," 76.

[112] In a related fashion, Wilhelm Reich claims "it would be wrong to speak of the 'transfer' of physiological concepts to the psychic sphere [or vice versa], for what we have in mind is not an analogy but a real identity: the unity of psychic and somatic function" (Reich, *Character Analysis*, 340).

[113] http://ask.metafilter.com/144861/Why-do-I-get-emotional-during-one-particular-yoga-pose, accessed May 19, 2013.

[114] Alan Finger, *Introduction to Yoga*, Yoga Zone DVD (Koch Entertainment, 2002).

release, multiple people describe their experiences of spontaneously crying (and occasionally laughing) when they are doing intense hip and hamstring stretching poses, particularly pigeon pose which stretches "the area from the butt to the knee."[115] As one person explains, "I burst into tears pretty much every time I do pigeon pose. At first, I thought I was weird—until this one class where we did pigeon and when I sat up at the end I saw that everyone was crying. Even now, years after I started doing yoga, it gets me, . . . bring[ing] up inexplicable, unplanned emotion."[116]

I do not wish to establish that biologically unconscious habits are located primarily in the hips (or anywhere else),[117] as if the body were a container with different compartments ("little shops") in which the unconscious can take up residence and store its stressful stuff. Even if there were empirical evidence of the connection between hips stretches and emotional outbursts—which, to my knowledge, has not yet been researched scientifically—the idea of locating biologically unconscious habits in a discrete area of the corpus misunderstands their relationship to the physiological body. We could say instead that the hips and hamstrings (which reach into the lower back) are a constellation of muscles and tendons crucial to the experience of strong emotions of, for example, fear and anxiety, and to the development of subsequent anxious and frightened emotional habits. When the eight-year-old Lee was about to be beat up by neighborhood boys, we should not understand him as feeling fear that eventually settled into his pelvis as he pushed the terrifying experience into his unconscious and then years later was released from "storage" during yoga class. Even if this account acknowledges some of the bodily aspects of fear, such as quickened breathing and elevated adrenaline levels, it construes Lee's fear as initially unrelated to his hips.

More helpful is to think of the muscles and tendons of Lee's hips as constitutive of Lee's fear itself, both initially and in an ongoing fashion. It's plausible to imagine that as Lee heard the other boys' threatening remarks and anticipated their first blows, not only did his blood pressure shoot up and his oxygen intake increase, but his gluteal muscles, thigh abductors, and hamstring muscles contracted strongly. While it's true that this bodily response could

---

[115] http://ask.metafilter.com/144861/Why-do-I-get-emotional-during-one-particular-yoga-pose, accessed May 19, 2013; see also the sources in note 2 above.

[116] http://ask.metafilter.com/144861/Why-do-I-get-emotional-during-one-particular-yoga-pose, accessed May 19, 2013. These anecdotes call to mind Wilhelm Reich's description of pelvic armor, the portion of muscular armor from the pelvic and gluteal muscles to the adductors of the thigh that blocks bodily energy especially by holding in rage and anxiety (Reich, *Character Analysis*, 389).

[117] Though many yoga teachers would. See, for example, one yoga instructor's comment that "the hips are said to be the place where we dump emotional baggage that we do not want to face, such as guilt, shame and grief" (Judy, "The Attic of the Body: A Workshop to Open and Release the Hips," March 29, 2013, http://www.yogawithjudy.com/, accessed February 12, 2015).

take place for life-preserving reasons, for example, to try to run away from the older boys, I want to resist flattening this account to merely the preservation of life.[118] Lee's contracting hip area also can be understood as a form of organic thinking and expression in response to the world, a kind of body language socially and emotionally composed of panic and terror. Lee's hips and hamstrings continued to be composed in this way, moreover, long after the beating ended. They never completely released their contraction, remaining tense and tight into Lee's adulthood. This is to say that their contracted state became habitual and that Lee's hips were constituted by unconscious emotional habits of contraction.

Based on what his hips told him that day on the yoga mat, Lee's emotional transactions with the world had long been characterized by the pulled-in tightness of fear and anxiety. As Lee explains while later reflecting on his yoga experience that fateful day,

> I realized I'd been living my life in fear of what 'big people' might do to me, probably since I was eight years old. A 'big person' was usually a male in a position of power or authority who could use his status to affect my life. Whether or not these authority figures were actual threats didn't matter, I perceived them as being capable of influencing me in ways that were destructive an coercive. I reacted to the imaginary threat by staying away from 'big people' or humoring them to protect myself from harm. . . . This defensive coping strategy manifested in a sense of helplessness that persisted into adulthood.[119]

The muscular habits of Lee's hips, which congealed and reenacted a social experience, greatly contributed to Lee's personal character as fearful. While Lee did not consciously experience his adult relationship with the world as frightening, his hips knew that the world was a terrifying place. This knowledge was not merely a retention or memory of a traumatic event. It also was a piece of information that guided Lee's life, an understanding of himself and the world that shaped his transactions with it. Changing that knowledge—which is to say, changing Lee's comportment toward other people and the world more generally—would require changing his hips.

Rather than understanding Lee's fear as hipless, we can view his hips as fundamental to his particular habits of fear. This understanding of Lee's experience suggests that different types of fear (and other emotions) are possible depending on which physiological habits constitute them. Many people hold

---

[118] As Elizabeth Wilson argues, "the flat topology of conventional biological knowledge" too often tends to reductively "think of organs only in terms of their utility for the preservation of life" (Wilson, "Gut Feminism," 76).

[119] Michael Lee, *Phoenix Rising Yoga Therapy: A Bridge from Body to Soul* (Deerfield Beach, FL: Health Communications, Inc. 1997) 15.

tension in their shoulders and upper back, for example—does this suggest that subtle but meaningful differences between hip-fear and shoulder-fear exist? I'm willing to bet yes, and at minimum I think the question is worth empirical investigation. This is due both to James's claim that "no shade of emotion, however slight, should be without a bodily reverberation as unique, when taken its totality, as is the [emotion] itself" and to the scientific studies documenting the difference between the chemical make-up of emotional and non-emotional tears.[120] Unfortunately the studies of tears to this date do not differentiate between different types of emotion—tears of sadness versus tears of anger, for example—but they do suggest that different bodily "reverberations" constitute different emotional experiences (whether consciously felt or not). Perhaps different areas of the body experience qualitatively different forms of fear and anxiety, as well as of positive emotions such as joy and gratitude.

A recent empirical study focusing on disgust supports this suggestion, demonstrating that "organ-specific physiological responses differentiate emotional feeling states."[121] At least two different forms of disgust can be differentiated based on physiological changes in the stomach and heart. Experience of disgust felt toward vomitus and repulsive food (which the study's authors call "core" disgust) is "associated with an increase in tachygastric responses in the stomach and right anterior insula activity [in the brain]," while disgust felt toward images of a human body being surgically opened (which the authors call "body-boundary-violation" disgust) is "associated with a reduction in parasympathetically mediated influences on the heart and activity in the left anterior insula."[122] We thus might distinguish between right-brain-stomach disgust and left-brain-heart disgust, each of which tends to occur via transaction with different types of social and material environments. Look at regurgitated food, and the rate of electronic current in your stomach (tachygastria) likely will increase as you experience disgust. Your feelings of disgust probably will be qualitatively different, however, as you look at a patient's bloody internal organs pulled outside of her body and the level of relax-and-repair cooperation between your heart and (parasympathetic) brain decreases.

Perhaps something like this is true of fear too. Fear experienced during a traumatic beating such as Lee underwent might be physiologically different than fear experienced, say, while watching a scary movie. Likewise, the fear of sexual assault might be different than the fear of racist violence. And when

---

[120] James, *The Principles of Psychology*, 450. I also think here of Reich's claim that "there is a specific 'pelvic anxiety' and a specific 'pelvic rage'" (*Character Analysis*, 389). According to Reich, "the pelvic armor is the same as the shoulder armor, inasmuch as it, too, holds bound in it impulses of rage as well as anxiety" (389).

[121] Neil A. Harrison, Marcus A. Gray, Peter J. Gianaros, and Hugo D. Critchley, "The Embodiment of Emotional Feelings in the Brain," *The Journal of Neuroscience*, September 22, 2010, 30[38]: 12878; available online at http://www.jneurosci.org/content/30/38/12878.full, accessed April 2, 2013.

[122] Harrison et al., "The Embodiment of Emotional Feelings in the Brain," 12883.

sexual assault and racist violence are one and the same event, as they often have been and are for African American women, perhaps that is yet another distinctive type of fear, not the addition of one fear based on sex/gender to another fear based on race. (It's a good bet that intersectionality has a great deal to offer philosophies of emotion.) In any case, it's likely that Lee did not consciously experience his tight hips as fear or any other emotion, at least not until the fateful day in yoga class described earlier. The fact that his lingering fear might have been unfelt does not necessarily mean it was unconscious, however, although I think it's likely in Lee's case that it was. Whether or not Lee's fear can be distinguished physiologically from other types of fear and even if his fear were non-conscious rather than unconscious, it can be understood as a psychic feature of his hips. The emotion of fear was intrinsic to his physiology and not secondary to it.[123] When his hips became emotional, this did not distort their "normal" physiological functioning by adding a psychological component to them. Involuntary muscle and tendon contractions are misunderstood when we think of them as "a simple mechanical action distinct from psychic or deliberative impetus."[124] "Normal" physiology is regularly and normally psychological because it is regularly and normally affective, and its affectivity is what makes possible its specifically emotional relationship to the world. Furthermore, "involuntary" cannot be equated with "non-psychological" even if its particular form of motivation and deliberation contrasts with that of conscious thought. Not everyone's hips are emotional—and the same could be said of the body more generally—but they are all affectively engaged with and attuned to the world, and that makes it possible for hips (the body more generally) to transact emotionally with the world.

The relationship between the physiological and the psychological is particularly pressing when considering the physiological incorporation of the effects of sexism and racism, as the following chapters will show. But already in Lee's case, we can see the important role of affective and emotional physiology in both causing and relieving a great deal of psychosomatic suffering. In one respect, Lee's physical injuries probably healed fairly quickly after the beating was over: a black eye, a bruised cheek, even broken bones . . . these go away within a few months. In another respect, however, the event endured much longer, for decades, in the physio-emotional tenor of the musculature of Lee's hips, pelvis, and hamstrings. When Lee's unconscious habits of hip fear finally were addressed through bodily movements and stretches, a new relationship with the world became possible for him.

---

[123] I follow here Elizabeth Wilson's claim that "while not all biological substrata are hystericized, a primitive kind of psychic action (motivation, deliberation) is nonetheless native to biological substance" ("Gut Feminism," 77).

[124] Wilson, "Gut Feminism," 80. Wilson is speaking of the gag reflex here, but her point about this biological event is the same as mine regarding the hips.

2

The Gut and Pelvic Floor

ON CLOACAL THINKING

[We need] an integrated vision of the gut and its foundation and
their interactions with the psyche and the past.

—GHISLAIN DEVROEDE, *CE QUE LES MAUX DE VENTRE*
DISSENT DE NOTRE PASSÉ

When Ginette was twenty-nine years old, she began a six-year ordeal of
outpatient and emergency medical treatment for her urinary problems.[1]
She reported symptoms that corresponded with pollakiuria, severe dys-
uria, interrupted micturition, and bladder retention, which means that she
had to urinate during the day with abnormal frequency (at least every two
hours), experienced severe pain and a burning sensation when urinating, and
couldn't urinate continually or fully empty her bladder.[2] The official diagnosis
was vesicourethral dyssynergia (or urethrismus), which is a lack of muscle
coordination (dyssynergia) in the bladder and urethra, thought to be caused
by a problem in the central nervous system.[3] Urethral dilation usually leads
to remission of this condition, or at least its symptoms, but in Ginette's case,
it had no effect. Her painful and life-disrupting symptoms continued, as did
frequent visits to the hospital and doctors' offices—until a nurse conducted
an extended medical interview and exam.

During that process, the nurse discovered an array of seemingly unrelated facts: (1) Ginette also was constipated, having a bowel movement only
once every two weeks; (2) Ginette suffered from dyssynergic defecation

---

[1] Ghislain Devroede, "Early Life Abuses in the Past History of Patients with Gastrointestinal
Tract and Pelvic Floor Dysfunctions," in volume 122 of *Progress in Brain Research*, eds. E. A. Mayer
and C. B. Saper (New York: Elsevier Science, 2000) 142.

[2] "Pollakiuria: Definition, Symptoms, Causes, Tests and Preventative Measure," 2012. http://
www.rayur.com/pollakiuria-definition-symptoms-causes-tests-and-preventive-measure.html,
accessed June 17, 2013.

[3] http://www.thefreedictionary.com/dyssynergia, accessed June 17, 2013; http://en.wikipedia.org/
wiki/Bladder_sphincter_dyssynergia, accessed June 17, 2013; http://medical-dictionary.thefreedic-
tionary.com/vesicourethral, accessed June 17, 2013.

(or anismus): when she pushed down as if to defecate, she simultaneously contracted her anus instead of relaxing it; (3) Ginette suffered from dyspareunia, which means that vaginal sexual intercourse was painful for her; (4) Ginette had cutaneous anesthesia: she could not feel painful or pleasant sensations on the surface of certain parts of her skin; and last but not least, (5) Ginette had a history of sexual abuse when she was an adolescent and young woman: first, by her older brother, who attempted vaginal penetration when Ginette was between eleven and fifteen years old; and then by her father, who kissed her on the mouth and fondled her breasts, until Ginette was twenty-two years old.[4]

How are Ginette's medical problems, physiological symptoms, and adolescent experiences related? This chapter tackles that question by examining the biological processes of the human enteric nervous system—the intestines as well as the esophagus and stomach, or more succinctly, the gut—and their relationship with the pelvic floor. I choose the gut because it is one of the most significant places in which the "external" world transacts with the "inside" of the body, and because it has been called "the second brain" due to its independent ability to regulate fundamental modes of engagement with the world, such as mood.[5] I also choose the gut because of its transactional relationship with the pelvic muscular structure that is marked by the urinary, genital, and lower intestinal tracts. As we will see, just as these three tracts are substantively and functionally integrated with each other, the gut also is substantively and functionally tied to genital and sexual experiences, including those of sexual abuse. The gut is a process of complex co-constitutive relationships between bodily organism and environment that can help us understand how habits formed as the result of sexism and male privilege are physiologically embodied.

My approach to the gut and pelvic floor develops what colorectal surgeon Ghislain Devroede has called *la pensée cloacale*, or cloacal thinking.[6] As I will explain in more detail later, the cloaca is the common cavity in fetal development that eventually differentiates into the urinary, the genital, and the lower digestive tracts.[7] Cloacal thinking considers the pelvic floor to be a psychosomatically integrated unit, appreciating the functional and co-constitutive relationships between the urinary, genital, and lower digestive tracts. It understands the boundaries between them to be fluid and refuses the sharp

---

[4] Devroede, "Early Life Abuses," 142; Ghislain Devroede, *Ce que les maux de ventre dissent de notre passé* (Paris: Payot & Rivages, 2002), 110, 115–116. Ginette is called "Geneviève" in *Ce que les maux de ventre dissent de notre passé*.

[5] Michael D. Gershon, *The Second Brain: A Groundbreaking New Understanding of Nervous Disorders of the Stomach and Intestines* (New York: Harper Paperbacks, 1999).

[6] Devroede, *Ce que les maux de ventre dissent de notre passé*, 109; Ghislain Devroede, "La pensée cloacale," http://www.crifip.com/articles/la-pensee-cloacale.html, accessed May 21, 2013.

[7] Devroede, "La pensée cloacale," http://www.crifip.com/articles/la-pensee-cloacale.html, accessed May 21, 2013.

anatomical divisions typically assumed by Western medicine and Western society more generally.

This refusal should not be restricted to the gut and pelvic floor. The human body as a whole is constituted by dynamic relationships between its various "parts," which are distinguished by fluid and permeable boundaries. In the spirit of Devroede's questioning of artificial anatomical divides, I thus will extend his notion of cloacal thinking to the entire human body and even to the bodies of different people. Just as there are no rigid boundaries between the tracts of the pelvic floor (including the lower gut), I will argue that there are no absolute divisions between the pelvic floor and the rest of the body (such as the breasts). Nor are there necessarily sharp divisions between the physiological functions of different people (such as mother and child). As we will see, the psychosomatic integration of the gut and pelvic floor can reach across generations, providing a kind of non-genetic inheritance of gut and pelvic floor maladies associated particularly with the sexual abuse of women.

The physiological functions of digestion and absorption provided by stomach and intestines offer a dramatic example of the transactional mingling of organism and environment. The food that comes "inside" the body helps constitute the body, and the body in turn helps constitute the world "outside" it with its waste matter, which in turn helps constitute the next round of food that enters the body, and so on. In this cyclical relationship, the gut is an ontological site and could be considered the most significant place "inside" the body with which the "outside" world comes into contact. Or rather, as the scare quotes around "inside" and "outside" indicate, perhaps the gut shouldn't be thought of as inside the body at all. In fact, biologists John B. Furness and Nadine Clerc claim that "the lining of the gastrointestinal tract is our largest *external* surface."[8] Neurogastroenterologist Michael D. Gershon elaborates:

> The space enclosed within the wall of the bowel, its *lumen,* is part of the outside world. . . . The gut is a tunnel that permits the exterior to run right through us. Whatever is in the lumen of the gut is thus actually outside our bodies, no matter how counterintuitive that seems. The body proper stops at the wall of the gut. Nothing is truly in us until it crosses that boundary and is absorbed; moreover, anything that moves across the intestinal wall in the reverse direction, into the lumen, is gone.[9]

---

[8] John B. Furness and Nadine Clerc, "Responses of Afferent Neurons to the Contents of the Digestive Tract, and Their Relation to Endocrine and Immune Responses," in volume 122 of *Progress in Brain Research*, eds. E. A. Mayer and C. B. Saper (New York: Elsevier Science, 2000) 159, emphasis added.

[9] Gershon, *The Second Brain,* 84.

These explanations of the gut's relationship with the outside world helpfully disrupt customary and misguided assumptions about the stomach and intestines. We can improve upon them, moreover, by thinking of the gut as in-between the inside and outside, where sharp boundaries between inside and outside break down into a dynamic relationship. Neither wholly contained inside the body nor wholly outside it, the gut is a vast place "inside" the body where the "outside" world is most intimately and busily engaged.[10] The wall of the gut, in particular, is a site of dynamic co-constitution in which what is "properly" body and what is "properly" world are necessarily and productively indeterminate.

The gut's engagement with the world takes the complicated form of simultaneously absorbing nutrients into the body and defending the body against bacteria and toxic substances that might have been ingested. To absorb nutrients, the gut must be welcoming and open to the "external" world, and for that reason it is lined with a highly permeable epithelial membrane.[11] But at the same time, its welcoming, permeable nature makes it extremely vulnerable, and so the gut must have a complex mechanism for monitoring and responding to its contents. "More extensive than those of any other organ" including presumably the brain, the gut has three control systems that determine how it should engage with the "external" world: "the gut immune system, in which 70% of the body's immune cells are found; the gastroenteropancreatic endocrine system, which uses more than 30 identified hormones; and the enteric nervous system, which contains of the order of 10^8 neurons."[12] One of those identified hormones is the neurochemical serotonin, which regulates mood and plays a significant role in depression and its relief. Over 95% of the body's serotonin is found not in the brain, but in the gut.[13]

Here we can begin to see what we could call the character of the gut. A person's gut immune, endocrine, and enteric nervous systems predispose a person to take up and respond to the world in particular ways. Of course, broadly considered, the gut does the same sort of thing for all people: digesting and absorbing food, and excreting the waste products it cannot use. But different guts can have different styles of doing this, different manners of welcoming (or not) the external world they take in. Some guts can be more and others less receptive of the outside world, or receptive and responsive to the world in different ways, and this can mean more than the obvious and simple fact that some gastrointestinal systems tolerate a broader range of foods

---

[10] See, in this context, Michael Pollan, "Say Hello to the 100 Trillion Bacteria That Make Up Your Microbiome," *New York Times*, May 15, 2013, http://www.nytimes.com/2013/05/19/magazine/say-hello-to-the-100-trillion-bacteria-that-make-up-your-microbiome.html?hp&pagewanted=all&_r=0, accessed June 10, 2013.

[11] Furness and Clerc, "Responses of Afferent Neurons," 159.

[12] Furness and Clerc, "Responses of Afferent Neurons," 159.

[13] Gershon, *The Second Brain*, xii.

than others. Take the example of bowel dysfunctions such as irritable bowel syndrome (IBS). IBS is a functional disorder, which means that there is no damaged or diseased organ to account for its symptoms of abdominal pain, diarrhea, constipation, bloating, and/or urgency.[14] IBS is associated with life stress (as distinct from physical stress, such as trying to lift an object too heavy to carry), and for that reason, until recently it was marginalized and dismissed by the medical community as a psychological, rather than medical, problem.[15] Guts with IBS have a distinctive character, a particular way of responding to—digesting and excreting—the food that they ingest, which is simultaneously psychological and biological. More specifically, guts with IBS are marked by a character that is uneasy with (some aspect of) the world. Furthermore, this particular gut disposition is more characteristic of women than men, though not exclusive to women, due to the disproportionate harmful effects of sexism and male privilege on girls and women.

To make sense of this last claim, two additional related facts about IBS are crucial. First, there is a high prevalence of a history of sexual abuse with the occurrence of gastrointestinal disorders. In a pioneering 1990 study of the connections between bowel dysfunction and a history of sexual abuse, 44% of patients with gastrointestinal disorders (constipation, diarrhea, and abdominal pain) reported a history of sexual abuse in childhood.[16] "Patients with functional disorders were twice as likely as those with organic disease to report a history of forced intercourse, and more than ten times as likely to report a history of frequent physical abuse," including ongoing sexual abuse in adulthood for half of the abused patients.[17] Perhaps then the second relevant fact will come as no surprise: gastrointestinal disorders such as IBS are prevalent in women on a ratio of about 2:1, and this ratio holds up "even after accounting for potentially confounding psychological and health care seeking gender differences."[18] Girls and women are more often the victims of sexual abuse than boys and men, and the rate of their abuse is higher than often is acknowledged. For example, the US Department of Justice reports that approximately 25% of college women have been victims of rape or attempted

---

[14] Bruce B. Naliboff, Lin Change, Julie Munakata, and Emeran A. Mayer, "Towards an Integrative Model of Irritable Bowel Syndrome," in volume 122 of *Progress in Brain Research*, eds. E. A. Mayer and C. B. Saper (New York: Elsevier Science, 2000) 413.

[15] Naliboff et al., "Towards an Integrative Model of Irritable Bowel Syndrome," 413.

[16] D. A. Drossman, J. Leserman, G. Nachman et al., "Sexual and Physical Abuse in Women with Functional or Organic Gastrointestinal Disorders," *Annals of Internal Medicine*, December 1, 1990, 113(11): 828–833.

[17] Devroede, "Early Life Abuses," 144. See also D. A. Drossman, N. J. Talley, J. Leserman et al., "Sexual and Physical Abuse and Gastrointestinal Illness—Review and Recommendations," *Annals of Internal Medicine*, November 15, 1995, 123(10): 782–794, and V. J. Felitti, "Long-Term Medical Consequences of Incest, Rape, and Molestation," *Southern Medical Journal*, March 1991, 84(3): 328–331.

[18] Naliboff et al., "Towards an Integrative Model of Irritable Bowel Syndrome," 414.

rape but that fewer of 5% of those women report the assault to the police.[19] Similarly, in the 1990 study mentioned above, "almost one-third of the abused patients had never discussed their experience with anyone, 60% had not discussed it with their family, and only 17% had informed their gastroenterologist."[20] A recent review of all research articles and observational data on the topic produced a clear scientific conclusion: "an abuse history is associated with gastrointestinal illness and psychological disturbance, appearing more often in women and patients with functional rather than organic, gastrointestinal disorders, is not usually known by the physician, and is associated with poorer adjustment to illness and adverse health outcome. Women are more often victims than men."[21]

Women can and sometimes do have different gastrointestinal habits than do men, and this is a biological, ontological detail that is inseparable from the political, historical, social, and other details about the contemporary world. Women's guts often have a different character or style of taking in and responding to the world when it includes what Andrea Dworkin has called "rapist cultures," which valorize male sexual aggression and normalize the sexual abuse of girls and women.[22] It is important, of course, to remember that cultures, rapist or otherwise, differ from place to place and nation to nation and also to note that rates of gastrointestinal disturbance vary across different countries.[23] Young boys also are victims of sexual aggression more often than one might think since they, like women and girls, are not (yet) considered full persons. The same could be said for men in prison and other situations in which the socially "acceptable" targets for male sexual aggression are not readily available. The situation is never as simple as a universal equation in which women + sexual abuse = gastrointestinal dysfunction. Nevertheless, the claims that women confront a sexist world and that social and cultural factors affect the frequency of gastrointestinal symptoms generally hold true. We thus can plausibly say that women's guts often have difficulty digesting and absorbing components of a sexist world that tends to be hostile to them, and this difficulty is as much a biological matter as it is a psychological one. "Digestion" and "absorption" are not metaphors in this claim. (Neither is "a sexist world.") The type of gut in question literally will not digest and absorb

---

[19] US Department of Justice, "Acquaintance Rape of College Students," 2002, https://cms.psu.edu/section/content/default.asp?WCI=pgDisplay&WCU=CRSCNT&ENTRY_ID=D308EFB3E0D D49E7A172FF3A9AE18285, June 15, 2013.

[20] Reported in Devroede, "Early Life Abuses," 144.

[21] Devroede, "Early life abuses," 145.

[22] See Andrea Dworkin's "Women in the Public Domain" (in *Women and Values: Readings in Recent Feminist Philosophy*, ed. Marilyn Pearsall [Belmont, CA: Wadsworth Publishing, 1986] 221–229) for a powerful account of the rapist culture in the United States. Dworkin uses the term "rapist culture" on page 229 of that essay.

[23] Douglas A. Drossman, ed., *The Functional Gastrointestinal Disorders: Diagnosis, Pathophysiology, and Treatment—A Multinational Consensus* (New York: Little, Brown, 1994) 119.

its food without abdominal pain, diarrhea, and/or constipation, indicating that it does not want to be constituted by a world that includes its (her) sexual abuse. By speaking of the gut's desire—"it does not want to be constituted"— as I simultaneously describe its digestive difficulties, I am arguing that we should not understand the gut by means of a conventional, biologically flat economy. That is an economy that ignores or neglects the psychological capacities inherent to human physiology.[24] With Elizabeth Wilson, I am arguing that "psychic action (motivation, deliberation) is ... native to biological" materiality and functioning.[25]

Take the example of constipation and suppressed anger. As discussed in Chapter 1, oppressed groups such as women and people of color are forbidden to express anger, and/or their anger is dismissed as irrelevant or irrational. Their anger tends to be seen as an intolerable act of insubordination, and so it often is suppressed or repressed by the oppressed person who feels it. Suppression and repression of any emotion has consequences, and one doesn't have to be a devotee of Freud to say that the repressed anger of an abused woman can be as much of a visceral as a psychological phenomenon. Constipation has been associated with the predominance of the sympathetic limb of the autonomic nervous system and with vagal suppression, which is suppression of the vagus nerve that innervates the muscles of the abdominal viscera.[26] So, too, has the suppression and repression of anger been associated with reduced vagal activity and sympathetic dominance. (Reduced vagal activity also has been documented in patients with functional dyspepsia and gastroesophageal reflux disorder.) As physiologist N. W. Read concludes, "these data suggest that symptoms indicating a psychovisceral attitude of resistance and hold-up are associated with sympathetic dominance."[27] An angry body that isn't allowed to express its anger can manifest its resistance to the world through its gut reactions. It can withhold itself, its contributions to the world, by withholding its feces. Avoiding a flat biological economy in appreciation of biologically unconscious habits, I would say that this withholding is a gut judgment of the world that something is wrong with it—with both the world and thus also with the gut (person) who is transactionally constituted in relationship with it.

---

[24] Wilson, "Gut Feminism," 83.

[25] Wilson, "Gut Feminism," 77.

[26] N. W. Read, "Bridging the Gap Between Mind and Body: Do Cultural and Psychoanalytic Concepts of Visceral Disease Have an Explanation in Contemporary Neuroscience?" in volume 122 of *Progress in Brain Research*, eds. E. A. Mayer and C. B. Saper (New York: Elsevier Science, 2000) 435. See also Emeran A. Mayer, Bruce Naliboff, and Julie Munakata, "The Evolving Neurobiology of Gut Feelings," volume 122 of *Progress in Brain Research*, eds. E. A. Mayer and C. B. Saper (New York: Elsevier Science, 2000) 197.

[27] Read, "Bridging the Gap Between Mind and Body," 435.

Of course, not every angry person or every abused woman is constipated. Positing an uncomplicated causal relationship between sexual abuse, repressed anger, and constipation would be woefully simplistic. People's lives and patients' symptoms are too specific and individual to be fully captured by broad characterizations of gut habits, and any generalization about women, sexual abuse, and gastrointestinal dysfunction is only that: a generalization that admits of many exceptions. But as neurobiologists, colorectal physicians, and gastroenterological specialists are documenting, there nonetheless remain "different styles of psychovisceral expression that are observed clinically," and given the importance of embodiment to human experience, we may ask, "why shouldn't the body (and particularly the gut) be able to express more subtle aspects of personality and feelings?"[28] (Indeed, one scientific study suggests that the effects of personality are greater than the intake in fiber in determining bowel functions.[29]) As Read claims, gastrointestinal dysfunction "may require us to look at symptoms, not [merely] as components of a medical diagnosis, but as highly individual expressions of emotional conflict. In other words, the symptom carries a meaning; it is a body language that needs to be understood."[30] An expression of a person's particular feelings and personality, gut function thus can be considered a physiological habit that also says something about the world "around" it. Gut function is a predisposition to transact with the world in particular ways that both contributes to a person's character and helps reveal her emotional well-being.

Depression offers another example of gut character, one that has gendered associations as well. Depression can be described both as an isolating breakdown of relationships with the world and other people and a biochemical imbalance (depletion) of neurotransmitters such as serotonin.[31] Women suffer depression more often than men, tend to develop depression at an earlier age than men, and tend to have longer lasting and more frequently recurring episodes of depression.[32] Depression typically is marked by symptoms that include problems with eating: most often a loss of interest in food, although sometimes an inability to stop eating. When a person is depressed, she becomes disconnected with the world, and that disconnection can be manifest in a gut refusal to take the world in. The depressed person has little interest in the "outside" world, one manifestation of which can be her body's having little interest in its largest "external" surface: the lining of the gastrointestinal tract. Alternatively, the depressed person who binge eats can be

---

[28] Read, "Bridging the Gap Between Mind and Body," 436, 434.

[29] Cited in Read, "Bridging the Gap Between Mind and Body," 436.

[30] Read, "Bridging the Gap Between Mind and Body," 432.

[31] Elizabeth Wilson, *Psychosomatic: Feminism and the Neurological Body* (Durham, NC: Duke University Press, 2004), 45.

[32] Roxann Dryden-Edwards and William C. Shiel, Jr., "Women and Depression," 2010, http://www.medicinenet.com/script/main/art.asp?articlekey=18987, accessed June 15, 2013.

understood as urgently trying to re-establish a connection with the world that she has lost, insistently using food to try to replace or compensate (hence overcompensate) for the relations with others that are missing in her life.

As we have seen in the example of gastrointestinal disorders such as IBS, the gut can be a key site for the working-through, both physiologically and psychologically, of a person's relations with others. We might say that relationships with other people become internalized in the habitual ways that the gut responds to the world it ingests. This phenomenon of transactional internalization also can be seen in the depressed person's refusal or failure to eat. A person's willingness or inability to put part of the world (food) in her mouth to digest and absorb is a form of her relationship with the world (other people). As Wilson has argued, this description of eating is not a mere metaphor for the internalization of social relationships, as if eating represented relationships with others and depression represented their interruption. Rather, Wilson suggests, "gut pathology doesn't stand in for ideational disruption, but is another form of perturbed relations to others—a form that is enacted enterologically."[33] In that case, the result is "a schema of depression in which the failure to eat doesn't represent a breakdown of connection to others, but is seen as a direct interruption to the process of remaining connected to others. The struggle to eat (or to stop eating) when depressed is a struggle to mediate difficult, attenuated, or lost relations to others and the outside world."[34]

This bodily form of perturbed relationships is not psychosomatic in the dismissive way that the term sometimes is used. To call a bodily ailment "psychosomatic" can be to brush it off as imaginary or—to say the same thing from some perspectives—as an offshoot of a psychical problem. As Devroede explains, "the medical community, in general, has a tendency to confuse imaginary diseases, i.e., fictitious disorders, with somatization disorders, which [are] really in the body."[35] Social epidemiologists Lisa Berkman and Ichiro Kawachi concur that the "distinction between 'psychosomatic' illness and other physical illnesses . . . is false. . . . The breakdown of this artificial dichotomy is critical to advancing [medical] knowledge in the coming decades."[36] In the case of depression, perturbed relationships with other people really are in the body just as reduced serotonin levels really are in the gut (and, secondarily, the brain). So, too, are the feelings of sadness and dejection that are the subjective hallmark of depression. "The gut is not immune to mental disease," Gershon explains, given that "an abnormality of the

---

[33] Wilson, *Psychosomatic,* 45.

[34] Wilson, *Psychosomatic,* 45.

[35] Devroede, "Early Life Abuses," 151.

[36] Lisa F. Berkman and Ichiro Kawachi, "A Historical Framework for Social Epidemiology," in *Social Epidemiology,* eds. Lisa F. Berkman and Ichiro Kawachi (New York: Oxford University Press, 2000) 4.

gut's own nervous system [can] be the cause of intestinal grief."[37] Gershon's *double entendre* when speaking of grief can be appreciated here as deliberate: the cramping pain of upset intestines simultaneously can be melancholic anguish. We could say that disturbed social relationships, low serotonin levels, and feelings of sadness are the very same thing considered from three different angles: social, biological, and psychological. All three considerations are functional, not substantive, distinctions regarding depression. Thus each consideration is inaccurate if it is thought to be ontologically separate or separable from the other. Depression is a biopsychosocial phenomenon in which low serotonin levels, feelings of profound sadness, and disconnected social relationships help constitute each other in an ongoing transactional spiral.

This explains why successful treatment of depression often depends on addressing multiple aspects of the syndrome at once. This usually takes the form of therapy combined with serotonin-selective reuptake inhibitor (SSRI) medications, addressing the psychological and biological dimensions of depression. But it also can take the form of working directly on the social, interpersonal relationships that the gut has with the world, namely through the act of eating with others. For example, in one man's account of his episodes of major depression, Andrew Solomon documents how he became emotionally frail, unable to sleep, disinterested in food, and increasingly isolated. Retching in the bathroom, Solomon felt as though his "acute understanding of [his] loneliness were a virus in my system. . . . I thought that the normal and real world in which I had grown up, and in which I believed other people lived, would never open itself up to receive me."[38] As Wilson explains, through its refusal to eat and vomiting when he did eat, Solomon's gut was "unable to take in the world, to let others pass through him and be absorbed."[39] Finding a way to get Solomon to take in the world was integral to his recovery. This happened when Solomon's father canceled all other plans to sit with his son at the dinner table, cut up his food, and talk and joke with Solomon as he fed him. Solomon was able to eat, which is to say that he was able to begin repairing broken social connections with the world. While Solomon also used SSRI antidepressants and psychotherapy to facilitate his recovery, his father's love, expressed through acts of feeding and eating, was crucial to changing the way that Solomon's gut worked, and thus also to changing his body's serotonin and other hormone levels.

It's not easy to specify why Solomon became depressed. (It probably never is.) It clearly had something to do his "confused sense of sexuality," which he describes as "my life's most impenetrable emotional challenge."[40] As Solomon explains with reference to his mother's and his own homophobia,

---

[37] Gershon, *The Second Brain*, 176, 177.

[38] Quoted in Wilson, *Psychosomatic*, 46.

[39] Wilson, *Psychosomatic*, 46.

[40] Andrew Solomon, *The Noonday Demon: An Atlas of Depression* (New York: Scribner, 2002) 41–42.

I have supposed that my first breakdown was tied to the publication of a novel that alluded to my mother's illness and death; but it was also a book with explicit gay content, and surely that too was implicated in the breakdown. Perhaps, indeed, that was the dominant anguish: forcing myself to make public what I had so long immured in silence. . . . [T]hough I [now] have a lot of positive emotion associated with my sexuality, I believe I will never escape fully from the abnegation.[41]

While Solomon's depressed gut apparently was not related to a history of sexual abuse, it nonetheless responded to a world that rejected and scorned him because he was gay. To take in that world would be to internalize its homophobia, which Solomon in fact did but which he also tried to expel. Solomon's broken biopsychosocial connection with the world was inseparable from his relationship with his mother, her death, and his self-abhorrence ("she hated what I was so much"[42]), and was repaired through his relationship with his father, his love, and their eating together.

My explanation to this point of why sexual abuse can result in gastrointestinal problems could apply to any situation or experience that a person (perhaps unconsciously) rejects or is angry about. It does not necessarily apply specifically to sexual abuse. The refusal to digest is a refusal of the world, whatever the particular state of a person's world. It can poison me, for example, with salmonella or with distressing news about the death of a loved one, and in either case I might vomit or have diarrhea as a way of expelling a world that I do not want to accept. But gut dysfunction tends to have a closer relationship with sexual abuse than with other social phenomena, a relationship on which I now specifically focus. It's helpful on this point to recall the 1990 study that strikingly found that almost half of all women with chronic gastrointestinal problems had experienced childhood sexual abuse. The statistical association between past chronic gastrointestinal problems and past sexual abuse is so strong that some doctors now treat chronic gut dysfunction as a possible symptom of sexual abuse and immediately broaden their medical exam and treatment accordingly.[43]

To better understand the strong connection between sexual abuse and gut dysfunction, I develop Devroede's notion of *pensée cloacale*. Cloacal thinking is a way of understanding the body holistically, not as fundamentally divided into separate parts that can be understood and medically treated in isolation from each other. For Devroede, cloacal thinking takes its cue from and is supported by the physiology of fetal experience. As he explains, "during

---

[41] Solomon, *The Noonday Demon*, 207.
[42] Solomon, *The Noonday Demon*, 207.
[43] Devroede, *Ce que les maux de ventre dissent de notre passé*, 110.

intra-uterine development, there is not, at first, a division between the urinary, the genital, and the lower digestive tracts, they all end in a common cavity: the cloaca."[44] The division between these three tracts is learned both medically and experientially, and the human body has early physiological experiences prior to this learning that mingle urinary, anal, and genital functions. Cloacal thinking considers those early experiences to be important to future pelvic floor functioning. It does not attempt to retreat or return to early fetal experience; the divisions that later develop between the urinary, anal, and genital tracts are physiologically real. But their reality is not that of rigid, impermeable borders that divide the tracts into isolated bodily compartments. It is a reality of physiological sharing, exchanging, and mingling with itself.

The shared world of the rectum, the vagina, and the urinary opening helps explain why sexual abuse in the vagina, for example, can manifest itself as a gastrointestinal problem, such as chronic constipation, diarrhea, abdominal pain, and other symptoms characteristic of IBS, Crohn's disease, and related gut maladies. It helps explain why Ginette could not fully empty her bladder; why she was constipated; and why vaginal intercourse and urination were painful experiences for her. I will say more about these symptoms below, but first I want to expand the notion of cloacal thinking to the entire body so that we can understand the relationship of all of Ginette's symptoms, including the lack of cutaneous sensation on her breasts and groin area. As we will see, the organic malleability and permeability characterizing the anal, urinary, and genital tracts also are intrinsic to other areas of the body. The body does not suddenly become a shared world at the point of the lower digestive tract. It is shared all along in different ways and to different degrees, and its world also can be mingled with that of other people.

To think cloacally about more than just the pelvic floor, let's begin with the digestive tract of an individual person, tarrying with the transition points between its different sections. The long tube that runs through the human body, from throat to anus, is psychosomatically co-constituted with other physiological organs and functions from the literal start, not just at its literal end. This is especially evident in the case of the fauces, or back of the throat.[45] The muscles and tissue of the fauces are involved in a number of different physiological activities: swallowing, of course, but the soft tissue at the back of the mouth also is involved in breathing (it is the entrance to the lungs), smelling, and hearing (the throat is connected to the ears and nose), tasting (while taste buds are on the tongue, up to 90% of taste occurs

---

[44] Devroede, "La pensée cloacale," http://www.crifip.com/articles/la-pensee-cloacale.html, accessed May 21, 2013.

[45] Wilson, "Gut Feminism," 80.

in the nose via smell[46]), and vocalizing (talking, singing, growling, groaning, and so on). The fauces tends to shift easily between these different functions, knowing how to close off the entrance to the lungs, nose, and ears when swallowing, for example, so that food goes down the esophagus instead of elsewhere. But as episodes of choking and snarfing (when chewed material or liquids are expelled from the nose) demonstrate, the fauces sometimes allows food to go in the wrong direction. What "wrong" means here, however, is merely that chewed food is not nutritive, and can even be harmful to the body if it enters the nose and especially the lungs. It does not mean that the fauces has somehow perverted its normal functioning by being an entry point to lungs and nose, rather than just to the esophagus and the stomach. The normal functioning of the fauces is plural and fluid. It inherently blurs the boundaries between the gut (esophagus, and then stomach and intestines) and the nose, ears, lungs, and mouth. The fauces marks a process/place where the gut and the head are entangled and cannot be sharply distinguished from each other.

For this reason, rather than thinking of the fauces as a switch point—as if the nose, ears, lungs, mouth, and esophagus were separate train tracks on which food, air, and other substances could run—better to think of it as a site where different organs come together in their co-constitution.[47] This doesn't mean that the nose and the ears, for example, are identical or that we have collapsed all differences between the mouth and the lungs. But it does mean that these physiological sites cannot be substantively separated from each other. In some respects, this is well recognized: breathing is not isolated in the lungs; it also involves the nose and mouth (and indeed the oxygen of the "outside" environment). Likewise, tasting is not segregated in the mouth; the nose also tastes our food when we eat. Perhaps less well known, however, are the hearing capacities of the nose and the tasting capacities of the ears, for example. When children in particular have nasal congestion, it can interfere with their hearing. This is due to the small size and horizontal positioning of their Eustachian tubes, which are connected to the back of the nose to ventilate the middle ear. When the nasal passages connected to the Eustachian tube are clogged, sounds tend to be muffled and one's ability to hear suffers.[48] Furthermore, as recent empirical studies have documented, the ears help us taste. For example, high-pitched music tends to make candy taste sweeter than low-pitched music does, and different vowel sounds consistently accentuate one or more of the four basic tastes of sweet, sour, salty, and bitter (for example, sweet tastes correspond to smoother vowel sounds than bitter

---

[46] The Smell and Taste Treatment and Research Foundation, http://www.smellandtaste.org/_/index.cfm?action=info.chemo, accessed May 30, 2013.

[47] Wilson uses the metaphor of switching (although not specifically with train tracks) in Wilson, "Gut Feminism," 80.

[48] http://www.entcare.com.au/blocked-nose-children-david-lowinger.html, accessed June 17, 2013.

and sour tastes do).[49] Given that lower pitched tones generally are easier to hear than higher pitched ones (because one can feel the vibrations of lower pitched sounds),[50] we can say without being confused that the world won't taste quite as sweet to a stuffy nose with hearing problems.

These cross-modal correspondences cannot be dismissed as instances of synesthesia, that is, as a so-called abnormal neurological condition that leads people to "incorrectly" experience one sense as another. They are too prevalent a phenomenon across the human population to be marginalized in this way. Or if we take the route of categorizing them as synesthesia, then we have to recognize that synesthesia is not abnormal or atypical. The blending and merging of sensory experiences are fundamental features of human physiology. As one pair of experimental psychologists ventures to ask in the wake of growing evidence of cross-sensory experience, "one important question in the field of multisensory perception still remains to be answered: Are 'true' synaesthesia and cross-modal correspondences qualitatively different phenomena, or are they manifestations of a more or less continuous spectrum of crossmodal links, possibly rooted in the same neurocognitive mechanism?"[51] I would argue against the strong neurocognitive bias suggested here. While the brain is important, it is not the only physiological mechanism that supports synesthesia. The physical location and intra-functioning of human sensory organs also is highly relevant. But the idea that synesthesia and cross-modal correspondences lie on a continuum nevertheless offers an attractive alternative to segregating the senses into five separate, isolated boxes. As neurologist Richard Cytowic explains, "synesthesia is a conscious peek at a neural process that happens all the time in everyone. . . . Synesthesia is not something that has been added [to synesthetes], but has always existed. A multisensory awareness is something that has been *lost* from conscious awareness in the majority of people."[52] Combining this view of synesthesia with what we know about the fauces, we can think of human physiology in

---

[49] Annie-Sylvie Crisinel, Stefan Cosser, Scott King, Russ Jones, James Petrie, and Charles Spence, "A Bittersweet Symphony: Systematically Modulating the Taste of Food by Changing the Sonic Properties of the Soundtrack Playing in the Background," *Food Quality and Preference*, April 2012, 24(1): 201–204; Klemens Knöferle and Charles Spence, "Crossmodal Correspondences Between Sounds and Tastes," *Psychonomic Bulletin and Review*, October 2012, http://www.academia.edu/1932968/Crossmodal_correspondences_between_sounds_and_tastes, accessed June 17, 2013.

[50] Hearing loss due to old age tends to target high-frequency tones, which are crucial for hearing human speech, especially that of women and children (University of Illinois Extension, http://urbanext.illinois.edu/wims/wims6c.html, accessed June 17, 2013). See also http://www.raisingdeaf-kids.org/hearing/sounds.php, accessed June 17, 2013.

[51] Knöferle and Spence, "Crossmodal Correspondences Between Sounds and Tastes," http://www.academia.edu/1932968/Crossmodal_correspondences_between_sounds_and_tastes, accessed June 17, 2013.

[52] Richard E. Cytowic, *The Man Who Tasted Shapes: A Bizarre Medical Mystery Offers Revolutionary Insights into Emotions, Reasoning, and Consciousness* (New York: G. P. Putnams Sons, 1993) 167, emphasis in original.

its entirety as a continuous spectrum of interlacing and cross-functioning modes and activities.

A holistic continuum of this sort does not mean that all bodily areas and functions communicate with each other in the same ways or to the same degree. Perhaps there are some areas and functions of the body that are so functionally or spatially removed from each other that, in practice, they do not communicate with each other at all. The answers to those questions must be developed in the context of particular bodily processes and physiological sites, rather than in the abstract. As we seek answers to those questions, however, we need to resist falling back into familiar habits of thinking that the body is fundamentally an assemblage of separate modules or parts, as the field of body mereology does (*meros* = parts). In the words of a trio of cognitive neuroscientists who are body mereologists, "the body is made up of parts. . . . The simplest scientific approach to bodily experience is a reductive one. We begin by assuming that the phenomenology of the perceiving and acting body is not a primitive fact, but can be analysed. We approach this analysis by considering how the phenomenology of the body can be broken down into a phenomenology of body parts."[53] In contrast to mereology, cloacal thinking is a useful heuristic device for both doctors and other medical specialists (Devroede's particular concern) and philosophers and other scholars (I would add). As we try to improve our understanding of the body, if we have to err on one side, the side to err on is that of looking for moments and means of interdependency and communication between physiological areas and functions. The importance of doing so isn't merely philosophical. It also is medical. As we will see, one of the things at stake in the question of cloacal thinking is alleviating psychosomatic suffering and improving psycho-gastrointestinal health.

Returning to the fauces, the view of human physiology for which I am arguing suggests that we shouldn't consider the process of vomiting to be the result of a malfunctioning fauces. The fact that the fauces can reverse the normal flow of digesting food from mouth to stomach, to stomach to mouth, is a manifestation of the fauces' amorphous agility, not a breakdown in its ability to regulate the train tracks. For one thing, when toxic food has been ingested, it's not a mistake for the fauces to cooperate with the esophagus and stomach to expel the food. But even in the example of food poisoning, vomiting should not be understood as merely a reversal of the traffic on the esophageal tract. The relationship and communication between the fauces, esophagus, and stomach are more complicated than this metaphor suggests. Vomiting makes vivid how the fauces as such (whether swallowing or vomiting) is "alive to a

---

[53] F. de Vignemont, M. Tsakiris, and P. Haggard, "Body Mereology," in *Human Perception from Inside Out*, eds. G. Knoblich, I. M. Thorton, M. Grosjean, and M. Shiffrar (New York: Oxford University Press, 2005) 147.

number of different ontogenetic and phylogenetic possibilities," as Elizabeth Wilson explains.[54] In large part, this is because the tissues of the fauces and pharynx are "'the embryological source of several important structures in vertebrates. For example, the breathing apparatus (gill pouches of fish and lungs of land animals) arises in this area.'"[55] Like the cloaca, the fauces is born of tissue that is not yet differentiated into distinct organs, in this case for breathing, speaking, and so on.[56] While it does take on these different forms, and their differences are meaningful, their distinct forms are functional, and their functioning occurs in a cooperative, co-constitutive manner in which faucal organs cannot be completely isolated or separated from each other.

This view of the fauces impacts not just how we understand a person occasionally vomiting from food poisoning, but also the bulimic person regularly vomiting to control her weight. As Wilson documents, the American Psychiatric Association characterizes bulimics as persons who can vomit "at will," but the will in question is more physiological than ideational.[57] Bulimics can vomit willfully not because they have mental powers to force the food up, but because their fauces communicates with their esophagus and stomach in different ways than the fauces of a non-bulimic generally does. For example, the gag reflex of bulimics often does not work in the same way that the gag reflex of non-bulimics does.[58] Bulimics do not gag when their fauces is stimulated (in this case, by inserting a plastic medical tube down their throat), suggesting that years of regular vomiting has altered the relationship that their fauces has with their esophagus and stomach. It's not that the fauces has messed up the directional switch between the mouth and stomach, but that "the gagging capacities of the fauces have borrowed from the pharynx and become more like swallowing; and ingestion has become a technique for expulsion rather than digestion."[59] As Wilson notes, when the fauces begins to communicate with other nearby organs in this way, bulimia becomes very difficult to treat successfully.[60] The typical arsenal of cognitive-oriented therapies often does not address the transformed morphology of the bulimic's fauces or its relationship with other organs.

Let's now move down the digestive tract to consider the relationship between the esophagus and the stomach and, in particular, the ring of muscles between them known as the lower esophageal sphincter. One of the important

---

[54] Wilson, "Gut Feminism," 80.

[55] *Gray's Anatomy* quoted in Wilson, "Gut Feminism," 80.

[56] The fauces and the anal portion of the cloaca also are similar in that their functions require the participation of the central nervous system. In between—from the pyloric sphincter to the anus—the enteric nervous system takes over (Gershon, *The Second Brain*, 87, 113).

[57] Wilson, "Gut Feminism," 79.

[58] Wilson, "Gut Feminism," 79–80.

[59] Wilson, "Gut Feminism," 81.

[60] Wilson, "Gut Feminism," 82.

roles of these muscles is to keep the stomach's contents, and stomach acid in particular, from flowing up into the esophagus. When that happens, gastroesophageal reflux disorder (GERD) can develop. GERD is characterized by painful symptoms of heartburn (a misnomer since the heart isn't directly involved), but it is a far more serious condition than the term "heartburn" suggests. This is because chronic GERD can lead to Barrett's esophagus, which designates a transformation in the cells that line the esophagus: metaplasia, or "change in form."[61] (GERD affects 40% of adults in the United States, of which 5%–20% will develop Barrett's esophagus.[62]) Bathed repeatedly with stomach acid, the esophageal tissue literally changes color and composition so that it is similar to stomach tissue. It is able to secrete mucus that protects the organ from the damaging acid.[63] The metaplasia of esophageal cells would seem like a good thing, and in fact people with Barrett's esophagus sometimes report an improvement in heartburn and other GERD symptoms. But left untreated, Barrett's cells can continue to change, becoming dysplasic, ranging from low-grade dysplasia (pre-cancerous) to high-grade dysplasia (cancerous). Statistically, high-grade dysplasia and thus esophageal adenocarcinoma develop in only 3.5% of all people with Barrett's esophagus, but they are associated with a mortality rate of greater than 90%.[64]

GERD damages the body, and it does so because the lower esophageal sphincter allows stomach acid to flow onto tissues that typically aren't typically prepared for it. GERD is an involuntary condition, most likely with an inherited component since GERD tends to run in families. (Note that "inherited" does not necessarily mean "genetic," as I'll elaborate later.) And yet there is something similar between the lower esophageal sphincter of a person with GERD and the fauces of a person with chronic bulimia. Each is a site of transition that functionally and substantively participates in the organs whose communication it facilitates. The lower esophageal sphincter is not precisely esophageal or stomachal but instead blends the two together. This is especially apparent in the case of GERD, when the sphincter allows so much communication between the stomach and esophagus that they start to be become indistinguishable. But the "abnormal" case of GERD is not a radical break from the "normal" relationship between the esophagus and the stomach.

---

[61] http://www.mayoclinic.com/health/barretts-esophagus/HQ00312, accessed June 17, 2013; http://www.nlm.nih.gov/medlineplus/ency/article/001143.htm, accessed June 17, 2013.

[62] Brian J. Reid, Douglas S. Levine, Gary Longton, Patricia L. Blount, and Peter S. Rabinovitch, "Predictors of Progression to Cancer in Barrett's Esophagus: Baseline Histology and Flow Cytometry Identify Low- and High-Risk Patient Subsets," *American Journal of Gastroenterology*, 2000, 95(7): 1669–1676, http://www.ncbi.nlm.nih.gov/pmc/articles/PMC1783835/, accessed April 5, 2013.

[63] http://www.virtualmedstudent.com/links/gastrointestinal/barretts_esophagus.html, accessed June 17, 2013.

[64] Reid et al., "Predictors of Progression to Cancer in Barrett's Esophagus," 2000, http://www.ncbi.nlm.nih.gov/pmc/articles/PMC1783835/, accessed April 5, 2013.

GERD is one extreme of a continuum in which the stomach and esophagus more or less blend with each other. GERD is a dangerous health condition; there is no doubt about that. But it is not different in kind from a healthy condition in which the lower esophageal sphincter opens and closes "normally." The extremity of GERD is not a perversion of the sphincter's functioning. It instead is an exaggeration of it in one particular direction, highlighting the malleability and the possibilities of the stomach-esophagus relationship that are inherent to the organs' physiology.

The same could be said for the other extreme of the stomach-esophageal relationship, when the lower esophageal sphincter doesn't open often, enough, or at all. In that case, the flow of communication between stomach and esophagus comes to a stop. Not only does acid not flow from stomach to esophagus, but chewed food also cannot pass the opposite direction from the esophagus to the stomach. Where does the food go? What can it do? It cannot remain in the esophagus long term. And so if the esophagus cannot or will not move the food downward to the stomach, then the food must come back up. The condition that marks this end of the stomach-esophageal continuum is known as achalasia (Greek for "failure to relax").[65] An esophageal motility disorder that occurs in the absence of cancer, fibrosis, or other explanatory causes, achalasia is characterized by both hypertension of the lower esophageal sphincter and peristalsis, which is the inability of the smooth esophageal muscles to move food downward.[66] Symptoms of achalasia include difficulty swallowing, chest pain, and especially regurgitation of undigested food.[67] Researchers do not know why otherwise healthy people develop achalasia. Possible hypotheses include damaged nerve cells in the esophagus that are attacked by the person's own immune system, making achalasia possibly another entry in the growing list of unexplained autoimmune disorders.[68]

It might be tempting to call achalasia a hysterical condition because of the psychosomatic nature of the failure to relax. Given the mind-body dualism that lurks in Freud's notion of hysteria, however, it is better to think of this end of the stomach-esophageal continuum as biologically unconscious regurgitation. The regurgitating person consciously knows that she is expelling food, of course. In fact, the regurgitation of achalasia tends to be more voluntary than vomiting, a kind of forced coughing up of food with an awkward hacking movement of the throat and upper chest, rather than with the wavelike contractions of the esophagus and stomach muscles. This is because

---

[65] http://emedicine.medscape.com/article/169974-overview, accessed June 17, 2013.

[66] http://emedicine.medscape.com/article/169974-overview, accessed June 17, 2017; http://my.clevelandclinic.org/disorders/achalasia/ts_overview.aspx, accessed June 17, 2013.

[67] http://my.clevelandclinic.org/disorders/achalasia/ts_overview.aspx, accessed June 17, 2013; http://www.medicinenet.com/achalasia/page3.htm, accessed June 17, 2013.

[68] http://my.clevelandclinic.org/disorders/achalasia/ts_overview.aspx, accessed June 17, 2013; http://www.medicinenet.com/achalasia/page2.htm, accessed June 17, 2013.

the esophageal muscles have stopped cooperating in the movement of food, as if they are frozen with uncertainty about what to do in the face of a sphincter door that is unexpectedly shut tight. The reasons for her physiological need to vomit, however, include anxieties and/or desires of which she probably is not consciously aware. Much like bulimia and also anorexia, this form of food expulsion illuminates through its extremity the way that all human physiological relationships to food—both "normal" and "abnormal" ones—are constituted by psychosocial factors and experiences.

To more quickly reach the end of the digestive tract, I'll pass quickly over the pylorus, which is the muscular valve that controls the passage of material between the stomach and the small intestine. It's worth briefly noting, however, the functional similarities between the pylorus and its uptown cousins. Like the fauces and the lower esophageal sphincter, the pylorus is a site of malleable transition and communication belonging to both its north and south neighbors. Most of the time, the pylorus ensures that chyme (partially digested foodstuff) moves from the stomach to the intestines, but in the case of pyloric stenosis, the pyloric muscles thicken so much that very little can pass through the valve.[69] The result is potentially life-threatening malnutrition and, more immediately, projectile vomiting since the stomach's contents have nowhere to go but back the way they came. Based on current medical knowledge, unlike problems with the fauces and the lower esophageal sphincter, pyloric stenosis is not a condition that develops over time. When it occurs, a person is born with it (although why some fetuses overdevelop their pyloric muscles is unknown). Nevertheless, pyloric stenosis reveals once again how a transformative malleability is fundamental to organic physiology. Bodily tissues can seamlessly exchange capacities with each other, in this case transferring the role of the intestines, colon, and rectum to evacuate chyme from the body to the stomach, esophagus, and mouth.

We now return to the end of the digestive tube: the rectum, which is the final five or six inches of the large intestine, and the anus, which is the rectum's opening to the "outside" world.[70] Like the fauces, the lower esophageal sphincter, and the pylorus, the anus regulates the flow of the external world through the body, in most cases by helping remove undigested solid matter from the body. Without this removal process, the body would become poisoned by its own waste. Just as we cannot live without breathing and eating, we cannot live without pooping. We defecate or we die. And yet sometimes the body refuses to defecate. Once again, like the fauces, the lower esophageal sphincter, and the pylorus, innate to the anus is the ability to reverse its "normal" function of directing food matter through the body. As in the

---

[69] http://www.nlm.nih.gov/medlineplus/ency/article/000970.htm, accessed June 17, 2013; http://medical-dictionary.thefreedictionary.com/chyme, accessed June 17, 2013.

[70] http://www.dartmouth.edu/~humananatomy/part_6/chapter_36.html, accessed April 5, 2013.

case of Ginette, the anus can become hypertensive, tightly constricting rather than opening when a person is consciously bearing down to defecate and the rectum is trying to move feces out of the body. This condition, known as anismus or dyssynergic defecation, is strangely similar to that of achalasia, in which there is a failure to relax. A person with anismus cannot get her anus to loosen up and cooperate with the movements of her rectum. The result tends to be severe constipation, often accompanied by intense abdominal pain.

The anus's relationship with the rectum is not the only important one that it has with surrounding organs and functions. Since the anus is an opening in the muscular floor that stretches from the front to the back of the pelvis, its relationship and communication with the urinary and genital openings are highly relevant to the anus's healthy operation. While the existence of the pelvic floor isn't news to anyone with basic knowledge of human physiology—and it certainly isn't news to doctors, nurses, and other medical professionals—its functional integration and co-constitution often is overlooked.[71] Urinating, defecating, and sexual and reproductive experiences can overlap, lend themselves to each other, and encourage or interfere with other. This co-constitutive relationship tends to be most obvious when something goes "wrong," as in the case of Ginette's urinary, anal, and other problems, but it is there all along, even when things are going "right" and one doesn't pay much attention to one's urination or defecation. Ginette's physiological condition isn't "wrong" in the sense of being foreign to the possibilities inherent in the human body. It is an atypical condition whose "abnormality" gives us a peek into the "normal," everyday relationships between urethra, anus, and genitals.

Ginette's urinary problems were diagnosed as "vesicourethral dyssynergia," and likewise her rectoanal problems typically would be called "dyssynergic defecation" or "rectoanal dyssynergia."[72] I avoid these terms, however, because they evoke a conventional, biologically flat economy that misunderstands—even eschews completely—the psychological capacities inherent to human physiology.[73] With Devroede, I prefer the terms "urethrismus" and "anismus," respectively, because the suffix "-ismus" indicates "functional disorders of a spastic or non-relaxing nature" that cannot be successfully treated with biologically flat medical approaches, such as simply administering pills or conducting surgery.[74] It's true that Ginette suffers from various forms of dyssynergia—the muscles in her pelvic floor are not well coordinated—but this description of her physiological condition is more

---

[71] Ghislain Devroede, "Front and Rear: The Pelvic Floor Is an Integrated Structure," *Medical Hypotheses*, 1999, 52(2): 147; Devroede, "La pensée cloacale," http://www.crifip.com/articles/la-pensee-cloacale.html, accessed May 21, 2013.

[72] Devroede, "Front and Rear," 148.

[73] Wilson, "Gut Feminism," 83.

[74] Devroede, "Front and Rear," 147, 148.

of a tautology than a diagnosis that might help her. Why can't her urinary muscles empty her bladder? Why aren't her rectum and anus coordinating to evacuate her feces? The answer, as "ismus" suggests, has something to do with an inability to relax. And given the integrated structure of the pelvic floor, that inability likely has something to do with the muscles around Ginette's vaginal canal. They, too, are likely to have difficulties knowing when and how to direct traffic in their region: when to relax and allow something in or out, when to constrict to prevent passage, and so on.

When Ginette's father began sexually abusing her as an adolescent, he would give her quarters so that she would "shut up" and not tell anyone about what he did.[75] When she told this to Devroede, he immediately exclaimed, "What an obedient little girl!" Ginette was puzzled by this response since she indeed, finally, was telling her doctors about the abuse, so Devroede continued, "But yes, he told you to shut up, and you closed up everything. You closed the exit to the urinary tract and you have urinary problems. You closed the vagina and you have pain at penetration during sexual intercourse. You closed yourself to pleasure and you never achieve orgasm. You closed your anus and you are constipated." Upon hearing this, Ginette burst into tears, flew into a fit of rage, and left the doctor's office, only to return eight hours later, collapsing into tears once again. When she calmed down, she told Devroede, "It's incredible! As soon as I began to cry, I felt that everything down below began to open up." As Devroede reports, Ginette's health soon began to improve: she no longer retained urine, no longer was constipated, and could achieve orgasm via vaginal penetration during sexual intercourse.[76]

Of course, Ginette's recovery was not so simple as crying and then immediately regaining healthy pelvic floor functioning. After her diagnosis of anismus and related problems, Ginette began a year-long schedule of eleven sessions of biofeedback to re-educate her perineum.[77] This process involves placing a probe in the rectum to detect which muscles are contracting and which are relaxing when the patient bears down as if to defecate. As the patient becomes consciously aware of what her anal muscles are doing, she can learn, through ongoing feedback from the rectal probe, to relax rather than contract her anus while attempting to defecate.[78] After one year, the communication—the dynamic pressure, tension, and reflexes—between Ginette's rectum and anus had changed so that they cooperated rather than fought against each other.

---

[75] Devroede, *Ce que les maux de ventre dissent de notre passé*, 110.

[76] Devroede, *Ce que les maux de ventre disent de notre passé*, 110–111, my translation.

[77] Devroede, *Ce que les maux de ventre disent de notre passé*, 116.

[78] Devroede, *Ce que les maux de ventre disent de notre passé*, 277. Devroede reviews the success rate and limitations of biofeedback therapy for anismus more broadly in Devroede, "Front and Rear," 149–150.

While not inaccurate, this description of perineal biofeedback still fails to fully capture the process by which Ginette's constipation was alleviated. Often during biofeedback sessions, Ginette declared that she could not feel the lower (pelvic) parts of her body but that she was beginning to feel them vividly at home, from time to time. As the sessions continued, Ginette began to verbalize (free associate) more and more while the rectal probe was in place. She spoke freely of her dreams and expressed a great deal of emotion while retraining her perineum.[79] The biofeedback sessions worked because they were as much a form of psychotherapy as a form of physical therapy. Ginette wasn't just retraining her rectal muscles; she also was reviving her "ability to feel the body as the place where the psyche lives."[80] As Devroede argues, this approach to biofeedback "is not compatible with an attitude that compares the technique of biofeedback therapy with the technique of repairing a car."[81] Treating the body like an inanimate machine, biologically flat methods of administering biofeedback misunderstand what physical therapy accomplishes because they misunderstand the "bio" with and to which it is providing feedback. Successful treatment of anismus depends on an appreciation of the body's biologically unconscious habits, and yet many technicians are not trained to provide psychological support to patients during the biofeedback process.[82]

In addition to biofeedback therapy, Ginette also participated in other forms of psychotherapy, including group therapy, hypnotic regression, dream analysis, and art therapy.[83] At one point, she sent a card and two dollars to her father with a note that simply said, "This is for the twenty-five cents."[84] She had chosen a card that featured a girl in front of a house that resembled her childhood home. After sending the card, Ginette experienced eight days of diarrhea, and then resumed normal bowel functioning. When the brother who had abused her eventually asked for her forgiveness, Ginette replied, "Even if I do that, my anus hasn't forgiven you yet."[85] (Ginette's retort is a brilliant illustration of physician Bessel Van der Kolk's claim that "the body keeps the score."[86]) Ginette's urinary problems eventually cleared up, as did her dyspareunia. The last symptom to disappear was her cutaneous anesthesia: even after Ginette could achieve orgasm during vaginal penetration, her breasts remained "frozen," as she described them, for some time. She began to

---

[79] Devroede, *Ce que les maux de ventre disent de notre passé*, 116.

[80] Donald Winnicott, quoted in Bessel Van der Kolk, *The Body Keeps the Score: Brain, Mind, and Body in the Healing of Trauma* (New York: Viking, 2014) 113.

[81] Devroede, "Front and Rear," 150.

[82] Devroede, "Front and Rear," 150.

[83] Devroede, "Early Life Abuses," 142.

[84] Devroede, *Ce que les maux de ventre disent de notre passé*,117, my translation.

[85] Devroede, *Ce que les maux de ventre disent de notre passé*, 118, my translation.

[86] Van der Kolk, *The Body Keeps the Score*.

regain sensation in her breasts around the time that her father asked for forgiveness and that Ginette openly grieved having never been loved by him.[87]

Ginette's case illuminates the thoroughly psychological and often unconscious dimensions of human physiology. As Wilson has argued regarding the gut in particular, "the aid given by the musculature of the intestines is not that of passive substrate awaiting the animating influence of the unconscious but, rather, that of an interested broker of psychosomatic events."[88] Ginette's experience supports extending Wilson's point to the pelvic floor, of which the gut is a part. When Ginette was sexually abused by her brother and father, her breasts and vagina were active psychosomatic participants in the traumatic event. Their physical involvement in the abuse was not that of being body parts touched by another person's body parts that then became unconsciously associated with the abuse. Nor, it should be said, were Ginette's breasts or vagina physically damaged during the abuse in the sense of being bruised or cut—which is not to say that they were not physically damaged. What "physical damage" means in Ginette's and similar cases is precisely what is at issue. A biologically flat attitude toward sexual abuse is incapable of comprehending not just the psychological harm, but also the physical harm that it does since the two are flip sides of the same psychosomatic coin.

Cloacal thinking helps us see how Ginette's urinary and rectoanal tracts were active psychosomatic participants in the trauma of her abuse, even though they were not directly targeted by her brother and father. They underwent the anxiety and tension experienced by the vagina as it closed itself off to say "no" to the abuse. They also were co-actors with the vagina when Ginette responded to her father's monetary bribe. And all three components of the pelvic floor coordinated with the skin of Ginette's breasts to strategize methods for coping with an abusive world. The character of her bodily tissues was to be constantly on guard and to numb themselves as a protective measure, just in case her muscular armor was breached. Ginette's anus, vagina, urinary tract, and breasts developed complex unconscious habits that allowed Ginette simultaneously to remain a dutiful daughter who obeyed her father's command to shut up and to disengage from sexual sensations and experiences so that she would be spared the psychosomatic pain of future sexual invasions.

Ginette was the mother of one son, but the reports of her medical case don't reveal anything about him or his gut functioning. It's fair to wonder, however, if the son experienced constipation, diarrhea, urinary incontinence, or other gut problems that manifested pelvic floor conflict similar to his mother's concerning when and whether to open up to or close off the "outside" world. This is because

---

[87] Devroede, *Ce que les maux de ventre disent de notre passé*, 119.
[88] Wilson, "Gut Feminism," 73.

gut dysfunction often follows along family lines.[89] It can do so, moreover, without involving genetic inheritance. While the field of psychoanalysis perhaps is best known for its insistence that unconscious fears, anxieties, and desires can be handed down across generations, surgeons and other medical professionals also have begun investigating the transgenerational, non-genetic inheritance of psychophysiological maladies. As Devroede claims, even as Western society tends to dismiss the significance of its elderly members, "these old people inhabit us. They have left traces in us."[90] Cloacal thinking encourages us to realize that, like the division of the pelvic floor tracts, separations between individual people are learned. Those separations are real, but they do not exhaust the realities of human relationships. The human body also has experiences prior to and apart from this learning that blur sharp boundaries between individuals and make possible psychophysiological communication between them.

We can see a concrete instance of this in the case of a seven-year-old boy named Charles, who was constipated from the very first week he was born.[91] By the time he was one month old, he was having only one bowel movement per week—an astonishingly low number given that newborns typically have very loose stool and are expected to have eight to ten bowel movements per day.[92] Because Charles was constipated when he was born and because he was a boy, an organic condition initially was suspected. The most likely diagnosis was Hirschsprung's disease, in which a person is born without nerve cells in the lower part of the large intestine and thus the intestinal muscles do not move waste matter downward to the rectum.[93] In that case, a straightforward surgical procedure should correct the condition. But after running the appropriate tests, it was clear that Charles did not have Hirschsprung's disease. His constipation was of a functional, rather than an organic nature. As additional tests confirmed, he had anismus. The amount of time that his fecal matter took to pass through the intestines was normal, but he contracted rather than relaxed his anal sphincter when he attempted to defecate.[94]

Before I move on to the rest of Charles's story, let me underscore that last point. As a newborn—*from the very first week of his life*—Charles suffered from a psychophysiological gut dysfunction.[95] How could that be so?

---

[89] To compound matters, Ginette's son, who was born before Ginette's treatment began, was named after her father at the insistence of Ginette's abusive husband, whom she later divorced (Devroede, *Ce que les maux de ventre disent de notre passé*, 115, 116).

[90] Devroede, *Ce que les maux de ventre disent de notre passé*, 94, my translation.

[91] Devroede, *Ce que les maux de ventre disent de notre passé*, 100.

[92] http://www.babycenter.com/404_how-many-bowel-movements-should-a-newborn-have-in-one-day_10014.bc, accessed June 17, 2013.

[93] Devroede, *Ce que les maux de ventre disent de notre passé*, 100.

[94] Devroede, *Ce que les maux de ventre disent de notre passé*, 101.

[95] While I have been unable to find details on other medical cases of infants with anismus as young as Charles, the North American Society for Pediatric Gastroenterology, Hepatology and Nutrition (NASPGHAN) Constipation Guideline Committee explains that "even in infancy, most

How could his anus already have developed biologically unconscious habits of anxiously fearing and shutting out the world? The details surrounding Charles's treatment, which involve his fusional relationship with his mother, provide an answer to that question. As a seven-year-old, Charles successfully underwent perineal biofeedback therapy, learning to relax rather than tighten his anus during defecation. At the beginning of early biofeedback sessions, when Charles's condition was beginning to improve, his mother, Jane, would announce proudly to the doctor, "We are less constipated now!"[96] As the sessions continued, Jane's choice of pronouns finally changed. Charles's doctor explains, "I gently made her understand that she was not constipated and that he [her son] is another person. The apprenticeship was slow and gradual before she passed from 'we' to 'he,' detaching him from her and bringing him into the world."[97] The gradual learning process that took place during the biofeedback sessions, which transformed Charles's relationship to the world, was as much his mother's as it was his own.

This point is highlighted by the events that followed Charles's biofeedback therapy. Charles no longer was constipated, but he became very angry and aggressive. His parents divorced, and Jane began psychotherapy, particularly concerning her own mother's dominance in her childhood family and the emotionally and psychologically incestuous relationship that Jane's father had with her. Charles experienced diarrhea during this time, leading his mother to exclaim, "It's mama that is the problem! When the mama is doing well, the son is doing well, and the reverse!"[98] When Jane tried to talk with her mother (Charles's grandmother) about her childhood, her mother would feign sleep and wouldn't discuss it. Shortly after and still refusing to talk with Jane about the past, Charles's grandmother began to attend a self-help group for sexually abused women.

---

constipation is functional" rather than the result of organic conditions such as Hirschsprung disease (Constipation Guideline Committee, "Clinical Practice Guideline: Evaluation and Treatment of Constipation in Infants and Children: Recommendations of the North American Society for Pediatric Gastroenterology, Hepatology and Nutrition," *Journal of Pediatric Gastroenterology and Nutrition*, 2006, 43: e11). Represented by two primary care pediatricians, one clinical epidemiologist, and five pediatric gastroenterologists, NASPGHAN developed its guidelines by reviewing and culling best practices from thirty years' worth of medical articles on constipation in infants and children. What is relevant for my purposes is that they excluded cases focusing on newborns less than 72 hours old ("Clinical Practice Guideline," e3). This seems to be because younger newborns with bowel dysfunction were assumed to have an organic disease, but that is an assumption worth questioning, in my view. (The committee does not explain the exclusion.) In any case, the apparently uncontroversial cutoff point of 72 hours demonstrates that infants as young as three days old are known in medical circles to suffer from non-organic bowel dysfunction—that is, while unusual, baby Charles's case is not unique.

[96] Devroede, *Ce que les maux de ventre disent de notre passé*, 101, my translation. I have provided a name for the mother for the ease of recounting Charles's story.

[97] Devroede, *Ce que les maux de ventre disent de notre passé*, 101, my translation.

[98] Devroede, *Ce que les maux de ventre disent de notre passé*, 102, my translation.

After his parents' separation, Charles divided his time between his mother's and his father's homes and developed divided bowel habits accordingly.[99] He had normal intestinal functioning during the days that he stayed with his father, and he was constipated during the days that he spent with his mother. Charles's doctor eventually learned that Jane also was constipated—the "we" she had used during Charles's biofeedback therapy was not entirely inaccurate, even though still inappropriate—and that all the children in her family of origin were. This is because at the smallest sign of a soft bowel movement, the children were forced to take a medicine to counter diarrhea. In addition to the medicine, another factor producing constipation was that to avoid this "treatment" (punishment) for defecating "improperly," the children tried not to defecate at all, leading to tremendous anxiety and panic when the inevitable need to defecate finally occurred. For her entire life, even after leaving her childhood home, Jane had been chronically constipated, and her bowel functioning was intimately related to the approval and disapproval of her parents. Her condition failed to respond to medical tests and treatments, which is not too surprising since it was not genetic (which some medical specialists suspected because of its lifelong duration) but rather familial.[100] Jane's bowel functioning finally became more regular when she began to talk with doctors about her childhood experience of enforced constipation.

Jane's experience of enforced constipation arguably was one of sexual abuse. This form of abuse is different from, for example, fondling the breasts, vaginal penetration, or rape. Enforced constipation might not seem particularly sexual because it involves the perineum. It does not directly involve the genitals, nor does it apparently generate overt sexual pleasure for the abuser, such as an orgasm. And it might seem exaggerated to call the situation one of abuse since on one description it merely involved regularly giving a child some over-the-counter medicine. Rape is a far more serious matter, one might say, and we undermine cases of real sexual abuse if we label deliberately constipating a child during potty training "abusive."

I agree that rape must be one of, if not the most, severe forms of sexual abuse. I do not wish to belittle the trauma of rape, nor do I wish to collapse all forms of sexual abuse into each other. But regularly and unnecessarily invading another person's body in order to control it, which is another description of what happened to Jane, also is abusive. And knowing what we do about the pelvic floor, we must acknowledge that the fact that the rectum and anus were involved rather than the vagina does not necessarily make the invasion non-sexual. Given that rape and other obvious forms of sexual abuse are as much, if not more, about domination as they are about overt sexual pleasure, we could say that a primary pleasure taken in sexual abuse is that of

---

[99] Devroede, *Ce que les maux de ventre disent de notre passé*, 102.
[100] Devroede, *Ce que les maux de ventre disent de notre passé*, 103.

bodily wielding power over someone else. This intertwining of power and sex in sexual abuse also is characteristic of "milder" forms of sexual abuse, such as the abuse Jane suffered. "The parental attitude toward the intestinal habits of their children is not sexually neutral," argues Devroede, which means "all forms of excretion thus can lend themselves to forms of abuse that are more of a symbolic order."[101]

What is unusual about Jean's experience as a child in North America in the mid-twentieth century is not that it included the abusive regulation of children's bowel functions, but that it reversed the typical pharmacological pattern of the abuse. The norm in that day and age, "as weekly as attending mass,"[102] was to give children laxatives, rather than constipating agents, to ensure that they defecated "properly." Whether through the use of laxatives or constipating agents, parents engaging in this norm kept tight control over their child's rectum and anus. The child didn't get a say in when or how to use this part of her pelvic floor. That decision remained firmly in the parent's hands.

More accurately, that decision typically remained firmly in the mother's hands. This detail points to the complicated—and complicit—relationship that women sometimes develop with a male-dominated society that encourages the abuse of females and other relatively powerless people. While we are not told which of Jane's parents administered the constipating agent (nor what form—oral or anal—the agent took), then as now, mothers, grandmothers, and other women tend to be the ones in charge of childrearing. While fathers and other men certainly might convey to their children (dis)approval for their (im)proper evacuation habits, it often was the mother's job to oversee the details of potty training. Thus "the impact of sexualization on the function of defecation by the parents" and the abuse that can accompany it are phenomena that often concentrate on the mother's relationship to her child.[103] "It is not rare, during a colonoscopy," Devroede explains, for him "to hear a patient speak of an invasive maternal comportment during their potty training: invasion of a titilating thermometer, of suppositories, of water enemas, or of the more oral method of laxatives."[104] Week after week, whether physically needed or not, the child's body was invasively controlled to open and shut as the parent/mother wanted, not as the child needed or desired. Through this practice, which was not uncommon in the United States at least until the 1950s, mothers participated in the domination of others encouraged by a masculinist and racist world. This is true even if they often did so out of a (perhaps unconscious) fear of failing to achieve the feminine ideal of being a perfect mother with a perfect child.

---

[101] Devroede, *Ce que les maux de ventre disent de notre passé*, 197, my translation.

[102] Devroede, *Ce que les maux de ventre disent de notre passé*, 102–103, my translation.

[103] Devroede, *Ce que les maux de ventre disent de notre passé*, 228, my translation.

[104] Devroede, *Ce que les maux de ventre disent de notre passé*, 228–229, my translation.

As Jean was talking about and recovering from her past history of enforced constipation, Charles meanwhile was becoming more and more enraged, even violent, at one point yelling at his mother and stabbing a knife into the kitchen table.[105] When he went so far as to angrily throw an ax at a summer camp instructor, something pivotal happened. Everyone, including his mother, was distraught, but something clicked for her in particular. Jane recognized and understood Charles's rage: it was the same rage that she felt. Or as Jane put it, "it was my rage that inhabited him, that he had made his own."[106] From a psychoanalytic point of view, we could say that Jane's/Charles' rage was like an activated hand grenade that had been passed down and finally exploded in their family.[107] The pin had been pulled when Jane was a child (and perhaps even earlier, in Jane's mother's life), but the explosion didn't occur until at least a generation later. The time delay can make the explosion seem unprovoked and thus irrational. When Charles acted out in violent rage, his behavior and feelings seemed incomprehensible to most people. There was nothing immediately associated with Charles (or apparently his camp counselor) to trigger them. Perhaps the problem was essentially Charles: was he revealing himself to be intrinsically unstable, even sociopathic? This misleading picture of Charles could result if we narrowly consider his behavior and emotions as that of a lone, isolated individual. Placed within the richer context of his family's history, in contrast, and appreciating the psychosomatic connections that can reach across generations, Charles's situation starts to make more sense.

After Charles's violent outburst at camp, Jane decided it was time to reveal and grapple with the big secret of her childhood, which was something other than—but perhaps, at least in her adult years, not unrelated to—her enforced constipation. When she was five years old, a priest who was an important friend of the family attempted to rape her. He had stripped her naked and was nude himself, just at the point of penetrating her, when her father walked in and saved her. To avoid scandal, however, Jane's father forbade her to speak of the event to anyone. It had to remain a secret, even from her mother, who beat Jane often and whom Jane feared would lash out if she knew what had taken place. Jane kept silent, describing herself as dead until the day when Charles attacked his camp counselor. At that point, Jane emotionally revived and finally felt the rage that had been repressed for decades: rage at the initial violation—rape—attempted by the priest, and rage at the following

---

[105] Devroede, *Ce que les maux de ventre disent de notre passé*, 103.

[106] Devroede, *Ce que les maux de ventre disent de notre passé*, 104, my translation.

[107] Bruno Clavier uses this metaphor to describe "the notion of a transgenerational phantom," which is produced by a trauma that a person cannot "metabolize, pass beyond, or transcend" and so she or he "expels" it to another family member (Clavier, *Les Fantômes Familiaux: Psychanalyse Transgénérationnelle* [Paris: Payot & Rivages, 2013] 49, my translation).

violation—silence—imposed by her family. And perhaps also rage at the other violation—of her anus—undertaken by her parent(s)'s constipating regime. In the process of Jane's return to therapy to deal with the rape, Charles's recurring constipation, as well as his anger and aggression, began to disappear.[108]

I hypothesize that Charles was born constipated because he inherited the condition from his mother. The muscles of his anus were already psychologically developed when he was born. Thus to understand his anismus, one must broaden the medical investigation to include his mother's psychophysiology. This is not, of course, the typical diagnostic procedure followed by Western medicine, but that might be why Western medicine has had a difficult time understanding and curing chronic gastrointestinal problems such as IBS and Crohn's disease. As Devroede comments in a related fashion, "It's clear that if a doctor asked a patient who consulted him because of a bad stomach what had happened to the patient's grandfather, the doctor would come off as crazy. And yet . . . We know today that the irritable bowel is learned, like the alphabet."[109] It might sound insane, but that's because of the misguided, atomistic individualism of Western medicine. It has recognized the contagious nature of, for example, the flu or the chicken pox, but not of physiological maladies that are highly animated by biologically unconscious habits. "We must stop seeing illness as an event that affects the sick person without affecting the people around him or her," as Devroede argues.[110] In particular, maladies of the gut often can be transgenerational. They can be handed down from grandparents to parents to children, much like family heirlooms are passed down, except that gut inheritances take place unconsciously. For a person to understand her own psychophysiological condition, she needs to grapple not only with what has happened to her in her lifetime, but also with "what the family milieu provided as ancestral heritage" when she was a child.[111]

As an adult, when pregnant with Charles, Jane was not consciously aware of the anxiety and rage she felt as a result of her traumatic childhood experiences. They nevertheless appear to have been transmitted to Charles while he was a fetus, a kind of ancestral heritage (reaching back at least to Charles's grandmother) passed down via endometrial lining and umbilical cord. Admittedly, since we don't know what the transmission mechanism is (or indeed, if there is one at all), all we can speak of in Charles's case is the appearance of transmission. We do know, however, that stress hormones, such as cortisol, can be passed from mother to fetus,[112] and so it is likely that

---

[108] Devroede, *Ce que les maux de ventre disent de notre passé*, 104.

[109] Devroede, *Ce que les maux de ventre disent de notre passé*, 174, my translation. The ellipses and pause are Devroede's.

[110] Devroede, *Ce que les maux de ventre disent de notre passé*, 303, my translation.

[111] Devroede, *Ce que les maux de ventre disent de notre passé*, 174, my translation, emphasis added.

[112] Richard C. Francis, *Epigenetics: The Ultimate Mystery of Inheritance* (New York: W. W. Norton, 2011) 142. Chapter 3 will take up stress hormones and fetal life in more detail.

a chemical story could be told about the effect of various hormones on the fetus's anal and other muscular development. (I also can't help think of the similarities between a pregnant woman's oral microbiome and her placental microbiome, mentioned in the introduction, although I don't know how to connect them to the case here. It's as if what Jane couldn't speak was transferred to Charles's fetal home.) Whatever the specifics—to my knowledge, we don't yet know why sphincter muscles sometimes become overly tight in the womb—what is important to realize is that the chemical and muscular story at work here is simultaneously a psychological one concerning the development of the fetus's biologically unconscious habits. We know that the fetus bodily recognizes things after it is born: the smell of its mother, the sound of her and others' voices.[113] The future adult that the fetus becomes almost certainly will forget these things, at least at a conscious level, but they nonetheless form "a mass of sensorial information that his [or her] body absorbs in the dawn of his [or her] senses."[114] What also is dawning in the fetal body are habitual ways of transacting with the world that are potentially emotionally and psychologically charged.

I suggest that this is true for all people, not just those who are born with anismus or other psychophysiological problems. Like the relationship of cross-modal correspondences and synesthesia, a continuum exists in human development between "normal" rectal habits and Charles's "abnormal" ones. Charles's illness has the ability to reveal aspects of human embodiment that often go unnoticed, to give us a peek at a process that happens for all fetuses that we usually aren't aware of. Contra Freud, strong affects experienced on a non-conscious or unconscious level are not, in themselves, a malady. They are native to biological life, at least at the human level. We thus should resist understanding the psychological nature of Charles's newborn anus as a deformity that occurred in the womb. It's true that his anus developed in a different psychophysiological way that most other anuses do and that his particular anal habits were harmful to his health. Those habits needed to change for the sake of Charles's future well-being. But their transformation was precisely that: a transformation, not an elimination of anal character. Treating Charles's illness did not mean discharging or abolishing his biologically affective habits, but rather altering them—which is to say, altering his relationship with the world and with his mother in particular. Those relationships improved only when Charles's gastrointestinal heritage was confronted: that is, when

---

[113] Stefano Vaglio, "Chemical Communication and Mother-Infant Recognition," *Communicative and Integrative Biology*, May–June 2009, 2(3): 279–281, http://www.ncbi.nlm.nih.gov/pmc/articles/PMC2717541/, accessed June 17, 2013; H. Varendi, R. H. Porter, and J. Winberg, "Attractiveness of Amniotic Fluid Odor: Evidence of Prenatal Olfactory Learning?" *Acta Paediatricia*, October 1996, 85(10): 1223–1227.

[114] Devroede, *Ce que les maux de ventre disent de notre passé*, 109, my translation.

his mother also addressed her pelvic floor's character and her biologically unconscious habits of anxiety and anger.

Cloacal thinking could be considered a description of how the body's biologically unconscious habits operate. The body relates to itself cloacally, refusing to compartmentalize itself or its functions, and this is particularly apparent in the case of trauma when bodily functions come to each other's aid and swap or share their jobs. The body's cloacal thinking doesn't collapse all bodily functions into each other. It understands their differences, even as it refuses to essentialize them. Not all gut habits are the same. It is significant, for example, that there is a much higher rate of past sexual abuse for patients with IBS than for patients with functional disorders of the upper gastrointestinal tract.[115] Both the anus (in the case of IBS) and the lower esophageal sphincter (in the case of achalasia) fail to relax, but their failure—which is to say, their refusal of the world—tends to have a different character. It unfortunately is difficult to be precise about the character of achalasia and other lower esophageal sphincter disorders since their relationships with various social maladies (for example, sexual abuse in the case of IBS) have not been studied as much as those of lower gut disorders. The rate of IBS among people with past sexual abuse (in contrast to the rate of sexual abuse among patients who seek treatment for IBS) also isn't often investigated or reported. But we know enough about the gut's unconscious biological habits to hypothesize that a biosocial-psychological factor, perhaps also a social malady, is relevant in the case of achalasia.

Finally, *pensée cloacale* is a form of thinking that would benefit Western medical practice. As Devroede has argued, the compartmentalization of urinary function, defecation, and sexuality makes it difficult for doctors and nurses to diagnose and treat patients (usually women) with various pelvic floor dysfunctions. Urologists, gynecologists, obstetricians, gastroenterologists, colorectal surgeons, psychologists, and doctors who treat sexual dysfunction—all tend to exist in separate medical worlds and not communicate with each other.[116] But the patient's symptoms and bodily experiences don't neatly divide up into isolated compartments. Especially in the case of gut abdominal pain and gut dysfunction, the medical failure to thinking cloacally has led to a great deal of unneeded surgery for women, especially vaginal/uterine procedures such as laparoscopy and hysterectomy.[117] "There exists an extraordinary clinical confusion between 'the front' and 'the back'" of the pelvic floor,[118] resulting, for example, in four times as much surgery for

---

[115] Devroede, "Front and Rear," 147.

[116] Devroede, "Front and Rear," 147.

[117] Devroede, "Early Life Abuses," 146; Devroede, "La pensée cloacale," http://www.crifip.com/articles/la-pensee-cloacale.html, accessed May 21, 2013.

[118] Devroede, "La pensée cloacale," http://www.crifip.com/articles/la-pensee-cloacale.html, accessed May 21, 2013, my translation.

sexually abused women as for non-abused women.[119] On average, a woman raped by her father will have eight surgical procedures, 70% of which will be unnecessary, and she will see eighteen non-psychiatric doctors and be hospitalized thirty times.[120]

We don't know exactly how many doctors and hospitals Ginette visited, nor how many times she was operated on. We do know that she endured years of pain and suffering because her condition was misunderstood and that this situation is not uncommon for women who are sexually abused. Why couldn't Ginette urinate normally? Why didn't her bladder and urethea muscles coordinate properly? The answer is not found in focusing mereologically on the urinary tract, just as the medical confusion between the "front" and the "rear" of the pelvis is not cleared up by establishing sharp boundaries between them. Isolating the functioning of Ginette's urinary tract from that of her anus and vagina (and breasts, moreover) only obscures the problem. To understand why her body was "shut up" means understanding the biologically unconscious habits of her gut, pelvic floor, and entire body. The character of a person's gut is at once physiological, psychological, and social, and it is formed through relationship with his or her past. Thinking cloacally would improve the medical treatment of women and victims of sexual abuse—and indeed, of all people, regardless of their gender or past history—but it will require physicians, nurses, biofeedback technicians, and other clinicians to adopt a more "holistic" view of medicine that appreciates the transactions between physiology and unconscious habit.[121]

We also don't know how exactly baby Charles inherited anismus from his mother while in the womb. Even if stress hormones such as cortisol were passed from mother to fetus (as we know they can be) and even if they can be chemically responsible for over-tightening a fetus's developing anal muscles (which we don't know much about), why would those hormones target Charles's anus in particular? Why not his lower esophageal sphincter or pylorus? To push the point further, why the digestive tract at all and not, for example, a set of relatively distant muscles such as those of the hands or feet? Perhaps one day a cloacal approach to medicine will give us answers to these questions. Lacking those answers for now, we nonetheless should not dismiss the uncanny similarity of Charles's and his mother's anismus. I want to underscore that point: there is so much that is unexplained about their case that it might be tempting to throw it out as an anomaly. But we should not use our lack (and often the biological flatness) of current medical knowledge as a reason to set aside odd or "crazy" sounding psychosomatic problems. Cloacal thinking urges us to investigate the medical possibility that Charles inherited

---

[119] Devroede, "Early Life Abuses," 147.
[120] Devroede, "Early Life Abuses," 147.
[121] Devroede, "Front and Rear," 147, 151.

the physiological effects of the sexual abuse that his mother experienced and that this inheritance was made possible by a shared psychosomatic world. This would be a transmission of a physiological affliction that is not genetic. (More soon on cases like this in Chapter 3.) Social phenonomena such as sexist oppression can have psychophysiological effects that ripple across generations, and recognizing this is important to healing everyone affected by them.

{ 3 }

The Epigenome

ON THE TRANSGENERATIONAL EFFECTS OF RACISM

When you're confronted with racism, that covert racism, your
stomach just gets like so tight. You can feel it almost
moving through your body; almost you can feel it
going into your bloodstream.

—KIM ANDERSON, *AFRICAN AMERICAN LAWYER AND MOTHER*

In 1990 Kim Anderson was six and a half months pregnant, in good health, eating well, exercising appropriately, and anticipating a healthy full-term baby. She unexpectedly went into labor two and a half months early, giving birth to her daughter Danielle, who weighed only two pounds and thirteen ounces. Danielle remained in intensive care while Anderson returned home, and as Anderson explains, "I remember getting home and being in the bathroom, just, I fell apart. You know, 'cause it's like I didn't get to take my baby home, you know. I remember just sort of falling apart."[1] As a severely premature baby, even if Danielle made it through the first few days, she still was at high risk of dying before her first birthday. And if she survived beyond one year, she had a high risk of subsequent health problems and learning disabilities, such as cerebral palsy, hearing loss, and visual, digestive, and respiratory problems.[2] But amazingly, Danielle pulled through and suffered no health or learning impairments due to her prematurity. In 2008, she was a healthy eighteen-year-old with aspirations of becoming a cardiologist and neonatologist. "It could have been so different," however, as Anderson underscores anxiously, "it could have been so different."[3]

While telling her story, Anderson mentions that Danielle was "a second-generation preemie," which leads her to "worry what would happen if

---

[1] Quoted in "Unnatural Causes: When the Bough Breaks," California Newsreel, 2008, page 2; http://www.unnaturalcauses.org/assets/uploads/file/UC_Transcript_2.pdf, accessed December 2, 2012.

[2] http://www.cdc.gov/features/prematurebirth/, accessed May 16, 2013.

[3] Quoted in "Unnatural Causes," 9.

[her] daughter delivered a preemie" in turn.[4] Concerned for Danielle's future, Anderson reflects, "You just don't want her to have to go through that and experience that, and wonder what the outcome would be."[5] It unfortunately is very likely, however, that Danielle would deliver prematurely if she became pregnant, making it (at least) three generations of premature birth for the women in Anderson's immediate family. (We aren't told if Anderson's mother also was born prematurely, but that fact would be relevant to my purposes here.) It's as if prematurity were inherited by Anderson's daughter and then could be passed down to Anderson's granddaughter as well. How could that be so? And why is it significant that this pattern of premature birth is occurring in the lives of African American women in particular?

We have already seen evidence in the context of sexual abuse that the physiological effects of psychosomatic trauma can be transgenerational. Baby Charles and his mother presented a striking case of the possible non-genetic inheritance of the effects of sexual abuse. Anderson's experience, in turn, raises the question of whether other forms of social trauma also might have inheritable biopsychosocial effects. This chapter continues to focus on non-genetic physiological heritability by examining how people of color can biologically inherit the deleterious effects of racism. As we will see, it's not just the effects of sexism and male privilege that can be passed down generationally. The harmful physiological impact of white supremacy and white privilege also can reach across multiple generations, from grandparents to their children and their grandchildren.

In at least one respect, of course, the general concept of transgenerational inheritance of the effects of racism is nothing new, at least not to critical philosophers of race and others who study—and often live—radical disparities in wealth across racial lines. On average, in the late 1980s, white people in the United States had twelve times the net worth of African Americans, in the form of property, savings, et cetera.[6] The gap only widened in the wake of the 2008 recession. In 2010, the median net household worth of white American families was twenty-two times that of black American families: $110,729 compared to $4,955.[7] The roots of this disparity reach far back in American history to the days of slavery, when black slaves did not own their labor and thus could

---

[4] Quoted in "Unnatural Causes," 9.

[5] Quoted in "Unnatural Causes," 9.

[6] Charles Mills, *The Racial Contract* (Ithaca, NY: Cornell University Press, 1997) 37–39.

[7] Tami Luhby, "Worsening Wealth Inequality by Race," *CNNMoney*, June 21, 2012, http://money.cnn.com/2012/06/21/news/economy/wealth-gap-race/index.htm, accessed December 10, 2012. See also Thomas Shapiro, Tatjana Meschede, and Sam Osoro, "The Roots of the Widening Racial Wealth Gap: Explaining the Black-White Economic Divide," Institute on Assets and Social Policy Research and Policy Brief, February 2013: 1–8, http://iasp.brandeis.edu/pdfs/Author/shapiro-thomas-m/racialwealthgapbrief.pdf, accessed June 25, 2013. Hispanic Americans and Asian Americans also saw their wealth inequality gap widen in comparison with white Americans; white families' net worth now is fifteen times that of Hispanic families and twice that of Asian families.

not profit from it, to the days of Reconstruction, when newly freed slaves did not receive their promised forty acres and a mule. These patterns have not disappeared, but currently the issue of economic transgenerational inheritance often is discussed without mentioning either race or centuries of white domination. While communities of color occasionally revive related questions concerning reparations to African Americans, Native Americans, and Japanese Americans, generally the subject of transgenerational inheritance is relegated to the seemingly color-blind realm of tax codes governing estate and inheritance taxes.[8]

Economic racial disparities constitute only one form of transgenerational racial inheritance, however. Another equally significant form is transgenerational racial inheritance along biological or physiological lines. We could call this phenomenon "racial disparities in health," in contrast (or actually, often in conjunction) with "racial disparities in wealth." As the biological and medical sciences increasingly are demonstrating, there exist significant differences in the general health of white and non-white Americans. For example, African Americans, Native Americans, and Pacific Islanders generally have higher rates of coronary artery disease, diabetes, stroke, HIV/AIDS, and infant mortality than do white Americans.[9] Health differences between black and white Americans in particular have been well studied in the United States, and thus we know that African Americans under fifty years of age are twenty times more likely to experience heart failure than white Americans in the same age group, and they have higher rates of the accompanying conditions of high blood pressure, obesity, kidney disease, and low levels of LDL or "good" cholesterol.[10] Racial health differences between black and white Americans persist, moreover, even after adjusting for differences in socioeconomic status.[11]

---

[8] Transgenerational inheritance also affects a person's "invisible capital," which includes the family connections and implicit knowledge that make it easier to succeed on the job market or as an entrepreneur (Chris Rabb, *Invisible Capital: How Unseen Forces Shape Entrepreneurial Opportunity* [San Francisco, CA: Berrett-Koehler Publishers, 2010]).

[9] Brian Smedley, Michael Jeffries, Larry Adelman, and Jean Cheng, "Briefing Paper: Race, Racial Inequality, and Health Inequalities: Separating Myth from Fact," (http://www.cmfp.org/MainMenuCategory/Library/ResearchResourceLinks/RaceRacialInequalityandHealthInequitiespdf.aspx, accessed November 30, 2012) 1. As a whole, Asian Americans also have better health outcomes than African Americans, Native Americans, and Pacific Islanders, but differences within this group should be noted. For example, Vietnamese and Korean American women have some of the highest rates of cervical cancer and Vietnamese American men die from liver cancer at a rate seven times that of white men (2–3).

[10] Katherine Kam, "Why Are African Americans at Greater Risk for Heart Disease?" 2010, http://www.webmd.com/heart-disease/features/why-african-americans-greater-risk-heart-disease, accessed November 30, 2012.

[11] Jonathan Michael Kaplan, "When Socially Determined Categories Make Biological Realities: Understanding Black/White Health Disparities in the U.S," *The Monist*, 2010, 93(2): 286; Michael C. Lu and Neal Halfon, "Racial and Ethnic Disparities in Birth Outcomes: A Life-course Perspective," *Maternal and Child Health Journal*, 2003, 7(1): 14; David R. Williams, Yan Yu, James S. Jackson, and Norman B. Anderson, "Racial Differences in Physical and Mental Health," *Journal of Health Psychology*, 1997, 2(3): 325–351.

These are health differences related to race, but just as accurate as labeling them *racial* disparities would be to call them *racist* disparities. Nowhere in the scientific world has this been recognized more forcefully than in the health sciences. As early as 1991, for example, a pair of American neonatologists called for "a shift of focus from 'race 'to 'racism' " in studies of racial health differences.[12] In the past decade, their request implicitly has been honored as various social and life scientists have documented the effects of racism on the physical and mental health of people of color, challenging the assumption that racial health differences can be explained by race apart from the phenomena of racial discrimination and racial prejudice. This shift in the health sciences is intensely disputed, however. Although some studies on race and health disparities increasingly are "unmask[ing] racism as a bona fide public health problem,"[13] large amounts of money and time are being devoted to the search for genetic causes of racial differences.[14] While the connection between racism and the risk of poor health isn't news to most people of color, it is profoundly changing the way that the life sciences is both thinking about the etiology of many diseases and grappling with questions of how to scientifically measure racial discrimination.[15]

As a briefing paper for the American Nurses Association recently has asked, "how does race get under the skin and influence our physiology if it isn't biological?"[16] The paper's authors rightly answer that it is not biology

---

[12] R. J. David and J. W. Collins, Jr., "Bad Outcomes in Black Babies: Race or Racism?" *Ethnicity and Disease*, 1991, 1(3): 240.

[13] Madeline Drexler, "How Racism Hurts—Literally," *The Boston Globe*, 2007, http://www.boston.com/news/globe/ideas/articles/2007/07/15/how_racism_hurts____literally/?page=full, accessed November 30, 2012; see also Nancy Krieger, "Does Racism Harm Health? Did Child Abuse Exist before 1962? On Explicit Questions, Critical Science, and Current Controversies: An Ecosocial Perspective," *American Journal of Public Health*, 2008, 98 (Supplement 1): S20–S25.

[14] Troy Duster, "Buried Alive: The Concept of Race in Science," in *Genetic Nature/Culture: Anthropology and Science beyond the Two-Culture Divide*, eds. Alan H. Goodman, Deborah Heath, and M. Susan Lindee (Berkeley, CA: University of California Press, 2003) 258–277; Duster, "Lessons from History: Why Race and Ethnicity Have Played a Major Role in Biomedical Research," *Journal of Law, Medicine & Ethics*, Fall 2006: 1–11; Katherine Kam, "Why Are African Americans at Greater Risk for Heart Disease?" http://www.webmd.com/heart-disease/features/why-african-americans-greater-risk-heart-disease; Nancy Krieger, "Stormy Weather: *Race*, Gene Expression, and the Science of Health Disparities." *American Journal of Public Health*, 2005, 95(12): 2155–2180; Sandra S. Lee, Barbara A. Koenig, and Sarah S. Richardson, eds., *Revisiting Race in a Genomic Age* (Piscataway, NJ: Rutgers University Press, 2008) 89–200; Pilar Ossorio and Troy Duster, "Race and Genetics: Controversies in Biomedical, Behavioral, and Forensic Sciences," *American Psychologist*, 2005, 60 (1): 115–128; and Dorothy Roberts, *Fatal Invention: How Science, Politics, and Big Business Re-create Race in the Twenty-First Century* (New York: The New Press, 2012) 104–122.

[15] Most studies have been done in the United States, but increasingly research is being performed in Finland, Ireland, South Africa, and New Zealand that demonstrates similar links between racism and negative health effects (Drexler, "How Racism Hurts—Literally").

[16] Smedley et al., "Briefing Paper: Race, Racial Inequality and Health Inequities," (http://www.emfp.org/MainMenuCategory/Library/ResearchResourceLinks/RaceRacialInequalityandHealthInequitiespdf.aspx, accessed November 30, 2012) 6. See also social epidemiologists Laura

alone that constitutes our body's physiology. Existing health disparities between races, for example, are not the result of any essential biological or genetic differences—indeed, in that sense, race does not exist—but rather are the result of being harassed, oppressed, and discriminated against because one is not white. As Anderson attests in the epigram above, when a person is the target of racial oppression, racism can move through his or her body, seeping into the bloodstream and wrenching the gut. We should understand Anderson literally: the experience she depicts is not merely metaphorical or figurative. The effects of racism include physiological changes for the people who confronted by it, changes that typically are very damaging to their physical and psychological health. The sociopolitical phenomenon of racism can be and often is a physiological, biological phenomenon. We thus need to develop ways to think about biology that neither assume it is radically divorced from the social nor completely collapse it into the social, and this need is especially acute in the case of genetics. But how exactly should we understand the relationship between biological genes and social environments? More specifically, how can the effects of racism be simultaneously social and biological such that they can get "under the skin" and into the bloodstreams of people of color? And how are these physiological effects sometimes inherited by subsequent generations, getting "under their skin," too?

I will draw primarily on the field of epigenetics to answer these questions, demonstrating how transgenerational racist disparities can be manifest physiologically and help constitute the chemicals, hormones, cells, and fibers of the human body. As anthropologists recently have explained, epigenetics "highlight[s] an important set of mechanisms by which social influences can become embodied, having durable and even transgenerational influences on the most pressing US health disparities."[17] Epigenetics thus can be used to demonstrate how racism can have long-lasting effects on the biological constitution of human beings that are not limited to the specific person who is the target of racism, but instead extend to that person's offspring. In this way, the field of epigenetics can help philosophers and others understand the transgenerational biological impact of social forces, such as racism. It reveals that the damage done by racism is far more extensive that critical philosophers of race might have realized, and also that interventions against racism must address not just the economic, geographical, social, and psychological, but also the biological aspects of human existence.

D. Kubzansky and Ichiro Kawachi, who ask, "How can social conditions that are external to the individual get inside the body to influence health? One pathway is through emotions" (Kubzansky and Kawachi, "Affective States and Health," in *Social Epidemiology*, eds. Lisa F. Berkman and Ichiro Kawachi [New York: Oxford University Press, 2000]) 213.

[17] Christopher W. Kuzawa and Elizabeth Sweet, "Epigenetics and the Embodiment of Race: Developmental Origins of U.S. Racial Disparities in Cardiovascular Health," *American Journal of Human Biology*, 2009, 21(1): 2.

One final point before I dive into the details. The topic of the biological durability of racism is somewhat somber and even dispiriting, but I want to underscore that "durable" is not the same thing as "permanent."[18] In my view, racism is far more extensive than generally is admitted—at least by most white people, and perhaps by some people of color, too—and will be far more difficult to eradicate than most (white) people think. This does not mean, however, that it can't be challenged successfully, at least in some situations some of the time. (I do not share Derrick Bell's view that racism is ineradicable, although I appreciate why he makes this claim.[19]) Precisely to improve the chances of success, it is important to confront the fact that white privilege and white supremacy are tough, stubborn, and invidiously resourceful. One reason they have been able to endure for so long is that they can repeat their effects transgenerationally in the physiological and biological processes of human life.

A major health disparity between black and white Americans is found in preterm birth rates, and because of the extensive and often severe consequences of preterm birth, I focus on it here. Preterm birth, which occurs when a baby is born at least three weeks before full term (forty weeks), is a leading cause of infant death and mortality. It also is associated with numerous, subsequent health problems in both childhood and adulthood, such as respiratory and heart problems (including cardiovascular disease and related maladies), cerebral palsy, intellectual disabilities, vision and hearing complications, and feeding and digestive problems.[20] African American women are 1.6 times more likely than white American women to give birth prematurely (thirty-seven weeks or earlier), and 2.9 times more likely to give birth very prematurely (thirty-two weeks or earlier).[21] An African American baby is more than twice as likely to die in the first year of his or her life than a white

---

[18] As do Kuzawa and Sweet, "Epigenetics and the Embodiment of Race," 10.

[19] Derrick Bell, *Faces at the Bottom of the Well: The Permanence of Racism* (New York: Basic Books, 1993).

[20] Michael C. Lu and Belinda Chen, "Racial and Ethnic Disparities in Preterm Birth: The Role of Stressful Life Events," *American Journal of Obstetrics and Gynecology*, 2004, 191: 692; Centers for Disease Control, "Premature Birth," 2012, http://www.cdc.gov/features/prematurebirth/, accessed December 3, 2012; Mayo Clinic, "Complications, 2011, http://www.mayoclinic.com/health/premature-birth/DS00137/DSECTION=complications, accessed December 3, 2012; Kuzawa and Sweet, "Epigenetics and the Embodiment of Race," 3.

[21] Lu and Chen, "Racial and Ethnic Disparities in Preterm Birth," 692; Mayo Clinic, "Premature Birth," http://www.mayoclinic.com/health/premature-birth/DS00137, accessed December 3, 2012. See also the data on race, maternal education, and infant mortality rates in Pamela Braboy Jackson and David R. Williams, "The Intersection of Race, Gender, and SES: Health Paradoxes," in *Gender, Race, Class & Health: Intersectional Approaches*, eds. Amy J. Schulz and Leith Mullings (San Francisco: Jossey-Bass, 2006) 142–143, and Leith Mullings, "Resistance and Resilience: The Sojourner Syndrome and the Social Context of Reproduction in Central Harlem," in *Gender, Race, Class & Health*, eds. Schulz and Mullins, 347, 363–364.

American baby.[22] This gap has not improved since the civil rights movement and the end of de jure Jim Crow, despite effects to increase African American women's access to prenatal health care.[23] In fact, it only has widened in the past fifty years: from 1.6 to 2.3 times a greater risk of mortality for African American children than white American children in the first year of their lives.[24] As one neonatologist has put it, "there's something about growing up as a black female in the United States that's not good for your childbearing health. I don't know how else to summarize it."[25]

What is this "something" that is so damaging to African American women's health? The official if somewhat unhelpful answer, provided by the US Centers for Disease Control (CDC), is that "the reasons for the differences between [the preterm birth rates of] black and white women remain unknown and are an area of intense research."[26] A significant portion of this research is searching for a "preterm birth gene" specific to African Americans.[27] Besides tending to work with an essentialist concept of race, this line of research is troubling because it "problematically conflates observed biological variation with inferred genetic contributions, and ignores evidence that social factors can have durable life-course and transgenerational effects on health."[28] The wrong-headed assumption made by the quest for a preterm birth gene is that biology is both synonymous with genetics and antithetical to all things social.

Two alternative, complementary approaches understand the relationship between the biological and the social in a more sophisticated fashion: epigenetics and weathering. Let me begin with the simpler concept of weathering, which signifies the gradual wearing down of the body's systems by stressors that accumulate over time.[29] These stressors can come from just about anywhere in a person's environment, from the more chemical or physical (for example, air pollution or intense physical strain) to the more social or interpersonal (for example, children's temper tantrums or an unreasonably demanding boss). As the body experiences more and more stress, it becomes

---

[22] Lu and Halfon, "Racial and Ethnic Disparities in Birth Outcomes," 13.

[23] Michael C. Lu, Milton Kotelchuck, Vijaya Hogan, Loretta Jones, Kynna Wright, and Neal Halfon, "Closing the Black-White Gap in Birth Outcomes: A Life-Course Approach," *Ethnicity and Disease*, 2010, 20:S2–62.

[24] Richard David and James Collins, Jr., "Disparities in Infant Mortality: What's Genetics Got to Do With It?" *American Journal of Public Health*, 2007, 97(7): 1191.

[25] Richard David in "Unnatural Causes: When the Bough Breaks," California Newsreel, 2008, 1; http://www.unnaturalcauses.org/assets/uploads/file/UC_Transcript_2.pdf, accessed December 2, 2012.

[26] Centers for Disease Control, "Premature Birth," http://www.cdc.gov/features/premature-birth/, accessed December 3, 2012.

[27] David and Collins, Jr., "Disparities in Infant Mortality," 1191, 1192.

[28] Kuzawa and Sweet, "Epigenetics and the Embodiment of Race," 9.

[29] Ryan Blitstein, "Racism's Hidden Toll," *Miller-McCune* 2009, http://www.psmag.com/health/racisms-hidden-toll-3643/, accessed December 3, 2012. Weathering also is referred to as a cumulative pathway mechanism (Lu and Halfon, "Racial and Ethnic Disparities in Birth Outcomes," 16–17).

more and more weathered, making it more and more prone to disease and chronic health problems.

The notion of allostatic load helps explain how environmental stressors get under the skin and have detrimental biological effects.[30] In contrast with homeostasis, allostasis is a type of physiological regulation in which the internal stability of an organism is maintained while the organism deals with a challenge or crisis. When the body undergoes a physical or social challenge, it temporarily produces extra hormones, such as adrenaline, that help the organism meet the challenge, and then ceases producing them when the challenge has passed. This would count as a manageable allostatic load. In the case of ongoing stress, however, the body doesn't stop its extra hormone production, resulting in a high allostatic load. It is as if the organism's allostatic capacities are forced into overdrive and never shut off, weathering the body's systems of regulation, which produces health problems such as cardiovascular disease, diabetes, and accelerated physiological (versus chronological) aging.[31] What forces them to do this is not, for example, some kind of genetic quirk, but a social environment that places too much stress on the physiological capacities of the organism.

Weathering helps demonstrate why many racial health disparities are in fact racist health disparities. While all people experience some stress from time to time, and white people also can have high allostatic loads from severe chronic stress, African Americans and many other people of color generally have to deal with a significant stressor that white Americans do not: being discriminated against because they are not white. Racism contributes to the excessive weathering of non-white bodies, leading to elevated rates of disease and accelerated aging in comparison with white Americans.[32] For example, based on differences in telomeres, which serve as a kind of biological "mitotic clock" that measures age, black women at ages 49–55 years are estimated to be biologically seven and a half years older than white women in the same age group.[33] The ongoing, even daily struggle of African Americans against white domination and white privilege means that their allostatic systems rarely get a break. They are like an engine that is gunned non-stop, burning out much more quickly than an engine that gets to rest from time to time.

---

[30] Blitstein, "Racism's Hidden Toll," 6.

[31] Blitstein, "Racism's Hidden Toll," 6.

[32] Arline T. Geronimus, Margaret Hicken, Danya Keene, and John Bound, "'Weathering' and Age Patterns of Allostatic Load Scores Among Blacks and Whites in the United States," *American Journal of Public Health*, 2006, 96(5): 826–833.

[33] Arline T. Geronimus, Margaret T. Hicken, Jay A. Pearson, Sarah J. Seashols, Kelly L. Brown, and Tracey Dawson Cruz, "Do US Black Women Experience Stress-Related Accelerated Biological Aging? A Novel Theory and First Population-Based Test of Black-White Differences in Telomere Length," *Human Nature*, 2010, 21(1): 19–38.

Weathering thus helps explain Kim Anderson's particular situation. A well-educated, health-conscious woman whose first baby was extremely premature, Anderson is an example of what has been called the "paradox of the well-off black mother."[34] Anderson and her husband enjoy(ed) a high socioeconomic status, and she ate well, exercised, didn't smoke or drink, and otherwise did everything "right" during her pregnancy. And yet she went into labor two and a half months early, delivering a daughter who weighed only two pounds and thirteen ounces.[35] It seems that this shouldn't have happened. Education and socioeconomic status are good predictors of infant mortality for women of any race, and the poorest women with the least education tend to be at greatest risk. Decrease poverty and increase education and infant mortality will drop, or so the thinking goes. Anderson's education, financial situation, and general good health should have protected her from having a preterm birth. But this rubric doesn't work for African American women the way it does for white American women. The rate of infant mortality for African American women with college degrees or higher is about three times higher than that of white women with the same level of education, and well-educated African American women have worse infant mortality rates than white women without a high school education.[36] The question thus is why doesn't higher socioeconomic status reduce the rate of preterm birth for African American women the way it does for white women in the same socioeconomic class?

The answer is not likely to be found in a preterm birth gene carried by African Americans but not white Americans. This is evident when one compares the rates of preterm birth of white women and African immigrants to the United States. If people of African descent carry a preterm gene, then African women who give birth shortly after immigrating to the United States should have a similar rate of infant mortality and preterm birth as African American women. But in fact, their rates are virtually identical to that of white American women. Even more striking is the fact that within one generation of living in the United States, the rate of infant mortality and preterm birth for African immigrant women climbs to that of African American women.[37] In other words, the problem is broadly environmental, not genetic: there is

---

[34] David and Collins, Jr., "Bad Outcomes in Black Babies," 238.

[35] "Unnatural Causes," 2; http://www.unnaturalcauses.org/assets/uploads/file/UC_Transcript_2.pdf, accessed December 2, 2012.

[36] "Unnatural Causes," 3–4; http://www.unnaturalcauses.org/assets/uploads/file/UC_Transcript_2.pdf, accessed December 2, 2012.

[37] "Unnatural Causes," 4; http://www.unnaturalcauses.org/assets/uploads/file/UC_Transcript_2.pdf, accessed December 2, 2012; David and Collins, Jr., "Disparities in Infant Mortality," 1193; Kuzawa and Sweet, "Epigenetics and the Embodiment of Race," 7. A similar phenomenon also occurs in the case of Hispanic immigrants to the United States (Sabrina Tavernise, "The Health Toll of Immigration," *New York Times*, May 18, 2013, http://www.nytimes.com/2013/05/19/health/the-health-toll-of-immigration.html, accessed June 10, 2013).

something about living as a black person in the United States that is bad for black women's reproductive health.

Above all, that something includes the stress of racism. For women of all races, stress hormones are a normal part of pregnancy and help trigger labor when the baby has come to term. Abnormally high levels of stress, in contrast, can limit fetal growth, contribute to uterine inflammation, and trigger premature labor.[38] The amount of stress experienced by a woman before her pregnancy is relevant, moreover. If a woman begins her pregnancy with a stress levels that are already unhealthily high, then the extra stress hormones produced during pregnancy can push her to the brink of labor sooner than they should. What counts is not just stress experienced during the nine months of pregnancy, but also accumulated stress across a woman's life course.[39] All women experience occasional stress, of course, and any particular woman can accumulate unhealthy levels of stress prior to a pregnancy. But what if a society routinely subjects a particular group of women to ongoing chronic stress, treating them as subpersons from birth forward? This describes the general situation of black women who live in white-dominated cultures, such as the United States, regardless of their socioeconomic status. Weathered by racism and thus beginning a pregnancy with a relatively high allostatic load,[40] even educated, well-off African American women have a high risk of preterm birth. And because babies who survive a preterm birth are more likely to have significant health problems, the racial stress experienced by African American women is not limited to them but "can have a life-long impact on African American families and their health."[41]

---

[38] "Unnatural Causes," 6; http://www.unnaturalcauses.org/assets/uploads/file/UC_Transcript_2.pdf, accessed December 2, 2012; Kuzawa and Sweet, "Epigenetics and the Embodiment of Race," 4; Lu and Chen "Racial and Ethnic Disparities in Preterm Birth," 692; Roberts, *Fatal Invention*, 139–140.

[39] Lu and Halfon, "Racial and Ethnic Disparities in Birth Outcomes," S2–62. See also Eric J. Brunner, "Toward a New Social Biology," in *Social Epidemiology*, eds. Lisa F. Berkman and Ichiro Kawachi (New York: Oxford University Press, 2000) 306–331.

[40] M. Guyll, K. A. Matthews, and J. T. Bromberger, "Discrimination and Unfair Treatment: Relationship to Cardiovascular Reactivity among African American and European American Women," *Health Psychology*, 2001, 20(5): 315–325; Lu and Chen, "Racial and Ethnic Disparities in Preterm Birth;" Roberts, *Fatal Invention*, 132–133; Michelle J. Sternthal, Natalie Slopen, and David R. Williams, "Racial Disparities in Health—How Much Does Stress Matter?" *Du Bois Review: Social Science Research on Race*, 2011, 8(1): 95–113; Cheryl L. Woods-Giscombé, "Superwoman Schema: African American Women's Views on Stress, Strength, and Health," *Qualitative Health Research*, 2010, 20: 668–683. Although Lu and Chen "found no significant interaction effects of race-ethnicity and stress on preterm birth" (698), the conclusion of their study was that the Pregnancy Risk Assessment Monitoring System (PRAMS) measures stress too narrowly. PRAMS includes only the stressful life events that occurred during the twelve months before delivery, and thus it "may not measure stress adequately, particularly those daily hassles, chronic stressors, or contextual factors that may be more pervasive in the lives of women of color" (698). It also should be noted that even when focusing only on the twelve months prior to delivery, "a modest effect between black race and traumatic stressors" was documented (691).

[41] "Unnatural Causes," 6; http://www.unnaturalcauses.org/assets/uploads/file/UC_Transcript_2.pdf, accessed December 2, 2012.

With the concept of weathering, we already can see how the effects of racism reach across a generation from mother to child. As Anderson recounts, when she enters a store and is tailed by a suspicious clerk because "they just see a black woman," the result is a surge of adrenaline and other stress hormones that caused her stomach to tighten and her heart rate to increase.[42] Experiences such as these, which are common for many African Americans, are not restricted to their immediate targets. The targets' children, such as Anderson's daughter, indirectly will undergo the experience as well. The experience continues in the children's lives, not just, for example, by hearing their parents talk about their confrontations with racism or by learning from their parents' strategies for surviving in a white-dominated world. Children also can undergo their parents' experiences in a more physiological fashion: children can experience their parents' racial discrimination through the bodily effects that it has on their own health while in the womb.

I want now to push this argument further, demonstrating how the biological dimensions of racism can replicate themselves across more than just one generation. This will entail a detour into the general principles of epigenetics before returning to the specific topic of racism. "Replicate" is not a metaphor here, and for that reason my use of the term might make some readers skeptical. Weathering may have significant health effects on a mother and her fetus, but at bottom, one might object, it is merely an instance of a fetus's environment impacting its development, not genuine biological replication across generations. The latter can happen only through genetic reproduction; that's what Darwin and Mendel are said to have taught us. The standard story is that Lamarck's theory of inheritance of acquired characteristics—for example, that giraffes' necks lengthened over a short number of generations so they could reach leaves on tall trees—was soundly defeated in the nineteenth century. So how could one credibly claim today that something broadly social and non-genetic, such as the effects of racism and white domination, can be biologically inheritable?

Coined in the 1940s and rooted in the word "epigenesis," the term "epigenetic" initially was used to oppose preformationism in debates about human development.[43] (Epigenetics also is different from, and sometimes opposed to genetics, which I'll take up shortly.) While preformationism argued that the human self was fully preformed at the moment of conception and thus merely needed to grow, an epigenetic perspective held that development is a gradual and creative process in which an organism comes to exist.[44] Various

---

[42] "Unnatural Causes," 7; http://www.unnaturalcauses.org/assets/uploads/file/UC_Transcript_2.pdf, accessed December 2, 2012.

[43] Richard C. Francis, *Epigenetics: The Ultimate Mystery of Inheritance* (New York: W.W. Norton, 2011) 136.

[44] Francis, *Epigenetics*, 120.

religious issues swirled around these two positions, but for my purposes here the important difference between them is the role that the environment plays (or not) in the formation of a human being. Preformationism effectively dismissed the environment as unimportant to human development. As the earliest, seventeenth- and eighteenth-century versions of preformationism held, whatever a human organism would essentially be when she or he became an adult, it was fully contained in the unfertilized egg. More sophisticated versions of preformationism emerged in the eighteenth and nineteenth centuries, arguing that a human development was a process of making "manifest" the being that was "latent" in the zygote, but the preformationist message was unchanged. Human development supposedly is a mere unfolding of what is already fully present, a process relatively independent of environmental transactions.[45]

Fast-forward to the twenty-first century, and one can find the ghost of preformationism alive and well in modern genetics. Nowadays, instead of the unfertilized egg or zygote, it is the gene—or more precisely, one's DNA (deoxyribonucleic acid)—that often is considered the already formed kernel of a human being. Somewhat oversimplified, each human organism allegedly has a genetic program for developing from conception to adulthood into the particular organism that she is, and her development does not depend in any essential way on material, social, or other environments. Of course, modern genetics recognizes that the environment contributes something to human development—think, for example, of the type and quality of food that a human being eats. A human organism couldn't develop (she would die) if she didn't eat. But her genes nonetheless dictate how her body will make use of the food she consumes: her metabolism, her ability to process glucose, and so on. Whether she becomes obese and/or develops diabetes, to continue the example, depends ultimately on what kinds of genes she inherited from her parents, not on her environment. On this view, the gene plays an executive role in the cell. It is something like a director of a theatrical production, unilaterally controlling the proteins (actors) and biochemicals (stagehands) of a cell that, in turn, work to fulfill the gene's goal.[46]

Epigenetics, in contrast, rejects the notion of an executive gene, and it does so by acknowledging the formative role that various environments play in cellular activity. Perhaps most straightforwardly, "epigenetic" refers to "somatically heritable states of gene expression... without alternations in the DNA sequence."[47] To explain this definition further, consider the gene in its "naked" state, which is DNA in its well-known form of the double

---

[45] Francis, *Epigenetics*, 120–121.
[46] Francis, *Epigenetics*, 18–19.
[47] Sang-Woon Choi and Simonetta Friso, "Epigenetics: A New Bridge Between Nutrition and Health," *Advances in Nutrition*, 2010, 1: 8.

helix. What is less well known, at least by lay people, is that the naked gene is something of a fable.[48] A gene is rarely if ever naked, which is to say that the double helix neither exists nor functions by itself. Chemically attached to it are various organic molecules that regulate its activity.[49] One of the most common forms of DNA regulation is methylation: a gene with methyl attachments (one carbon atom and three hydrogen atoms) is said to be methylated.[50] Methylation can occur in varying degrees. We can think of methyl attachments as something like power knobs, turning down (or even off) certain genes in some cases, and turning up other genes in other cases.[51] The more methylated a particular gene is, the more its expression is inhibited, and vice versa.[52] Thus, for example, when the genes in mice contributing to both coat color and various health problems (such as obesity, diabetes, and cancer) are unmethylated—that is, turned up—the mice have yellow coats and significant health problems. When the same genes are highly methylated—that is, turned down/off—the mice have both darker coloration and no health problems associated with obesity, diabetes, or cancer.[53]

How do genes become methylated or demethylated? While methyl attachments and detachments can be a product of happenstance, often they occur because of environmental factors. For example, diet tends to play a significant role in epigenetic processes. When the mice with inadequate methylation of the relevant gene were fed a diet high in a methyl donor, such as folic acid, the coat color of their offspring darkened and their offspring suffered less from obesity, diabetes, and cancer.[54] (Epigenetics thus is related to why pregnant women are advised to take folic acid supplements.) Environmental factors contributing to methylation include not just elements of the physical and chemical environment, such as the food one eats and the pollution one intakes, but also social exchanges and interactions. Competitive experiences in sports or work, for example, can raise testosterone levels affecting gene expression, just as psychological trauma and chronic stress can influence genes expression via the elevation of corticotropin-releasing hormones (CRH) that stimulate cortisol production.[55]

---

[48] It also turns out to be something of a fable that each person has only one DNA sequence, identical across each of their cells. Many people, perhaps especially women who have been pregnant, "contain genetic multitudes" and even have the genomes of other people in their bodies (Carl Zimmer, "DNA Double Take," *New York Times*, September 16, 2013, http://www.nytimes.com/2013/09/17/science/dna-double-take.html?hpw&pagewanted=all&pagewanted=print, accessed November 15, 2014).

[49] Francis, *Epigenetics*, xi.

[50] Francis, *Epigenetics*, 6.

[51] Kuzawa and Sweet, "Epigenetics and the Embodiment of Race," 4.

[52] Francis, *Epigenetics*, 46.

[53] Francis, *Epigenetics*, 82–83.

[54] Francis, *Epigenetics*, 85.

[55] Francis, *Epigenetics*, 29, 33, 39–40.

The existence of methylation and other epigenetic processes helps shatter the myth of the executive gene. A human organism's material and social environments can play as significant a role in cellular activities determining health, weight, appearance, and so on, as her DNA does. (While conventional evolutionary biologists in particular might not agree with this claim, I would argue that scientists work with a very narrow range of tools if/when they limit themselves to genetic processes.[56]) Considered as part of a team that includes its epigenetic attachments, genes are poorly understood in terms of unilateral causation. They can be an effect as well as a cause of environmental, non-genetic factors.[57] We thus could claim that "epigenetic processes occur at the interface of our environment and our genes," which is to say that our cells—our bodies—are dynamically co-constituted by things both "inside" and "outside" us.[58]

The case of the under-methylated mice does more than just shatter the myth of the executive gene, however. It also provides an example of epigenetic inheritance. Epigenetic modifications to genes can and do occur within the lifetime of a single being, continuing well after the developmentally crucial periods of birth and childhood.[59] This is medically significant since it means it is conceivable that pathological epigenetic expressions could be changed or even reversed. But epigenetic events are not always or necessarily contained within a single being. They can be passed from one generation to another, as when the folic acid eaten by under-methylated mice changed the biochemistry of their pups. How is it that epigenetic processes can be transgenerationally inherited?

There generally are three forms of epigenetic transgenerational inheritance, ranging from more or less direct, with "direct" meaning that "the epigenetic mark is transmitted directly from parent to offspring through sperm or egg."[60] The most indirect form of epigenetic transgenerational inheritance occurs via the repetition of similar environments and social contexts in subsequent generations. In this case, the environment that triggers the (de)methylation or other alterations of a particular gene is reconstructed anew for each generation, producing epigenetic effects for offspring that are similar to those of their adult caregivers. The most powerful environment for this type of

---

[56] Thanks to an anonymous reviewer for providing this point.

[57] Francis, *Epigenetics*, 76, 124, 159.

[58] Francis, *Epigenetics*, xi. In this context, the "second genome," which is the genetic information carried by the hundreds of bacterial species that constitute the "microbiome" in the human gut, also is relevant. See Michael Pollan, "Say Hello to the 100 Trillion Bacteria That Make Up Your Microbiome," *New York Times*, May 15, 2013, http://www.nytimes.com/2013/05/19/magazine/say-hello-to-the-100-trillion-bacteria-that-make-up-your-microbiome.html?hp&pagewanted=all&_r=0, accessed June 10, 2013.

[59] Francis, *Epigenetics*, 47, 74.

[60] Francis, *Epigenetics*, 158.

epigenetic inheritance is the so-called maternal or uterine environment. For this reason, indirect epigenetic inheritance is similar to the phenomenon of weathering. In the case of epigenetic inheritance, however, the extra cortisol that a pregnant female produces when she is stressed does more than trigger early labor. It also changes some of the epigenetic markers on the fetus's DNA. When the mother's stress hormones are transmitted to the fetus through the placenta, they program—or overtax—the fetus's stress axis, also known as the HPA axis (for the hypothalamus, pituitary, and adrenal glands). The "axis" between these three endocrine glands is the set of influences and inter-relations between them: neurons in the hypothalamus produce a particular hormone (corticotropin-releasing hormone, or CRH) that leads to the pituitary gland to produce another hormone (corticotropin, or CT), which in turn stimulates the adrenal gland to release stress hormones such as cortisol.[61] The result of the mother's stress hormones' influence on the fetus's HPA axis is something like a fetal post-traumatic stress disorder (PTSD): "the elevated cortisol levels experienced by the fetus permanently adjust the settings of the stress axis of the fetus in a way that makes it more sensitive and hyperrespon-sive to subsequent stressful events."[62] The adult that the fetus then becomes is more likely to experience psychological difficulties, including actual PTSD, when exposed to significant stress.

Without performing specific tests on Kim Anderson's daughter, we have no way of knowing if she inherited the effects of her mother's racist envi-ronment via epigenetic changes. We do know, however, that something like this occurred in the case of German children whose mothers were pregnant during the Holocaust and American children whose mothers were pregnant during the September 11 World Trade center attacks. The German children were more prone to PTSD even though they had no direct experience of the Holocaust, and the American children were born with elevated stress responses and a hypersensitive stress axis, making them more susceptible to anxiety and depression than children whose mothers did not experience PTSD while pregnant.[63] The difference between these two examples and Anderson's situation lies in the duration of the stressful event in question. Because they were distinct events or time periods, the Holocaust and September 11 did not contribute to weathering in the same way that ongoing quotidian racism does. Nevertheless, the Holocaust and September 11 illustrate the repetition of a stressful/traumatic environment across two generations, producing simi-lar epigenetic effects for each of them. As in the case of the Holocaust and September 11, it is probable that the racism experienced by Anderson (and many other African American women) was a cortisol-producing situation

---

[61] Francis, *Epigenetics*, 39–40.
[62] Francis, *Epigenetics*, 42.
[63] Francis, *Epigenetics*, 43; Kuzawa and Sweet, "Epigenetics and the Embodiment of Race," 6.

that epigenetically changed their fetus's stress axes, producing deleterious psycho-physical results.

It also is probably that this pattern will repeat itself in the third generation, at least absent social, medical, or other interventions to change a person's stress response. Offspring with hypersensitive stress axes tend to become parents who create environments for their offspring that will elevate their children's (the grandchildren's) cortisol levels in turn.[64] For one reason, a pregnant woman who has an overtaxed stress axis (courtesy of the uterine environment when she herself was a fetus) will in turn have elevated cortisol levels in her uterus that can be transmitted to her fetus via the placenta.[65] In other words, Anderson's future grandchildren via Danielle are at risk of having overtaxed stress axes regardless of her daughter's experiences with racism and even if racism were abolished before the grandchildren were even conceived.

A second reason is that an overtaxed stress axis also affects parenting styles. As the above study of methylated mice also demonstrated, mice with a hyperresponsive stress axis do not lick their babies as much as parents with a healthy stress axis do. This is significant since baby mice that are licked amply have higher levels of a particular nerve growth factor (NGFI-A) that, when bound to glucocorticoid receptors (GR) in the brain, epigenetically change the responsiveness of that gene for the better. The higher the NGF level, the less sensitive one is to cortisol, which reduces levels of CRH and results in a dampened (that is, more resilient) stress axis.[66] In sum, mouse pups of poor lickers tend to develop the same overtaxed stress axis that their parents (and grandparents) have, and so the cycle repeats itself. Similar results have been found in studies on captive gorillas and rhesus monkeys.[67] Epigenetic effects related to the genes associated with stress sensitivity can be inherited transgenerationally through the replication of post-natal as well as uterine environments. This means that Anderson's stress levels might contribute to a parenting style that makes her daughter more sensitive and less resilient to racist (and other forms of) stress.

I will return shortly to the contentious issue of parenting styles, but before I do, it is important to note that biases exist in epigenetic research just as they do in any scientific field. There is no such thing as objective science if "objective" means a viewpoint that is independent of any particular perspective or interests. This is not necessarily cause for relativistic alarm, nor is it reason to dismiss what can be learned from epigenetics and other sciences.

---

[64] Guerry, John D., and Paul D. Hastings, "In Search of HPA Axis Dysregulation in Child and Adolescent Depression," *Clinical Child and Family Psychology Review*, 2011, 14(2): 135–160..

[65] Francis, *Epigenetics*, 42.

[66] Francis, *Epigenetics*, 45–46, 69.

[67] Francis, *Epigenetics*, 69.

In and of itself, bias is not problematic. In fact, it is unavoidable given that human beings are in and of the world, not little gods hovering outside it. As embodied, perspectival human beings, we can still judge better and worse ways of understanding the world.[68] The more important question to ask about genetics thus is not *whether* it is biased, but *which* particular biases have contributed to it and *whose* interests they tend to serve. The biases present in epigenetics do not necessarily invalidate the field, but they need to be unearthed, acknowledged, and critically countered by other perspectives.

For example, in my discussion of the pup-rearing methods of methylated mice, I referred to *parental* styles of licking, when in fact the scientific studies explicitly examined and discussed *maternal* styles of licking. Paternal styles of parenting in mice and other mammals, especially their connections to the stress responses of their offspring, have not been studied much to this point, as if they are irrelevant to the subject of childrearing.[69] This fact reflects a male-privileging bias in the human world, carried over to the worlds of other mammals such as mice, that the job of caring for offspring is properly the work of the females of the species. This bias is in need of feminist critique, not just politically and ethically but also epistemologically. Perhaps there are different ways in which methylation is triggered in newborns and young children given different parenting styles commonly adopted by men and women. Or perhaps parenting is just parenting and there are no meaningful differences in methylation patterns in offspring based on the gender of the parents. Rather than myopically focusing on maternal styles and the so-called maternal environment (as if pregnant women and mothers weren't persons, but an atmospheric condition or landscape instead), scientists should reformulate both their implicit assumptions and their explicit hypotheses about gender and parenting so as to expand our understanding of epigenetic inheritance.

Equally as pressing is the need to interrogate racist stereotypes of people of color that could influence both epigenetic research and its subsequent interpretations. For example, in the nineteenth century craniology sought to prove scientifically the innate intellectual inferiority of people of color, and in the late twentieth century Richard J. Herrnstein and Charles Murray's inflammatory book, *The Bell Curve*, appealed to genetics for much the same

---

[68] Feminist standpoint theory is well known for its examination of scientific objectivity. See, for example, Sandra Harding, *Whose Science? Whose Knowledge? Thinking from Women's Lives* (Ithaca, NY: Cornell University Press, 2001) and Donna Haraway, *Simians, Cyborgs and Women: The Reinvention of Nature* (New York: Routledge, 1991). See also Chapter 2 of Charles Mills, *Blackness Visible: Essays on Philosophy and Race* (Ithaca, NY: Cornell University Press, 1998), and Chapter 6 of Shannon Sullivan, *Living Across and Through Skins: Transactional Bodies, Pragmatism, and Feminism* (Bloomington: Indiana University Press, 2001).

[69] Francis, *Epigenetics*, 73.

end.[70] In the case of epigenetics, stereotypes of the black family as broken and dysfunctional are particularly problematic. They probably date back to the days of chattel slavery, but they were given a kind of official credibility with Daniel Patrick Moynihan's 1965 publication of "The Negro Family: A Case for National Action" on the part of the United States Department of Labor.[71] In the name of advising the federal government how to improve the lives of black Americans, Moynihan's report diagnoses black families as pathological. "At the heart of the deterioration of the fabric of Negro society is the deterioration of the Negro family," Moynihan writes, "it is the fundamental source of the weakness of the Negro community at the present time."[72] Because black families are broken, they are perpetuating problems of poor education, poverty, illegitimate births, dependence on welfare, and (most problematic of all, for Moynihan) female-headed households in the black community. Moynihan blames slavery for initially breaking black families, but the fact remains for him that merely by growing up in a black family, a black child is being socialized in an unstable, pathological environment that ensures the replication of black inferiority from generation to generation. According to Moynihan, before real headway can be made against racial inequalities, black families must be repaired so that they have the same high degree of stability as white families.

Bluntly put, one of the dangers of epigenetic research in connection with race is that it could be wielded as scientific "proof" of the diseased or broken black family. This danger is not intrinsic to the field of epigenetics. Epigenetic inheritance can and does happen for people of all races and, moreover, it encompasses health benefits, not just health problems. But because epigenetics and the stereotype of the broken black family share the theme of socially and environmentally caused problems being passed down generationally, epigenetics might be seen as offering physiological evidence of the validity of the stereotype. Perhaps it is not black people's fault—one could say it is the fault of a racist environment, just as Moynihan pointed a finger at chattel slavery—but they nonetheless are a sick people. For that reason, they are biologically inferior to white people, so the well-worn story goes. In fact, they are so fundamentally ill that they can pass down their disease to the next generation of black children regardless of what the future social environment is like.

---

[70] Stephen Jay Gould, *The Mismeasure of Man* (New York: W. W. Norton, 1981); Richard J. Herrnstein and Charles Murray, *The Bell Curve: Intelligence and Class Structure in American Life* (New York: Free Press, 1996).

[71] Daniel Patrick Moynihan, "The Negro Family: A Case for National Action," US Department of Labor, 1965, http://www.dol.gov/oasam/programs/history/webid-meynihan.htm#.UMXrOKXjfpA, accessed December 10, 2012.

[72] Moynihan, "The Negro Family," Chapter 2, http://www.dol.gov/oasam/programs/history/moynchapter2.htm#.UMcoKaXjfpA, accessed December 11, 2012.

The echo of white supremacist eugenics here is loud, clear, and alarming. There is no way to sidestep this fact, and so it needs to be faced head-on. As the quantity and scope of epigenetic research increases, biological and health scientists need to be in critical dialogue with each other and with feminists, critical philosophers of race, and other scholars about how echoes of white supremacy and white privilege could be impacting their research. They also need to be mindful and vocal about how politicians, health specialists, academics, and others might take up and (mis)construe their work. There are no guarantees to be offered or found, no way to ensure that racist, sexist, and other pernicious stereotypes won't fundamentally shape the "breakthrough" scientific era of epigenetics.[73] But epigenetics does not have to be eschewed for that reason, and it indeed can be part of a critical race and feminist arsenal for combating racism by fully comprehending its extent. Simply put, whether we like it or not, the social often becomes durably and transgenerationally biological. Epigenetics shows us one way that this happens.

We can see this once again in the second general form of transgenerational epigenetic inheritance, which is genomic imprinting. Genomic imprinting is considered the more direct of the two indirect forms of epigenetic inheritance because it is not dependent on uterine or post-natal environments. It nevertheless does not involve direct transmission of epigenetic attachments from parent to offspring. The epigenetic attachments in the offspring from its parent(s) are re-established anew. What is distinctive about genomic imprinting is that this reiterative process happens during the development of sperm and eggs.

During the body's process of making sperm or eggs and also shortly after fertilization of an egg by sperm, most epigenetic marks contributed by the female and male parents are erased, bestowing each zygote with a fresh set of naked DNA to clothe anew.[74] This process is called epigenetic reprogramming, and it is why epigenetic processes once were thought to begin and end within a single lifetime. We now know, however, that the epigenetic slate isn't always wiped clean during sperm and egg production. In the case of imprinted genes, the epigenetic marks (for example, degrees of methylation) are erased from the sperm or egg, but they subsequently are restored before the sperm or egg matures.[75] This means that the methylation patterns inherited from the parent(s) are present at the point of fertilization. All genes then must undergo a second round of epigenetic reprogramming prior to implantation, but what is significant about imprinted genes is that their epigenetic attachments

---

[73] D. Kennedy, "Breakthrough of the Year," *Science*, 2002, 298: 2283; S. Baylin and K. Schuebel, "The Epigenomic Era Opens," *Nature*, 2007, 448: 548–549.

[74] Francis, *Epigenetics*, 86.

[75] Francis, *Epigenetics*, 111.

withstand this process. The result is that "by the time the embryo implants, imprinted genes are already epigenetically fixed in their expression pattern."[76]

The fact that imprinted genes survive epigenetic reprogramming can be good news since they are responsible for a great deal of crucial developmental work in the fetus prior to birth. But the situation is grimmer when the imprinted genes in question are linked to major health problems. Environmental toxins such as endocrine disruptors, for example, can have a significantly negative impact on imprinted genes.[77] Chemicals such as polychlorinated biphenyls (PCBs) and bisphenol A, used in the production of clear durable plastics, and weed killers and fungicides, used in many lawn care products, can produce kidney disease and immune system problems and, in males, prostate cancer, abnormal testes, defective sperm, and low fertility. They do this by disrupting physiological processes that involve hormones, in this case by mimicking (and thus overdosing on) estrogen. What is especially alarming about endocrine disrupters is that their effects are transgenerational. Male rats that were exposed as fetuses to the fungicide vinclozolin not only suffered from defective sperm and low fertility, but their male pups and grand pups did, too, even though they were not exposed to fungicides. The fungicide "alter[ed] the imprinting process during sperm development,. . . not only alter[ing] normal imprints but establish[ing] new ones in parts of the genome that are not usually imprinted."[78] This imprinting pattern survived epigenetic reprogramming not just once, but for at least *four generations* of male offspring.[79] Although the parent(s)' methylation patterns had to be reconstructed in their offspring's sperm or eggs, genomic imprinting offers a stunning example of the transgenerational reach of the physiological effects of social and environmental forces.

Perhaps even more powerful, however, is the third form of transgenerational epigenetic inheritance: the direct transmission of methylated genes from one generation to another, without any erasure (and thus no re-imprinting) of epigenetic attachments. Direct epigenetic inheritance is much more common for plants than for mammals. This is because the epigenetic reprogramming in plants is far less extensive or effective than it is in mammals.[80] But there is compelling evidence of direct epigenetic inheritance in mammals, including human beings. One of the best cases comes

---

[76] Francis, *Epigenetics*, 111.

[77] Francis, *Epigenetics*, 113–114. For additional discussion of the transgenerational epigenetic effects of environmental toxins, see Zaneta M. Thayer and Christopher W. Kuzawa, "Biological Memories of Past Environments: Epigenetic Pathways to Health Disparities," *Epigenetics*, July 2011, 6(7): 1–6.

[78] Francis, *Epigenetics*, 115.

[79] Francis, *Epigenetics*, 115.

[80] Francis, *Epigenetics*, 90. Epigenetic attachments can survive epigenetic reprogramming in plants for hundreds of generations, making plants' epigenetic inheritance almost as stable as their genetic inheritance.

from the methylated mice discussed above. The folic acid that the mother mice consumed not only changed their pups' appearance and health via their experience in the womb. It also changed the pups' epigenetic attachments independent of the uterine environment. When the fertilized eggs of yellow (severely under-methylated) mother mice were transferred to the wombs of dark (sufficiently methylated) mice, the offspring remained yellow. And when the offspring who had received folic acid in the womb and thus were darker colored became mothers themselves, their offspring (the "grand-pups") also were darker colored, even though they did not receive any methyl supplementation in utero.[81] The upshot is that neither the methylation of the pups' relevant genes nor the methylation of the grand-pups' relevant genes was an effect of their own consumption of methyl donors while in the womb. The folic acid consumed by the mother mouse had a direct effect on the composition and activity of the genomes of both her children and her grandchildren. A particular methyl-DNA combination was inherited from her by at least two subsequent generations.[82] This type of inheritance was not genetic because the DNA itself did not mutate. It is, in other words, an instance of physiological transgenerational inheritance on a non-genetic level.

In human beings, the study of true epigenetic inheritance is quite recent, but scientists are beginning to question whether it is involved in a certain form of colon cancer.[83] Historical evidence from Sweden also offers an interesting case of epigenetic inheritance, although it is difficult to be certain whether it is an instance of genomic imprinting or true inheritance. An isolated Swedish population that keeps very accurate records of crop harvests and calorie consumption per person occasionally experienced severe famine, and scientists found that the grandsons of men (on their paternal side only) exposed to famine before they were adolescents experienced less cardiovascular disease than the grandsons whose paternal grandfathers did not experience famine as pre-pubescent boys.[84] In other words, severe malnutrition undergone by their paternal grandfather meant better heart health for Swedish men.

There are two significant aspects of this case to underscore. First, the grandfathers did not experience famine while they were fetuses, and second, the cardiovascular health effects in question were not transmitted to Swedish men from their maternal grandfathers. The grandsons' health effects thus cannot be attributed to the nutritional stress experienced by

---

[81] Francis, *Epigenetics*, 85.

[82] See also recent research on the transgenerational transmission of early life trauma through sperm in mice, in Katharina Gapp, Ali Jawaid, Peter Sarkies, Johannes Bohacek, Pawel Pelczar, Julien Prados, Laurent Farinelli, Eric Miska, and Isabelle M. Mansuy, "Implication of Sperm RNAs in Transgenerational Inheritance of the Effects of Early Trauma in Mice," *Nature Neuroscience*, May 2014, 17(5): 667–671.

[83] Francis, *Epigenetics*, 87.

[84] Francis, *Epigenetics*, 89.

their great-grandmothers while they were pregnant, nor can it be attributed to the repetition of a similar environment (nutritional or otherwise) in the womb from one generation to another. Something more directly affecting the grandsons' genome appears to have been passed down to them from their grandfathers via their fathers, presenting a strong case of possible true epigenetic inheritance in human beings. One admittedly cannot be one hundred percent sure how direct the epigenetic inheritance was in this case. For example, it is possible that the relevant epigenetic markers were erased and re-imprinted during the maturation of the father's sperm. But because unlike women's ovaries, men's sperm matures during adolescence, we at least know that uterine epigenetic reprogramming was not involved. As other studies on the epigenetic effects of pre-pubescent boys' smoking confirm, "there is a general [epigenetic] mechanism for transmitting information about the ancestral environment down the male line."[85] In the Swedish case, it's a fairly strong hypothesis that the DNA in the grandfathers' sperm was altered epigenetically by the famine as the grandfathers went through puberty and—even more significantly—that this alteration was maintained in their sons' sperm, which later contributed to the biochemical makeup of the grandsons. The evidence for true epigenetic inheritance is compelling, even if not (yet) complete. It is very possible that the effects of social experiences can be directly, biologically handed down from one generation to another.

In both its direct and indirect forms, the notion of epigenetic inheritance radically disrupts customary notions of biological heritability. It tends to blur the line between extrinsic and intrinsic biological causes of heritable traits, especially in the case of direct epigenetic inheritance. The field of epigenetics does this by dismantling sharp divisions between the innate (biology) and the acquired (culture). Those divisions tend to cluster in the following ways. If a physiological condition is

Innate, then allegedly	Acquired, then allegedly
* a person is born with it.	* it develops after birth.
* it doesn't change or is difficult to change.	* it is relatively easy to change or eliminate.
* it has a genetic (DNA) cause.	* it is environmental, not genetic.
* it can be biologically inherited.	* it is not biologically heritable.

[85] John Cloud, "Why Your DNA Isn't Your Destiny," *Time*, 2010: http://www.time.com/time/magazine/article/0,9171,1952313,00.html, accessed November 30, 2012. Further support of this claim is found in Katharina Gapp, Ali Jawaid, Peter Sarkies, Johannes Bohacek, Pawel Pelczar, Julien Prados, Laurent Farinelli, Eric Miska, and Isabelle M. Mansuy, "Implication of Sperm RNAs in Transgenerational Inheritance of the Effects of Early Trauma in Mice," *Nature Neuroscience*, April 14, 2014, http://dx.doi.org/10.1038/nn.3695, accessed April 15, 2014. Gapp et al. demonstrate that mental illness due to trauma can be passed down to second and third generations of mice via epigenetic changes transmitted through sperm.

But the line between the innate and the acquired is not as sharp as these two columns suggest. One can be born with a physiological condition, such as a predisposition to cardiovascular disease or cancer due to under-methylated genes, that is non-genetic and yet inherited. Is the disease that may develop from that condition innate or acquired? Either answer oversimplifies and thus misconstrues the situation. Feminists and critical philosophers of race need a different way to think about physiology and heritability.

To find another way, the line between the genetic and the environmental must be understood as permeable and fluid since, as we have seen, DNA does not exist apart from its epigenetic markers. In addition, our under-standing of "environment" must be stretched beyond present environ-ments to include the environments of our recent ancestors, environments that we did not directly experience and yet whose effects physiologically inhabit us. The dualism between the innate and the acquired misunder-stands the role of time and history, as much as it misconstrues the relation-ship of biology and culture. Epigenetics illustrates how the past of one's ancestors materially constitutes one's present, which then gives direction to one's future. The present cannot be adequately understood—or, in a medical context, treated—isolated from the past. A person's experience is not fully her own. It also is that of her parents, grandparents, and other family members. This means that a person's health also is not fully her own. Whether healthy or dysfunctional, a person's psychophysiological condition is profoundly impacted by that of her ancestors. The causes of premature birth in African American communities, for example, cannot be narrowly located in the (current) environment, even though they do not involve changes in DNA structure. Their location in the ancestral past is why we can say simultaneously that they are environmentally caused *and* that they are independent of current environments. The fact that recently past environments can alter the human genome means that if we wish to retain a distinction between the innate and the acquired, that difference must be functional—a difference of degree, not kind, that is relevant in some situations but not universally.

Whether or not a case of true epigenetic inheritance, the Swedish fam-ine offers a powerful example of a socio-historical event producing health effects physiologically inherited at least two generations after the event. While the grandsons of the famine survivors did not directly experience the famine, it is as if their bodies nonetheless remember its hardships. This is not an instance of conscious memory of the past, but a non-conscious (perhaps even unconscious) bodily retention of the past's effects. And the same general point could be made for other instances of epigenetic inheritance, indirect and direct alike. As one pair of scientists has put it, epigenetic attachments can be thought of as "biological memories of past environments."[86] Memories of the Swedish famine persisted across generations, even if they were buried in the chemical makeup of the genome, not known or remembered consciously but nevertheless expressed and experienced via a person's cardiovascular health.

The nature of epigenetic memory can be surprising. Why would famine produce better health, not worse, in subsequent generations, for example? After all, in a different famine inflicted upon the Dutch by the Germans during World War II, people exposed to severe malnutrition in the womb during the first trimester experienced greater levels of heart disease and obesity, while those exposed during the second trimester had more lung and kidney disease, and those in the final trimester tended to suffer from glucose intolerance.[87] What accounts for these epigenetic differences? The answer to this and many other questions about epigenetics isn't always clear,[88] but what is evident is that, courtesy of our bodies, past social environments and situations can be vibrantly alive in the present. Epigenetics thus gives striking new meaning to William Faulkner's famous comment that "the past isn't dead. It isn't even past."[89] The past bodily lives on—is "re-membered"—in our epigenetic markers.

This observation resonates with an American Indian practice of gathering the tribe together when a tribe member is sick. As Ghislain Devroede explains, members of a tribe "come together as a group for healing when one of them is sick and is considered a spokesperson of a pervading illness that is overtaking him."[90] This practice would have been appropriate for treating baby Charles, for example. We could say that Charles was something of a spokesperson for a social illness that surrounded him as much as was physiologically inside him, an illness that was not fully or solely his own. He began to recover only when the larger group to which he belonged, and his mother in particular, began to heal. To treat Charles's past—which included his mother's childhood experiences—as irrelevant when trying to cure Charles's anismus would be to allow the harmful effects of past sexual abuse to continue unchecked.

---

[86] Thayer and Kuzawa, "Biological Memories of Past Environments," 1. K. Kim et al. also speak of epigenetic memory in "Epigenetic Memory in Induced Pluripotent Stem Cells," *Nature*, 2010, 467(7313): 285–290. See also Christopher W. Kuzawa and Zaneta M. Thayer, "Timescales of Human Adaptation: The Role of Epigenetic Processes," *Epigenomics*, 2011, 3(2): 221–234, especially page 229.

[87] Francis, *Epigenetics*, 4. For more on epigenetics and the Dutch famine, see "Prenatal Exposure to Famine May Lead to Persistent Epigenetic Changes," 2008, http://www.sciencedaily.com/releases/2008/10/081030110959.htm, accessed June 20, 2013.

[88] For more on the challenges to investigating gene-environment interactions, especially from the "environment" side, see Miun J. Khoury and Sholom Wacholder, "Invited Commentary: From Genome-Wide Association Studies to Gene-Environment-Wide Interaction Studies—Challenges and Opportunities," *American Journal of Epidemiology*, 169 (2): 227–230.

[89] William Faulkner, *Requiem for a Nun* (New York: Random House, 1951) 81.

[90] Ghislain Devroede, *Ce que les maux de ventre disent de notre passé* (Paris: Payot & Rivages, 2002) 303, my translation.

Likewise, Kim Anderson's premature delivery of her daughter was an event shaped as much by her ancestors' lives as by her own choices and actions. Anderson's reproductive health was not fully or solely her own. It belonged partially to her mother, and perhaps even her grandmother, and the racist environments they inhabited. Her daughter Danielle thus could be seen as a spokesperson for a social malady—white domination—that surrounded and helped constitute her ancestors. To consider Danielle's past in the form of her mother's and grandmother's experiences as irrelevant to her premature birth would be to allow the harmful effects of racism to go unnoticed.

The past lives on in our physiological health. The lines between the past and the present are blurred on this account, in other words. While we can make abstract distinctions between the effects of past and present racism, in practice—in our lived biology—such distinctions might be difficult, even impossible to make. This can be a chilling thought given the years of racism that mar the past of the United States (and many other countries). It means, for example, that the stress and trauma of de jure Jim Crow continue to live, even though it ended in the 1960s. Its health effects likely persist physiologically, not only in the biochemistry of African American people who were adolescents in the 1950s, but also in the biochemistry of their children and grandchildren. An epigenetic legacy could explain why Kim Anderson, herself a premature baby, gave birth prematurely to her daughter Danielle. Of course, ongoing racism and de facto Jim Crow also can be blamed for contributing to the high rates of infant mortality and cardiovascular disease experienced by African Americans. But it is not just the racist present that is harming contemporary African American women, such as Kim and Danielle. It also is the racist past experienced by their ancestors.

Given what we know about the Swedish famine, it's possible that African American males also are involved in the epigenetic transmission of the effects of racism. Due to the importance of the uterine environment in producing indirect epigenetic change through altered somatic and/or sex cells, we might have thought that if Anderson had given birth to a son instead of a daughter, then the ancestral effects of white domination would come to an end in her family line. Her family would be free of one part of the legacy of white supremacy and white privilege. (Ongoing racism and de facto Jim Crow would likely still cause health problems for African Americans of all classes, of course.) But since changes to epigenetic markers can be transmitted through sperm, it is possible that some of the harmful effects of racism would be transmitted down a male line of Anderson's family. If she had a son, his sperm could be epigenetically affected by Anderson's racial/racist weathering, which in turn could affect that son's children. Anderson's grandchildren via a son could "re-member" her experiences with racism, just as her grandchildren via Danielle might do.

If the past lives on epigenetically, then our present will become the past that endures in our children's, and perhaps even their children's, biochemistry. The racism that mars our society today will not necessarily stop there, in other words. It likely will impact the lives of several generations to come, physiologically and medically as well as economically, possibly through direct paternal as well as direct maternal lines. This implication of epigenetics is distressing. But there is an additional facet to this observation about the past, one that offers a measure of hope to those who wish to eradicate racism. The effect of changes made today might not always be immediately apparent, but they can make a significant difference in the future. While a reduction in institutional and individual prejudice against adult people of color could improve their health by reducing stress levels, it is not likely to completely eliminate a person's existing major health problems, such as cardiovascular disease, associated with years of enduring a heavy allostatic load. A severely weathered body does not rebound in this way; this is the bad news. (It also marks a moment to guard against racist stereotypes of the broken black person. The point here is the opportunity offered by the future, not that the present is unimportant or somehow "unsalvageable.") Even if adult African American health were only marginally improved by reducing racism, however, the good news is that such a reduction made today is likely to significantly benefit the health of their future children and grandchildren.

In particular, the persistence of the past and present in the future means rethinking the scope and significance of prenatal care. Activities such as avoiding smoking and drinking alcohol and eating healthily and taking vitamins remain important, but we need to appreciate that "the benefits of prenatal care for improving birth outcomes may be more intergenerational than immediate."[91] Anderson's case highlights how what counts as prenatal care for women of color needs to be expanded transgenerationally. It's not just a matter of nine months of healthy living and regularly visits to the obstetrician. The relevant issue also is that broad-scale racial justice is needed to close the racist gap in birth outcomes. Reflecting on the fact that African American women who had prenatal care still have higher rates of infant mortality than white women who received none, some health specialists have concluded that "to expect prenatal care, in less than 9 months, to reverse the impact of ... cumulative allostatic load on [African American] women's reproductive health, may be expecting too much. . . . Prenatal care as currently prevails may do too little too late to have a major impact on [racial] disparities in birth outcomes."[92] Seemingly non-medical aspects of contemporary black people's lives, such as urban renewal, improved schools, and better educational

---

[91] Lu and Halfon, "Racial and Ethnic Disparities in Birth Outcomes," 25.
[92] Lu and Halfon, "Racial and Ethnic Disparities in Birth Outcomes," 21.

opportunities, are closely tied to the health and well-being of future generations of African Americans and thus should be considered part of prenatal care.[93]

Anderson's case also provides an opportunity to clarify the relationships between non-conscious and unconscious habits and between emotion and affect. Comparing Anderson's situation to that of baby Charles helps us see that the line dividing non-conscious and unconscious habits and the one dividing emotion and affect are not necessarily very sharp. Biologically unconscious emotional habits clearly were at work in baby Charles's illness. Even though Charles was a newborn, his anismus revealed that his transactions with the world already included emotions of fear and confusion about how open to others he should be. These were emotions of which he was unaware because, as a fetus and then newborn, Charles was developmentally incapable of consciously comprehending them. This unawareness was more than merely non-conscious. The root causes of Charles's anismus did not just happen to go unnoticed by him because of his young age. Charles's physiological habits of anismus were a form of bodily knowledge of the past that actively resisted conscious awareness, even as it non-linguistically voiced his mother's pain and anger.

Anderson's situation is somewhat different. To begin, Anderson's epigenetic habits are best characterized as affective rather than as emotional, and they were unfelt rather than felt: a person does not consciously feel his or her genes methylating or a chemical hormone adhering itself to his or her DNA. These processes nonetheless are part of what William James called the bodily sounding board, which reverberates with the world, not just echoing it but replying to it in a dynamic call-and-response relationship. Recalling the extension of Catherine Malabou's notion of cerebral auto-affection to the entire body, we could say that epigenetic markers are part of a person's epigenomic auto-affection. They are part of being a living being, which is to say that they are how an organism maintains a living attachment to itself and its processes through its epigenome. This epigenomic attachment means that an organism is invested in remaining this particular being, rather than dying and disintegrating back into the soil, while simultaneously engaging in reciprocal, invested relationships with other beings and environments. (The notion of epigenomic investment does not entail an atomistic view of the organism, in other words.) It is not a misuse of the term "affect" to describe the nature of living attachments and investments, even if those affective relationships take place at the level of the epigenome.

---

[93] Michael C. Lu, Milton Kotelchuck, Vijaya Hogan, Loretta Jones, Kynna Wright, and Neal Halfon, "Closing the Black-White Gap in Birth Outcomes: A Life-Course Approach," *Ethnicity and Disease*, 2010, 20: 62–76.

Are Anderson's epigenomic habits unconscious as Charles's animus was, or merely non-conscious? Put another way, it is easy to understand epigenetic marking as non-conscious; people certainly are not consciously aware of the process of epigenetic marking taking place in their own bodies. But could it ever make sense to say that a chemical marker attached to a person's DNA is an affective relationship with the world too painful for a person to acknowledge and thus one that actively attempts to resist conscious awareness? This characterization of epigenetic markers as unconscious might appear too strong, even farfetched. At best, epigenetic habits like Anderson's would seem to be non-conscious: something that she usually doesn't think about and that can function quite well without her conscious awareness, but whose existence she can bring to conscious attention if she (or her doctors) need to.

As counterintuitive as it might initially seem, however, I think it is worth considering the possibility that epigenetic habits could be unconscious in some cases.[94] I do not wish to claim a priori that every affect (or every emotion, for that matter) of which a person is not consciously aware necessarily is unconscious. Not all bodily changes and movements are constituted by relationships with the world that are painful or shameful to acknowledge consciously. Sometimes a bruised muscle is just that: a bruised muscle and nothing more. Breaking down biology-cultural dualisms doesn't entail seeing repressed trauma or forbidden desire in every bodily twinge. While I agree with Nancy Krieger that "bodies tell stories that people cannot or will not tell, because they are unable, forbidden, or choose not to tell," I acknowledge that some bodily processes hum along non-consciously without being an extra-linguistic mouthpiece for an unspeakable past.[95]

But at the same time, I would caution that we don't always know when a bodily process or state is trying to tell a story that is forbidden to tell. As contemporary scientists like Krieger, following Freud, teach us, forbidden stories are very good at hiding within seemingly unimportant or trivial physiological conditions. For this reason, I think an agnostic attitude toward bodily processes is called for: we often don't know when those processes are psychosomatic, rather than "merely" physical symptoms. This would be an attitude that does not automatically see hidden trauma in every runny nose but that also admits the possibility that a runny nose could mean something other than the presence of a cold virus. Just as we don't fully know what bodies can do, we don't always know what bodies are trying to say.[96] Remaining open

---

[94] Linking epigenetics with psychoanalysis, Bruno Clavier explicitly describes epigenetics as a form of emotional transmission across generations, in Clavier, *Les Fantômes Familiaux: Psychanalyse Transgénérationnelle* (Paris: Payot & Rivages, 2013) 50.

[95] Nancy Krieger, "Embodiment: A Conceptual Glossary for Epidemiology," *Journal of Epidemiology & Community Health*, 2005, 59: 350.

[96] Cf. Gilles Deleuze, *Spinoza: Practical Philosophy*, trans. Robert Hurley (San Francisco: City Lights Publishers, 2001) 17–18.

to the idea that physiological processes such as epigenetic marking could be unconscious would help feminists and critical philosophers of race attune themselves to the frequency on and across which bodies sometimes communicate their stories.

By hypothesizing that at least some epigenetic habits could be unconscious, a configuration of the physiological body and its relationship with the (sexist and racist) world would emerge that is helpfully different from the one that has been handed down to us via long-standing biology-culture dualisms. For example, thought as unconscious, a body's marking its genes in a particular way and then handing down those habits to the next generation could be seen as a form of physiological resistance to efforts to acknowledge and change them. More specifically, in Anderson's paradigmatic case, the epigenetic process of marking her genes with race-based stress could be seen as a product of racism that then attempts to perpetuate itself and thereby actively resist efforts to change or eliminate it. The fact that this resistance happens chemically, via epigenetic markers and triggered by hormones that are invisible to the human eye, does not make it any less psychological or any less social. Thinking of epigenetic habits as unconscious could help feminists and critical philosophers of race to sweep away remaining bits of mysterious mind-stuff from our understanding of racism and sexism and to appreciate how unconscious resistance to recognizing and eliminating oppression is biopsychosocial through and through.

Human beings are composed through our transactions with our environments; the fresh insight provided by epigenetics is that those environments are not just contemporary but also historical ones.[97] Social environments inhabited by one's ancestors can constitute the person that one is today, and this can occur physiologically via inherited chemical and hormonal markers that affect the expression of one's genes. The fight against racism thus needs to be waged on biological and medical levels, as well as economic, political, aesthetic, and other social terrain. Or rather, since no rigid lines separate the biological and the social, we could say that due to the existence of racist health disparities, the medical already is implicated in political struggles against white domination. By illuminating the transgenerational scope of racism, epigenetics can be a useful ally in that fight.

---

[97] Kuzawa and Thayer, "Timescales of Human Adaptation," 222.

The Stomach and the Heart

ON THE PHYSIOLOGY OF WHITE IGNORANCE

> Whites . . . experience genuine cognitive difficulties in recognizing certain
> behavior patterns as racist, so that quite apart from questions of motivation
> and bad faith they will be morally handicapped simply from the conceptual
> point of view in seeing and doing the right thing.
>
> —CHARLES MILLS, *THE RACIAL CONTRACT*

In this chapter, I turn to some of the physiological effects of racism on white
people. In particular, I return to the stomach of Brittney, my white under-
graduate student presented in the Introduction, and I also examine another
bodily organ strongly associated with affective and emotional experience, the
heart. While these are not the only areas of white bodies that can be constituted by racism, the stomach and the heart provide vivid illustrations of
how white people's physiology can be shaped by white domination. They also
provide excellent examples of how white ignorance can function on a physiological level. Sometimes the physiological effects of racism on white people
are unpleasant for them to experience, as in the case of Brittney's stomach,
while other times white people don't notice their effects at all, as tends to
be the case for the heart. But in both cases, a kind of racialized knowledge,
grounded in white ignorance and white physiology, is at work.

Brittney defiantly insisted that she experiences visceral tension when
she is alone at night and encounters a black man. The situation she testi-
fied to in my class is similar to the elevator effect well described by George
Yancy. When alone in an elevator with Yancy, who is an African American
man, white women regularly even if unintentionally tense up: their bodies contract and tighten inward (along with their handbags) as if to pull
away from and protect themselves against Yancy and, Yancy reports, they
suddenly seem dry mouthed and to have difficulty swallowing, as if they
are a bit nauseous.[1] Like Brittney, perhaps many white women who have

---

[1] George Yancy, *Black Bodies, White Gazes: The Continuing Significance of Race* (Lanham,
MD: Rowman and Littlefield, 2008), 5.

undergone the elevator effect would defend their physiological reactions to black men as having nothing to do with racism. For starters, they might say, their reactions were automatic, not deliberate or willed. They did not choose to tense up; their bodies just did it. And moreover, they might insist, their bodies did it in reaction to an objectively alarming situation. As feminists have argued, women in the United States live in a rapist culture, which doesn't mean that every man is a rapist.[2] What is means instead is that boys and men are socialized into a form of masculinity that celebrates sexual aggression and violence against women, and that this socialization has harmful effects on women. In a rapist culture, women are right to be cautious—even scared—when they are in an isolated place that leaves them vulnerable to sexual assault. Their bodily tension in the elevator has a lot to do with our society's sexism and male privilege, they might conclude, and not with any racism on their part.[3]

The rapist culture in the United States is not a figment of Brittney's imagination. This does not mean that every woman will be raped at some point in her lifetime—although about one in six will be—but that the glorification of men's sexual aggression as a "normal" part of masculinity entails that a "natural" part of life as a women in the United States (and elsewhere) is to take steps to protect oneself from sexual assault.[4] The misguided ways that many white women take those steps, however, demonstrate that a racially biased fear tends to govern their thinking about prevention of assault. It leads them to myopically focus on strategies for warding off an attacker in a dark parking lot (such as using mace, car keys, or even their high-heeled shoes to fight back), rather than strategies for how to safely navigate an alcohol-fueled fraternity party. Given that approximate 75% of all sexual assaults against women in the United States, including rape, are committed by acquaintances, neighbors, family friends, or even close relations (husbands, boyfriends, fathers, uncles, brothers, and so on), and given the dogged persistence of de facto racial segregation in the United States, which means that white people tend to be related to, live near, party with, hang out with, and otherwise acquaint themselves with other white people—given all this, the objectively alarming situation that most white women face regarding sexual assault is in their own homes,

---

[2] Andrea Dworkin, "Women in the Public Domain," in *Women and Values: Readings in Recent Feminist Philosophy*, ed. Marilyn Pearsall (Belmont, CA: Wadsworth Publishing, 1986) 221–229. See also Jackson Katz, *The Macho Paradox: Why Some Men Hurt Women and How All Men Can Help* (Naperville, IL: Sourcebooks, 2006).

[3] Yancy documents a number of other excuses and rationalizations for the elevator effect often made by white people in George Yancy, *Look, a White! Philosophical Essays on Whiteness* (Philadelphia: Temple University Press, 2012) 155.

[4] Rape, Abuse, and Incest National Network (RAINN), http://www.rainn.org/get-information/statistics/sexual-assault-victims, accessed June 11, 2013; Dworkin, "Women in the Public Domain," 221–229.

apartment complexes, dorm rooms, college campuses, and neighborhoods.[5] It objectively, statistically, is not with a stranger. It is not in a random elevator or on an empty street. And it is not with black men. This is not to trivialize the stranger rapes that take place. Taking precautions, for example, when walking home alone at night is a smart thing for a woman to do. It instead is to point out that, just like many other aspects of life in the United States, sexual assault and rape generally are racially segregated in the United States.

These statistics are important, but they do not, by themselves, constitute an adequate response to Brittney. In fact, they are some of the statistics about sexual assault that the course with Brittney included, but they did very little to relax her stomach at the thought of encountering a black man while alone. We might say the statistics about assault spoke to Brittney's brain but not to her stomach. (Even this explanation, however, isn't quite accurate, nor is it fair to the brain since the brain is characterized by much more than conscious belief.) How can feminist and critical philosophers of race speak effectively and persuasively to the unconscious habits of white people? How might they be heard by white people's hearts and stomachs? More specifically, what might feminist and critical philosophers of race say or do that could help transform white people's physiological racist habits, rather than encourage them to cling defensively to the felt certainty of their white privileged experience (as I believe my teaching assistant's response to Brittney unfortunately did)? This is a difficult task since, as Charles Mills states in the epigraph above, white people often are incapable of understanding their behavior as racist due to the white ignorance required by the racial contract. I believe that Brittney genuinely didn't understand what was ethically objectionable about her fear of black men. This is not solely, or perhaps even primarily, a cognitive difficulty, however. Like most contemporary white ignorance/knowledge, her emotional "knowledge" that black men are threatening operated primarily on a non-cognitive, bodily level.

As I shift in this chapter from examining the harms of racist oppression in the bodies of African American people to examining their unjust benefits in the bodies of white people, let me emphasize that I am not claiming that white people are oppressed. Quite the contrary. Brittney's visceral reactions to black men, for example, are a gastrointestinal enactment of white people's racist domination of black people, not any kind of evidence of a "black peril" against white people. Systems of oppression can and do have physiological effects on the oppressor as well as the oppressed, even if those effects tend to be very different for the two groups. This fact does not mean that the oppressor has now become the oppressed, a fellow victim of some impersonal system of oppression, for example. In the case of racism, white people are not victims of

---

[5] Rape, Abuse, and Incest National Network (RAINN), http://www.rainn.org/get-information/statistics/sexual-assault-offenders, accessed June 11, 2013.

white domination because their stomachs and hearts are affected by and involved in their attempts to maintain white superiority. But the point is that their stomachs, hearts, and other bodily organs and functions *are* involved. White people's physiological bodies are and historically have been involved in their attempts to dominate and degrade people of color, and this fact needs to be recognized if we are to adequately address racism's operation outside the realm of conscious belief.

When trying to change white people's racist attitudes and comportments, critical philosophers and other theorists of race often start in the wrong place by focusing on conscious beliefs. We might think, as the early W. E. B. Du Bois did, that if we could just provide accurate information that would eliminate white people's misconceptions about African Americans, then their mistaken belief in white supremacy would dissolve. And if more information alone isn't enough to do the trick, then it can be supplemented with moral injunctions that use guilt and shame to get white people to change their minds about people of color. In either case, faulty beliefs about people of color are the supposed culprits. But as Du Bois himself later realized, white ignorance of people of color isn't accidental, and it isn't likely to be changed by moral exhortations. It is a product of white people's unconscious racial habits, which have deep roots and are strongly invested—albeit not consciously—in maintaining the economic, psychological, and global domination of people of color.[6] White misunderstandings of people of color, and of race more broadly, are part of what Mills has called an epistemology of ignorance that enables and even requires white people to know the world in systematically distorted ways.[7]

White ignorance is not an accidental feature of the world—although it likes to be understood in this way. If white people's (mis)understandings of the world seem like a product of happenstance, then they can appear relatively harmless and easy to correct. Sure, one might say, white people might have gaps in their knowledge about people of color, but their ignorance isn't significant and doesn't have any major impact on the world. White ignorance is much more devious and malign than this peaceful description depicts, however. "Imagine," as Mills urges, "an ignorance militant, aggressive, not to be intimidated, an ignorance that is active, dynamic, that refuses to go quietly—not at all confined to the illiterate and uneducated but propagated at the highest levels of the land, indeed presenting itself unblushingly as *knowledge*. . . ."[8] Because white ignorance functions as

---

[6] W. E. B. Du Bois, *Dusk of Dawn: An Essay Toward an Autobiography of a Race Concept* (New York: Schocken Books, 1984) 296.

[7] Charles Mills, *The Racial Contract* (Ithaca, NY: Cornell University Press, 1998) 18, 93. See also Shannon Sullivan and Nancy Tuana, eds., *Race and the Epistemologies of Ignorance* (Albany: State University of New York Press, 2007).

[8] Charles Mills, "White Ignorance," in Sullivan and Tuana, eds., *Race and Epistemologies of Ignorance*, 13, emphasis in original.

official knowledge of "invented Orients, invented Africas, invented Americas, with a correspondingly fabricated population, countries that never were, inhabited by people who never were—Calibans and Tontos, Man Fridays and Sambos," it tends to be extremely powerful and effective.[9] It helps generate and secure a white-dominated world that is comfortable for and flattering to white people.

The phantastic epistemic creations produced by white ignorance generally do not hinder white people. In fact, they are incredibly functional: they allow white people to socially, psychologically, financially, and physically thrive at the expense of people of color.[10] Yet at the same time, as Mills argues, the phantasies of white ignorance ethically handicap white people. They produce tremendous obstacles for the ethical behavior of white people, toward people of color in particular but also toward other white people at times.[11] It's not just that the racial contract contains rigorous epistemological clauses, in other words. Its twisted epistemological requirements also entail a particular relationship to the world that is highly unethical. The resulting handicap is twofold. Even as they might thrive in other respects, white people are largely incapable of behaving ethically, especially with regard to racial matters, *and* they generally cannot see or understand themselves as unethical and thus they have little chance of changing their behavior for the better.

According to Mills, white ignorance is primarily a cognitive dysfunction. Even as he insightfully examines the "microspace of the [raced] body" and the perception of black bodies in particular as "moving bubble[s] of wilderness," white people's distorted understandings of non-white bodies (and the world more generally) are never themselves described as embodied. They are mental. As in the epigraph above, Mills invokes the cognitive in claiming "*white misunderstanding, misrepresentation, evasion, and self-deception on matters related to race* are among the most pervasive *mental* phenomena of the past few hundred years, a *cognitive* and moral economy psychically required for conquest, colonization, and enslavement."[12] The inverted epistemology of the racial contract is "a particular pattern of localized and global cognitive dysfunctions" requiring "a certain set of structured blindnesses and opacities."[13] Those blindnesses are "not, of course, due to biology, the intrinsic properties of [a white person's] epidermis, or physical deficiencies in the white eye," but to a pattern of white cognitive (mis)perception that systematically distorts the world for the ends of white domination.[14]

---

[9] Mills, *The Racial Contract*, 18–19.

[10] Mills, *The Racial Contract*, 18.

[11] See Thandeka, *Learning to Be White: Money, Race, and God in America* (New York: Continuum, 2007) on white parents' "child abuse" of withdrawing love from a white child who does not conform to white supremacy.

[12] Mills, *The Racial Contract*, 19; I italicized "mental" and "cognitive," all other italics are Mills's.

[13] Mills, *The Racial Contract*, 18, 19.

[14] Mills, "White Ignorance," 18.

In contrast, I want precisely to invoke biology to understand the operations of white ignorance. Not in the sense that white people necessarily have
deficiencies in their retinas or optical cones, but in the sense that their racialized blindness can be located in the opacities of their physiology. This claim
appreciates Du Bois's shift to understanding white domination as unconscious, which in turn resonates strongly with Mills's vibrant description of
white ignorance as aggressive, active, and dynamic. It also complements José
Medina's call for "unmasking and dismantling the racial ignorance hidden in
the ideology of color blindness [which] requires that we see through the ruse
of vision, and that we put sight on the same plane as hearing, smelling, tasting, and touching."[15] But it pushes further than all three to posit that white
people's unconscious habits of white privilege are physiological, not just narrowly psychological or even phenomenological, and they are not restricted to
or even primarily located in vision. Human physiology from the nose down,
so to speak, is where a great deal of supposed non-bodily aspects of human
existence is located.

Phenomenological analyses of racial embodiment have developed helpful
understandings of the operations of white privilege and white supremacy.[16] As
in the case of Maurice Merleau-Ponty, however, phenomenology's approach
to embodiment often is set in opposition to biology, going so far as to argue
for "a foreswearing of science."[17] This dismissal is problematic given that racism can help constitute white people's biochemical makeup and activities: for
example, their serotonin and other neurotransmitter levels, the activity patterns of their autonomic nervous system, their predisposition for gastric
tachyarrhythmia, their levels of hormone production, and so on. We might
say that the tenets of the racial contract need to be examined not just mor-
ally and epistemologically, but also biologically. To be fully effective, critical
philosophy of race needs to be in conversation with the medical sciences: car-
diologists, neurobiologists, gastroenterologists, psychoneuroimmunologists,
and other medical and health professionals who understand human biology
and physiology well.

What then do we learn from these conversations? The first thing is that
they can be difficult to begin because of the invisibility of whiteness and white
privilege in most biomedical literature. This invisibility is terribly ironic, of

---

[15] José Medina, "Color Blindness, Meta-Ignorance, and the Racial Imagination," *Critical
Philosophy of Race*, 2013 1(1): 49.

[16] See, for example, Linda Martín Alcoff, "Toward a Phenomenology of Racial Embodiment,"
Radical Philosophy, 95, May/June 1998: 15–26, included in Alcoff, *Visible Identities: Race, Gender, and
the Self* (New York: Oxford University Press, 2006); Shannon Sullivan, *Revealing Whiteness: The
Unconscious Habits of Racial Privilege* (Bloomington: Indiana University Press, 2006); and Yancy,
Black Bodies, White Gazes.

[17] Maurice Merleau-Ponty, *Phenomenology of Perception*, trans. Colin Smith (London: The
Humanities Press, 1962) viii.

course, given that white people continue to be the main subjects of medical research—unless the research focuses on race, and then it often omits white people. The primary focus of the medical sciences when they study race and racism tends to be on the detrimental health effects of racial discrimination and oppression for people of color. For example, hypertension, high blood pressure, poor cardiovascular activity, and other physiological conditions associated with increased mortality rates have been linked with incidents of racial hostility and socioeconomic stress experienced by African Americans and other racial minorities in the United States.[18] What is virtually never discussed is the flip-side of this research's conclusions: that the relatively good health of many white Americans—lower incidence of hypertension, high blood pressure, and so on—can be considered a product of white privilege rather than a neutral or "normal" physiological condition.[19] While white people sometimes are mentioned as a racial group in medical studies, they very rarely are discussed there as a group of people who systematically benefit, medically and otherwise, from their race. Categories of race sometimes are used in the medical and life sciences, in other words, and occasionally even racism is acknowledged as a problem that people of color confront, but the topic of white domination's effect on white people is largely absent.

And yet it hovers in the margins of at least some scientific studies, which makes it possible to hypothesize about the operations of white privilege and domination in the physiology of white people. With Brittney in mind, consider the example of nausea, a queasy or tense feeling in the stomach that is a control mechanism inhibiting food intake and sometimes producing vomiting. What is interesting about this control mechanism is that it is not merely physiological. It also is psychological and, as psychologist R. M. Stern explains, "it [sometimes] occurs in threatening situations that have little to do with eating."[20] While perhaps initially puzzling, this characteristic of nausea turns out to make sense: when threatened, the body's autonomic nervous system (ANS) activity changes in ways that decrease or even stop gastric motor activity.[21] The stomach and intestines stop digesting their contents, in other words, and so it's not a good idea to keep putting food into them. In the face of a threat—which can be a toxic piece of food, or it can be a threat having

---

[18] Carol D. Ryff and Burton H. Singer, "The Role of Emotion on Pathways to Positive Health," in *The Handbook of Affective Sciences*, eds. Richard J. Davidson, Klaus R. Scherer, and H. Hill Goldsmith (New York: Oxford University Press, 2003) 1086. See also David R. Williams, "Race, Socioeconomic Status, and Health: The Added Effects of Racism and Discrimination," *Annals of the New York Academy of Sciences*, 1999, 896: 173–188.

[19] One rare exception is the excellent essay by Jessie Daniels and Amy J. Schulz, "Constructing Whiteness in Health Disparities Research," in *Gender, Race, Class and Health: Intersectional Approaches*, eds. Amy J. Schulz and Leath Mullings (San Francisco: Jossey Bass, 2006) 89–127.

[20] R. M. Stern, "The Psychophysiology of Nausea," *Acta Biologica Hungaria*, 2002, 53(4): 590.

[21] Stern, "The Psychophysiology of Nausea," 590.

nothing to do with food whatsoever—the body has a control mechanism to keep the stomach and intestines empty while they are not functioning.

While the different nausea thresholds of white, Chinese, and African American people are briefly discussed in Stern's study, topics of racism and white domination are never explicitly broached. The non-food-related "threats" that are mentioned in the study are public speaking and acting in a play. But the specific phenomenon of threat is used to explain the psychophysiology of nausea, and I suggest that racial threats, both real and perceived, fall into the category of menacing situations that can contribute to nausea. When a person feels threatened because of a racial situation, as Brittney did, her physiology can be altered: chemical levels can change, gastro-motor activity can cease, impacting the absorption of nutrients that help constitute her flesh, bones, and blood, et cetera.

This is true for anyone in a threatening racial situation, whatever his or her race. Although I am focusing here on white people who experience themselves as racially threatened, I must underscore that historically and presently white people themselves are the primary group that poses a threat to other people. White people almost exclusively are the terrorizing force that uses race to menace people of color, not the other way around. I am not flattening the racial terrain with a turn to white people's physiology, nor am I treating as identical, for example, the real threat of white lynchers and the perceived threat of black men as experienced by Brittney. What I am claiming is that white domination has different but nonetheless constitutive effects on the biology of white people and people of color, and that the end of white domination will require not just significant financial, legal, educational, and political changes, but also psychophysiological transformations. White people's mistreatment of people of color as inherently inferior is found in all kinds of registers, not just the physiological, but it manifests itself in the latter domain, too. As long as white women's stomachs seize up in fear of black men, we know that white privilege and white supremacy continue to "invisibly" thrive.

Another example of the raced character of white people's stomachs is the historical one of white people's general refusal to eat with African Americans during the period of legalized racial segregation in the United States. Like interracial sex, interracial dining has long been a concern of systems of white domination (and the two practices aren't unrelated from that perspective).[22] In antebellum and especially de jure Jim Crow United States, who ate with whom was a matter of much attention and grave concern. More specifically, white people's eating with black people was a serious violation of the racial etiquette of white domination. Interracial eating was not allowed on pain of severe physical punishment, perhaps even lynching, in the case of black

---

[22] Jennifer Ritterhouse, *Growing Up Jim Crow: How Black and White Southern Children Learned Race* (Chapel Hill: University of North Carolina Press, 2006) 30.

people. In de jure Jim Crow America, black people might purchase food from the same restaurants and drugstores as white people, but they were expected to stand at the rear of the counter and take their food outside (or perhaps into the restaurant kitchen) to eat it.[23]

Codes of racial etiquette were (and are) binding on the dominant as well as the subordinate,[24] which meant that white people who violated interracial eating taboos were subject to significant social censure. But the taboo against interracial eating was not solely enforced from without. It was so deeply ingrained in the habits of white lives that many white people experienced intense revulsion at the thought of eating with African Americans. As one white woman wrote in 1947 when reflecting back on her childhood, "often we spoke of the sin it would be to eat with a Negro. Next to 'intermarriage' this was a most appalling thought. It was an unthinkable act. . . . In the whole roster of Southern taboos ['eating with Negroes'] was nearly the most sacred. It was a grievous Southern sin for which were allowed no mitigating circumstances."[25] Another white woman explained in 1904 that "if anything would make me kill my children, it would be the possibility that niggers might sometime eat at the same table and associate with them as equals."[26] And a white woman living in Mississippi in the 1890s explained that "the colored people all love me where I live. Some would almost give their right hands to help me if I asked them. But I would starve to death before I would eat a crust of bread at a table with one of them."[27]

The essence of Jim Crow etiquette is found in white people's unrelenting demonstration and enforcement of black people's alleged inferiority. But the question remains, why was interracial eating central to this demonstration? Why did white people so vehemently reject the idea of eating with black people? After all, the taboo against interracial eating was highly hypocritical: white people were fully aware and accepting of the fact that black people prepared and served the food that white people ate, both at home and in restaurants.[28] How could white people say they preferred their own death and the death of their children to the act of eating with black people? The answer I propose is that a white person's refusal to eat with a black person was part of her racist rejection of black people's constitution of herself. The segregation enacted in restaurants, dining cars, and dining rooms and kitchens in white homes was not merely geographical. Nor was it only political, in terms

---

[23] Bertram Wilbur Doyle, *The Etiquette of Race Relations in the South: A Study in Social Control* (Chicago: University of Chicago Press, 1937), 146.

[24] Doyle, *The Etiquette of Race Relations in the South*, xx.

[25] Katherine Du Pre Lumpkin, quoted in Fred Hobson, *But Now I See: The White Southern Racial Conversion Narrative* (Baton Rouge: Louisiana State University Press, 1999) 45, 49.

[26] Ritterhouse, *Growing Up Jim Crow*, 42.

[27] Doyle, *The Etiquette of Race Relations in the South*, 150.

[28] Ritterhouse, *Growing Up Jim Crow*, 42.

of the socio-legal-political question of whether black people were treated as equal or inferior to white people. It also was ontological: it was a matter of what parts of the "outside" world would be taken into white bodies to help constitute them.

Of course, this refusal failed: black people and other people of color do help constitute who and what white people are. But its failure does not change the fact that white people have tried mightily to convince themselves that they are ontologically separate from people of color, and taboos against interracial eating historically were a significant part of that effort. White people long have been "eating the other," as bell hooks charges, in terms of culturally appropriating, enjoying, and commodifying their music, clothing, dance, food, and more.[29] But at the same time that white people are willing and even eager to consume blackness, they ironically have been unwilling historically to eat *with* the other. Dabbling in blackness evidently is not threatening to white people when it serves their pleasure as consumers. Outside that context, however, proximity to black people in the form of literally eating with them has troubled white people's sense of racial superiority.

The white refusal to be constituted by black people was not merely a conscious decision. Especially as this refusal concentrated on the question of interracial eating and drinking, it also was a visceral habit, a biological manifestation of racism in the gut that wouldn't allow interracial eating on (stomach) pain of nausea, loss of appetite, and related symptoms. This suggestion is admittedly speculative. I am unaware of any medical research on white people's gastrointestinal reactions to racial situations, culinary or otherwise. (There does exist research on the cardiovascular system and cognitive control brain regions of white people with high levels of racial bias, who tend to experience interracial interactions as distressing and threatening.[30]) But as one historian of the de jure Jim Crow South has argued, white people's belief in white superiority "may have operated at a visceral level, [a white person's] gut reaction telling him that [eating or] drinking after a black person was somehow dirty and defiling."[31] The stomach can possess a racialized and racist affective knowledge in which the conscious mind does not necessarily participate.

The idea that the stomach can be a physiological site of unconscious knowledge is further supported by discourses on emotion from the early modern period, when "you are what you eat" had not yet been conquered by

[29] bell hooks, "Eating the Other," in *Black Looks: Race and Representation* (Boston: South End Press, 1999). See also Greg Tate, *Everything but the Burden: What White People Are Taking from Black Culture* (New York: Harlem Moon, 2003).

[30] Jennifer A. Richeson and Sophie Trawalter, "Why Do Interracial Interactions Impair Executive Function? A Resource Depletion Account," in *Journal of Personality and Social Psychology*, 2005, 88(6): 934–947.

[31] Ritterhouse, *Growing Up Jim Crow*, 127.

the rival ontology in which "I think, therefore I am."[32] For a pre-Cartesian subjectivity, "thought and feeling reflect, and [were] grounded in, the stomach's physiological functions—functions directly related to and imbricated with psychological experience."[33] Rather than or in addition to knowing if someone was of a like mind, "a person might wish to know someone's stomach or learn if he or she were of the same stomach, while to do something against one's stomach was to do something against one's wishes."[34] Such visceral knowledge was used in particular to create and maintain early modern social hierarchies based on gender, ethnicity, and class.[35] While these usages now are largely obsolete, or at least no longer consciously invoked, they reveal that the stomach's reactions to what one eats and with whom one eats historically have been a socially and politically important matter. Although the particular information provided by the stomach has changed over time, we "postmoderns" are not so different from pre-Cartesians when it comes to the cultural importance of visceral knowledge. The stomach continues to play a role in upholding social hierarchies, including contemporary racial hierarchies that benefit white people.

Given, as we saw in Chapter 2, that the gut is a key site for the transaction of body and world, of biology, psychology, and society, it perhaps is not surprising that white people's racism and their racist habits of engaging with the world can be found in their stomachs. Racism does not merely take the form of thoughts and ideas, such as the thought that black people are inferior and dangerous to white people. It is not only found in unreflective and/or unconscious bodily behaviors, for example, in the elevator effect. It also can be found in the elevator-bound white woman's gastrointestinal tract: the "difficulty swallowing, . . . dry mouth, [and] nausea" that Yancy describes,[36] as well as the eventual constipation (from the digestion-slowing effects of adrenaline on the stomach and intestines[37]) that her racist fear and anxiety can produce. The character of the stomach can be racist, and white people's racist stomachs have contributed to their habitual ways of engaging with the world, with black people and other people of color in particular.

The next example of the hidden physiological dimensions of white privilege that I examine—in this case, specifically white class privilege—focuses on the heart and brings out the raced and racist benefits to white people's health. It is

---

[32] Jan Purnis, "The Stomach and Early Modern Emotion," *University of Toronto Quarterly*, 2010, 79(2): 816. See also David Hillman and Carla Mazzio, *The Body in Parts: Fantasies of Corporeality in Early Modern Europe* (New York: Routledge, 1997), especially Chapters 12 and 13.

[33] Purnis, "The Stomach and Early Modern Emotion," 804.

[34] Purnis, "The Stomach and Early Modern Emotion," 803.

[35] Purnis, "The Stomach and Early Modern Emotion," 814.

[36] Yancy, *Black Bodies, White Gazes*, 5.

[37] http://digestive.niddk.nih.gov/ddiseases/pubs/yrdd/, accessed June 18, 2013.

because of those benefits that I shift focus from the stomach to the heart, but the shift also makes sense recalling the link between the two organs assumed to exist in pre-Cartesian times. As with the stomach, in early modernity internal bodily organs such as the heart played an important role establishing the character and identity of people via their emotions. The heart and the stomach in particular had some meanings in common, especially concerning courage. For example, in 1588 Queen Elizabeth I rallied her English troops against the Spanish Armada by proclaiming, "I know I have the body of a weak and feeble woman, but I have the heart and stomach of a king, and a king of England too."[38] Like the stomach, the heart can be a site for the incorporation of various social and political positionalities, as early moderns appreciated.

Recent empirical research unintentionally reveals that white class privilege tends to have positive effects on the health of white people's hearts. This claim may seem puzzling since, as mentioned above, the benefits of white privilege to white health are virtually never discussed in contemporary neurocardiological studies. To see white privilege at work in them, one must read with an eye for something that, in a significant respect, is not there. This does not mean, however, that white privilege is a foreign topic being artificially inserted into the research. It is not the case, as the familiar accusation goes, that racism never would have been an issue if the critical philosopher of race and/or person of color had not introduced it.[39] Something like a gestalt shift is necessary: we need to change what we are looking for when we read. While the study examined below says nothing about the health effects of white privilege for middle- and upper-class white people, the topic simultaneously is included, written with the very same words that don't speak of it.

Dubbed the "heart brain" because of its sophisticated intrinsic nervous system, which "enables it to learn, remember, and make functional decisions independent of the cranial brain," the heart affects not just the body's autonomic regulation, but also its emotional and affective processing.[40] Afferent neuronal signals travel from the heart to the brain, affecting the central nucleus of the amygdala, which is a key emotional center.[41] This means that early modern and contemporary folk associations of the heart, with affects such as courage, love, compassion, and spirituality, can be understood as more than metaphorical or figurative.[42] These other-directed emotions and

---

[38] Quoted in Purnis, "The Stomach and Early Modern Emotion," 800.

[39] Many people of color and probably every critical philosopher of race have been accused of this at least once. For an example in print, see Yancy, *Look, a White!* 138.

[40] Rollin McCraty and Doc Childre, "The Grateful Heart: The Psychophysiology of Appreciation," in *The Psychology of Gratitude*, eds. Robert A Emmons and Michael E. McCullough (New York: Oxford University Press, 2004) 232.

[41] McCraty and Childre, "The Grateful Heart," 233, 235.

[42] McCraty and Childre, "The Grateful Heart," 230.

states of being are associated by some psychologists with both an appreciative openness to the world and a complementary sense that the world is open to you. Both experiences of openness, moreover, are correlated with a physically healthy heart brain. A heart brain that is functioning optimally is the physical manifestation of an open relationship to the world.

Evidence of the heart brain's optimal functioning can be found in the rhythms and patterns of a person's heart rate, as indicated by its tachograms (indicating heartbeats per minute) and its power spectral density (indicating the frequency, or the specific electric current, of the beating heart).[43] Consider three different cases: one of negative emotions such as anxiety, frustration, or anger; a more neutral case of relaxation; and finally a case of positive emotions such as appreciation. As we will see, the terms "negative" and "positive" here correspond with the harmful or beneficial physiological effects of various emotional and affective states. For example, when a person is angry, her heart rate tends to be fast, erratic, and characterized by rhythms in the low frequency band of the power spectrum (0.0033–0.04 hertz). This type of heart rate decreases parasympathetic activity in the ANS (autonomic nervous system), which is significant because the parasympathetic branch of the ANS regulates sleeping, digesting, and other bodily activities associated with rest and relaxation.[44] If the balance in the ANS tips too often away from the parasympathetic and toward the sympathetic branch, the latter of which stimulates "fight or flight" responses to danger, the body doesn't have enough time or energy to renew and repair itself. The result of this imbalance tends to be health problems associated with chronic anxiety and stress, such as cardiovascular disease and antecedent conditions such as hypertension.[45] In contrast, when a person is relaxed and not angry, her heart rate pattern tends to be relatively slow, less erratic, and marked by increased power in the high frequency band (0.15–0.4 hertz). Correspondingly, parasympathetic activity in the brain also increases.[46]

The sympathetic branch of the ANS should not be thought of as simply opposed to the parasympathetic branch, however. The relationship between the two branches actually is one of complementarity since the constant, basic activity of the sympathetic branch is crucial to the body's ability to maintain its internal stability (homeostasis). The ideal physiological situation thus is for the two branches to be synchronized, and this takes place when the heart rate is highly ordered and smooth. This type of heart rate tends to occur when a person feels positive emotions such as appreciation. When a person

---

[43] McCraty and Childre, "The Grateful Heart," 237.

[44] McCraty and Childre, "The Grateful Heart," 233.

[45] Simon C. Malpas, "Sympathetic Nervous System Overactivity and Its Role in the Development of Cardiovascular Disease," *Physiological Reviews*, 2010, 90(2): 513–557.

[46] McCraty and Childre, "The Grateful Heart," 237.

experiences the emotion of appreciation or gratitude, her parasympathetic activity increases and coordinates with the activities of the sympathetic branch. The rhythms of the appreciative heart are not identical to those of the relaxed heart, however. While both are marked by increased parasympathetic activity in comparison to the angry heart, the appreciative heart oscillates at a different frequency (0.04–0.14 hertz, centering around 0.1), one that allows better resonance and coherence across different physiological systems.

When a person feels grateful or appreciative, her entire biological system tends to pulse in smooth coordination with itself. The result of such synchronization is health benefits such as "increased efficiency in fluid exchange, filtration and absorption between the capillaries and tissues" and other physiological changes that increase "systemwide energy efficiency and metabolic energy savings."[47] Sometimes this event is described subjectively as an experience of increased "flow," of clarity, creativity, and invigoration, in which blockages and barriers in one's life have (at least temporarily) dissolved.[48] The feeling is one of possibilities opening up, along with the physical and emotional energy to pursue them. As a corresponding study argues, while negative emotions "narrow people's ideas about possible actions," positive emotions "widen the scope of attention, broaden repertoires of desired actions,. . . and increase openness to new experiences."[49] This can be a spiritual experience for some, in which one feels an increased connection with other people and the world at large. Whether spiritual or not, however, positive emotions such as appreciation have been linked scientifically to increased physiological efficiency, "substantiat[ing] what many people have long intuitively known: positive emotions bolster one's ability to meet life's challenges with grace and ease, optimize cognitive capacities, sustain constructive and meaningful relationships with others, and foster good health."[50]

So, the primary study's authors ask, why aren't more people doing something to pursue positive emotions on a day-to-day basis? Their answer provides a trigger for the gestalt shift needed to reveal white class privilege:

> Why do genuine positive emotional experiences remain transient and unpredictable occurrences for most people? We propose that a main factor underlying this discrepancy is a fundamental lack of mental and emotional self-management skills. In other words, people generally do not make efforts to actively infuse their daily experiences with greater emotional quality because they sincerely do not know how.[51]

---

[47] McCraty and Childre, "The Grateful Heart," 238.

[48] McCraty and Childre, "The Grateful Heart," 231–232.

[49] Barbara L. Fredrickson, "Promoting Positive Affect," in *The Science of Subjective Well-Being*, eds. Michael Eid and Randy J. Larson (New York: The Guilford Press, 2008) 450.

[50] McCraty and Childre, "The Grateful Heart," 249.

[51] McCraty and Childre, "The Grateful Heart," 241.

The authors proceed to offer a number of feedback techniques, or "interventions," that can improve emotional experience by increasing awareness of and altering heart rates and frequencies. These can be sophisticated "heart math" techniques or as simple as deep breathing exercises, which modulate the heart's rhythm and thus can change one's emotional-neurological state. [52]

The authors' suggestions are intriguing, and in many respects their overall research program integrating emotions, cardio-physiology, and neurology is both medically and philosophically important. It provides a concrete example of how to non-reductively appreciate the medical-physiological aspects of human emotional life. But it is woefully focused on the individual isolated from the social-political world, which enables the authors to offer extremely white-washed guidance for improving human emotional-cardio health. By "white-washed," I mean saturated with white class privilege. Whether or not the authors are white or come from race and/or class privileged backgrounds (I do not know, nor is it necessarily important to know), their interventions implicitly address only the emotional-cardio difficulties of middle- and upper-class white human beings and exclude those of people of color. They focus on people who are not regular targets of racism and who do not daily benefit from the "invisible" ease and comfort in life provided by white class privilege. In that way, the authors' suggestions suffer from white solipsism, erasing or ignoring the lives and health of those who are not white.

To better see the white class privilege at work in this study, consider an all-too-common experience for African Americans of being presumed to be intrinsically criminal. George Yancy powerfully describes the phenomenon of hearing the click of a car door being locked by a white person inside when he or she sees a black person on the street. Much more than just a simple sound, the click is "part of a racial and racist web of significance" that constructs "the occupants' sense of themselves as 'safe' (and white) [which] is purchased at the expense of denigrating the black body as unsafe."[53] If the clicks could speak, we could hear them establish the ontological stability and epistemological credibility of white identity: "*Click* (innocent) . . . *Click* (reliable). *Click* (*our* white space) . . . *Click* (civilized). *Click* (law abiding)."[54] White people's security and comfort are established in opposition to the dangerous black person, "fragment[ing] my existence and cut[ting] away at my integrity," as Yancy explains.[55] The same clicks proclaiming white goodness simultaneously tell him and all black people—for they, too, can hear the clicks outside the car—that they are subpersons: "*Click* (thug), *click* (criminal), *click*

---

[52] McCraty and Childre, "The Grateful Heart," 243–246, 236.

[53] Yancy, *Look, a White!* 31.

[54] Yancy, *Look, a White!* 31.

[55] Yancy, *Look, a White!* 33.

(thief)" and, ultimately, "*Click, click, click, click, click* (nigger, nigger, nigger, nigger, nigger)."[56]

This is not an isolated or atypical experience for black people in the United States. In addition to the clicking experience, the elevator effect powerfully described by Yancy is all too common in the lives of black men.[57] Brent Staples also writes in a similar fashion of the handbag-clutching march white women assume when they see him on the street.[58] In a related vein, Cornel West has documented his experience with the police in Princeton when he was "Driving While Black": he was stopped three times in ten days for driving too slowly in an upscale residential area.[59] Something similar happened as recently as 2013, when an African American graduate student with whom I work was pulled over on the Virginia interstate while driving the speed limit, hassled for a while as the white police officer couldn't find any expired registrations, and finally let go with a warning for appearing to have windows that were tinted a shade too dark. On the racial flip-side, Tim Wise, a white man, describes the surprise on a white police officer's face when Wise rolled down the darkened window of his beat-up, anti-David-Duke-bumper-stickered car when he also was stopped for no apparent reason.[60] As the officer fumbled to find an explanation for pulling Wise over, it was clear to Wise that he was targeted because his car marked him as black. (In Wise's case, the officer finally discovered that Wise's insurance had expired two weeks earlier, but after giving Wise a ticket, the officer proceeded to explain the steps for how to have the ticket thrown out.) Finally, I offer the corresponding, ubiquitous experience of black people being tailed by store clerks or plainclothes officers when they do their shopping. As Yancy explains, the "presumptive innocence" granted to white people spares them this unnerving and infuriating experience. A white person "can walk into stores [or drive down the street] without anyone doubting the integrity of his [or her] character and intentions."[61]

These incidents might seem (especially to white people) to be minor, even trivial—after all, there no longer are any physical or legal obstacles in the United States to a black person's entering an elevator or a store, for example, and traveling to the desired floor or making the needed purchases. And these incidents don't come close to comparison with the police shooting of

---

[56] Yancy, *Look, a White!* 33.

[57] Yancy, *Black Bodies, White Gazes,* 5. While not in an elevator or directed at black men, my experience as the only white person on a city bus in Birmingham portrays from the white side, so to speak, the white bodily tension of which Yancy speaks (see Sullivan, *Revealing Whiteness*, 98–101).

[58] Brent Staples, "Just Walk on By: A Black Man Ponders His Power to Alter Public Space," *Ms.,* September 1986, 54.

[59] Yancy, *Look, a White!* 44–45. See West's account of the experience in Cornel West, *Race Matters* (Boston, MA: Beacon Press, 1993) x–xi.

[60] Discussed in Yancy, *Look, a White!* 45–46. See Tim Wise, *White Like Me: Reflections on Race from a Privileged Son* (Brooklyn, NY: Soft Skull Press, 2005) 39.

[61] Yancy, *Look, a White!* 164.

Michael Brown in Ferguson, Missouri, or the chokehold death of Eric Garner in New York. What is the big deal about an unfriendly clerk or an uptight elevator companion, one might ask? The answer is that in seemingly small details such as these lies a particular world that contemporary black people are forced to inhabit, one that is substantially different than the world inhabited by white people and one, moreover, that helps make possible more spectacular events such as Brown's and Garner's deaths. The worlds of white and black people are not always, or perhaps never, the same, even though black and white people might inhabit (sometimes, anyway) the same physical space. "To be white in a white world," as Yancy reveals, "is to be extended by that world's contours. The world opens up, reveals itself as a place called home, a place of privileges and immunities, a space for achievement, success, freedom of movement."[62]

The world generally is not open to black people in this way. Even when they are not, for example, tailed by a clerk or stopped by a cop on a given day, the possibility that they could be is ever present, adding to every excursion into the public sphere an element of anxiety. As Yancy explains, black people are "exposed to a daily enactment of white racialized drama" that undercuts their efforts to "secur[e] existential and psychological safety in a white racist world."[63] Whether in a store, at work or school, or merely walking down the street, they do not get to arrive on the scene as white people do, "with socially fortified . . . identities that are certain of who they are" and whose "psychic integrity" is not at risk.[64] As a result, even though de jure Jim Crow laws have long been removed from the books, the world is not a smooth space of easy passage for black people in the way that it generally is for white people. The world presents obstacles to black people at just about every turn.

Even though these obstacles often aren't physical, their effects can be. Kim Anderson, the African American women discussed in Chapter 3, captures this point well as she elaborates on her experience of being tailed:

> So nobody, when I walk in a store, nobody says, "Oh, that's Kim Anderson, African-American, female lawyer, went to Columbia," they just see a black woman. I was in a store once, just walking around thinking I was going to buy a pair of jeans. This clerk's following me around. So I said, "Why are you following me around? I'm not going to steal anything. Leave me alone. I'm not going to take something." When you're confronted with racism, that covert racism, your stomach just gets so tight. You can feel it almost moving through your body; almost you can feel it going into your bloodstream.[65]

---

[62] Yancy, *Look, a White!* 45.
[63] Yancy, *Look, a White!* 156.
[64] Yancy, *Look, a White!* 131.
[65] Quoted in "Unnatural Causes: When the Bough Breaks," California Newsreel, 2008, 7; http:// www.unnaturalcauses.org/assets/uploads/file/UC_Transcript_2.pdf, accessed December 2, 2012.

When Anderson describes racism coursing through the veins and tissues of her body, she is right. It's highly likely that the emotional tension she felt in the store was simultaneously a physiological event in which cortisol and other stress-related hormones elevated her heart rate and stimulated the sympathetic branch of her ANS, as well as altered some of her epigenetic markers connected with the risk of preterm birth.[66] The "outside" of the social world should not be thought of as sharply divided from the "inside" of her body. The racism "outside" Anderson's body simultaneously was "inside," possibly altering her not just her epigenetic attachments but also her heart brain.

One might object that experiences like Anderson's are not unique and that white people are confronted with similar obstacles and health risks as people of color. For example, white people often don't feel safe or welcome in predominantly non-white neighborhoods and, as Brittney would testify, they too can feel stress coursing through their bodies, for example, when confronted by a "threatening" black man. But these are not the same kinds of experiences, neither socially nor physiologically, and this is so for at least three reasons. First, Brittney's tense stomach is the result of an occasional, rather than a chronic, stressor, and occasional stresses do not have much, if any, of a negative effect on a person's health. As we saw in Chapter 3, it is the daily weathering of chronic, ongoing stresses that presents a significant health concern. A second, related reason is that white people generally get to choose when to enter non-white worlds, while people of color often are forced economically, geographically, and otherwise to travel to white worlds. A white person's stress upon entering a non-white world thus tends to be avoidable as well as episodic, unlike that of a person of color coerced into entering the white world. Third, white people's discomfort in non-white neighborhoods is more of a curtailment of their ontological expansiveness than it is an instance of so-called reverse discrimination.[67] White people tend to assume that they should be psychosocially comfortable in any space of their choosing, and they are offended when that racial "right" is violated. The indignant anger of a white person who isn't welcome in a non-white space is not the same thing as the stressed anxiety of a black person who is perceived as intrinsically criminal.

Even if we allowed that white people can be racially discriminated against, however, they do not experience negative health effects as non-white people do when they are the targets of racial discrimination. A recent study comparing African American and white American women—one of the rare empirical studies that make white privilege visible—demonstrates that subtle

---

[66] Salynn Boyles, "Stress Hormone Predicts Heart Death: High Cortisol Levels Raise Risk of Heart Disease, Stroke 5-Fold," *WebMD Health News*, 2010, http://www.webmd.com/heart-disease/news/20100909/stress-hormone-predicts-heart-death, accessed January 29, 2013.

[67] For more on white people's ontological expansiveness, see Sullivan, *Revealing Whiteness.*

forms of racial discrimination raised the blood pressure levels and affected the cardiovascular health of the black, but not the white, women.[68] The study controlled for numerous variables, including interpersonal mistreatment or antagonisms, to ensure that stress due to racial discrimination was targeted. It also distinguished between subtle and blatant forms of racial discrimination, discovering that blatant forms did not affect cardiovascular functioning. While initially surprising, this discovery fits with other research that shows both that negative emotions such as anxiety and anger have been linked with coronary heart disease in particular and that "chronic minor stress may be more strongly related to adverse health outcomes than are major stressors that occur infrequently."[69] In the case of a blatant form of racial discrimination, the unfair treatment would be obvious to virtually everyone, the perpetrator would be widely condemned, and the victim would receive strong social support.[70] Subtle, "invisible" forms of racial discrimination, in contrast, can lead to higher stress levels because of their ambiguity. It is precisely the "trivial" character of many forms of contemporary racism, in combination with its daily relentlessness, that makes contemporary racism so harmful to black health. It also makes the effects of Anderson's stress very different than those of Brittney's fear.

Returning to the heart brain study after revealing its false universalism, we now can give its central question a twist. If the study allegedly applies to all people, then we can ask: Why don't *black* people more often cultivate positive emotions and better heart health? And the answer that critical philosophers of race would provide is not that they don't have sufficient mental and emotional self-management skills. That answer is both obtuse and insulting to people of color. It's that black people are constantly battling racism. The primary "intervention" needed to improve African American people's affective-cardio health thus is not heart rhythm feedback training, but interrupting white domination. This is not to deny that stress-management techniques might be helpful to black people, but appealed to outside any social-political context, they treat only the symptom, not the real problem. More sinisterly, they even can exacerbate the real problem by making black people's hypertension and other heart maladies seem like the result of their individual failure as members of a particular racial group. (The racist stereotype of the broken black family rears its ugly head again here.) The real

---

[68] Max Guyll, Karen A. Matthews, and Joyce T. Bromberger, "Discrimination and Unfair Treatment: Relationship to Cardiovascular Reactivity Among African American and European American Women," *Health Psychology*, 2001, 20(5): 315–325.

[69] On the first point, see Laura D. Kubzansky and Ichiro Kawachi, "Affective States and Health," in *Social Epidemiology*, eds. Lisa F. Berkman and Ichiro Kawachi (New York: Oxford University Press, 2000) 231. On the second point and quote, see Guyll et al., "Discrimination and Unfair Treatment," 322.

[70] Guyll et al., "Discrimination and Unfair Treatment," 323.

problem is not the insufficient affective skills of African Americans, but white people and their institutional and (inter)personal habits of white supremacy and white privilege. Once one acknowledges the ongoing existence of racism, the "invisible" theme of white class privilege in this empirical study becomes apparent: the affective-physiological body addressed in it is a body that does not have to worry about the daily stresses and hassles of contemporary, de facto Jim Crow racism. It is a middle- to upper-class white body with the affective-cardio problems typical of middle- and upper-class white people.

The study's covert white privilege perhaps isn't too surprising given the history of the field of cardiology in the United States. Founded in the 1910s and 1920s, cardiology was thoroughly racialized from the outset in terms of who was thought to suffer from cardiovascular disease. Black Americans allegedly did not get heart disease, or at least not the emblematic form of it, which is coronary disease.[71] Only white people, especially white men, did, and so cardiology focused exclusively on them. The explanation for this exclusion is not found in an overt policy or declaration that the field of cardiology should omit black Americans. It instead lies in a combination of the racialized narrative told about modern development and the racialized distinction made between two types of heart disease, infectious and non-infectious. Examples of infectious heart disease include syphilitic and rheumatic heart disease, while non-infectious heart disease is arteriosclerotic due to degenerative causes.[72] Although half of the cases of heart disease in the 1920s were infectious, it was non-infectious heart disease that was on the rise in the early twentieth century, and that explained the increasing overall rate of heart disease in the United States.[73] Degenerative heart disease was considered to pose the greatest threat to America's future heart health, and thus the new field of cardiology chose to concentrate on it. "Genuine" heart disease was (and is) coronary and degenerative, not the result of a contagious infection.

Why was degenerative heart disease on the rise in the early twentieth century? The culprit was thought to be modern progress and civilization. As Western society became more civilized, the pace and productivity of life increased.[74] This generally was perceived as a beneficial and welcome change, but it also had an unfortunate side effect on the health of civilized people. The increasing stress and strain of living in a modern, industrialized world taxed their nervous systems. The responsibilities and demands of being a modern citizen increased, as did the need for complex planning, organization, and coordination. Ambition and hard work paid off, but they tended to take a

---

[71] Anne Pollock, *Medicating Race: Heart Disease and Durable Preoccupations with Difference* (Durham, NC: Duke University Press, 2012) 29.

[72] Pollock, *Medicating Race*, 30, 31.

[73] Pollock, *Medicating Race*, 31.

[74] Pollock, *Medicating Race*, 34.

biological toll. While civilized people could be proud of the modern world they helped build, the stress of building it often damaged their cardiovascular system. The field of cardiology thus implicitly was founded to offset or repair the harms caused by modern society. Even though the increasing rate of coronary heart disease was distressing, the "degeneration" from which civilized people suffered was never synonymous with "regression." It instead was a physiological manifestation of the heights to which civilized societies had progressed.

As will come as no surprise to critical philosophers of race, the category of "civilized" almost always is reserved for white people, and this pattern holds true in the specific case of heart disease. The ambitious hard workers who suffered from the strain and stress of creating a new future for America were middle- to upper-class white people, especially white men. (White women were seen as more susceptible to regrets about the past, and thus to developing cancer, conceived as an illness that strikes civilized, modern people in particular.[75]) People of color, and especially black Americans, allegedly were not capable of the "brain" work that civilization required. They were too simple, too carefree, and too childlike. (Lower class white people also were not thought to be capable of this kind of work, but not because of their supposedly innate constitution.[76]) As physician and president of the American Heart Association (1933–1934) Stewart R. Roberts pointedly and somewhat wistfully explained in a 1931 essay,

> The white man, particularly those living lives of stress in urban conditions of competition, work and strain, makes his little plans and lays up cares and riches and takes much thought of the morrow; the negro knows his weekly wage is his fortune, takes each day as it is, takes little or now thought of the morrow, plays and lives in a state of play, hurries none and worries little. What must it be to live unhurried, unworried, superstitious but not ambitious, full of childlike faith, satisfied, helpless, plodding, plain, patient, yet living a life of joy and interest?[77]

Likewise, but in a more resentful tone, Roberts laments the attitude of his black maid when she won't answer the ringing telephone. Rather than see her lack of effort as a form of resistance to her oppressive situation, Roberts takes her inaction as a sign of her intrinsically passive constitution. As Roberts complains,

---

[75] Pollock, *Medicating Race*, 35.

[76] Their "failure" was more offensive because it was avoidable, even though it might be partially be the fault of black contagion, i.e., "catching" what black people have/are. For more on lower class white people and "white trash," see Chapter 1 of Shannon Sullivan, *Good White People: The Problem with Middle Class White Anti-Racism* (Albany: State University of New York Press, 2014).

[77] Quoted in Pollock, *Medicating Race*, 34.

I strain, she lives with the day. She illustrates the advantages of being uneducated, untutored, unambitious, just one who by nature has been born
with "an internal adjustment—to change her soul into an attitude of acceptance." But I meet difficulties every day, and many times a day, and try
much or little to change and correct the difficulty externally rather than to
adjust myself to it internally.[78]

The white-invented world of Calibans, Tontos, Man Fridays, and Sambos is
in full evidence here. Roberts's maid is a sidekick—albeit an allegedly lazy,
rather than reliable one—an accessory to the white people (Roberts) who are
the central characters in the (his)story. The ignorant knowledge produced by
this invented world had a profound impact on the science of heart disease
(as well as just about everything else). Given their allegedly essential comportment as relaxed and accepting of the world, black people were designated
as constitutionally incapable of developing coronary heart disease.

In addition to the perceived black constitution as childlike and unambitious,
so-called black infectiousness also explains why the burgeoning field of cardiology excluded African Americans. In the white imaginary, blackness not only was
imbricated with carefree laziness, but it also was inseparable from contagious
infection. Civilized members of the United States were sanitary citizens, and
black people were neither civilized nor sanitary.[79] They were closely tied to vene-
real infections and (a lack of) sexual hygiene, contagious diseases that tended to
define blackness during the early twentieth century.[80] The association of blackness with contagious infection made it seem natural that black people would suffer from syphilitic, rather than coronary heart disease. Their hearts were highly
susceptible to contagious rather than degenerative maladies. "Germs gathered
toward the bottom of social hierarchies, [while] coronary disease collected up,"
and this difference impacted the kind of medical care that each group should
receive.[81] Black people didn't warrant a sophisticated new branch of medical science for better heart health, as white people did. They merely needed to practice
better hygiene to curb their infectious nature. Cardiology thus implicitly was
founded as a racialized medical field exclusively for middle- to upper-class white
people, particularly white men. It has a long history of dismissively misunderstanding the heart health of African Americans.

Of course, white people of all classes can suffer from chronic stress
and associated negative emotions, and it's important to mark differences
in white health across class and wealth lines. Poor and lower class white
people generally do not experience the same existential and financial

---

[78] Quoted in Pollock, *Medicating Race*, 35.

[79] Pollock, *Medicating Race*, 39.

[80] Pollock, *Medicating Race*, 39.

[81] Pollock, *Medicating Race*, 35.

comfort that middle- and upper-class white people do. But as Anderson's comments in particular illustrate, the class-race privilege in question here cannot be reduced to class. Across a number of health problems, racial differences between black and white Americans in particular persist even after adjusting for differences in socioeconomic status.[82] Both education- ally and financially, as lawyers and university professors, Anderson, West, and Yancy all have the cultural and economic capital to count as middle class (or perhaps higher). Nevertheless, their class status is not enough to protect them from racial harassment or to provide them with socially forti- fied and respected identities. In contrast, the health problems of poor and lower class white people occur against a backdrop of relative existential and psychological security provided by their whiteness, even if their level of security is significantly lower than that of middle- and upper-class white people.[83] Poor and lower class white people might be anxious, frustrated, or angry because of, for example, their job or their life prospects, but their status as a full person is not subtly and constantly put into question solely because of their race.[84]

Isn't that a good thing, however? Isn't it is an important ideal of racial justice struggles that no one should be oppressed because of his or her race? One might object that the body in this study isn't a specifically raced or classed body, but a general body relevant to the ideal health of all people. In a world free of race and class oppression—a world to be embraced by feminists and critical philosophers of race, after all—questions of cardio-emotional health will still arise and will need to be addressed. Especially given medi- cine's racist past (and present), shouldn't we welcome a medical perspective that treats all people as equal, demonstrating how everyone can benefit from heart rhythm feedback and other heart brain health techniques?

The answer is no—not because black people should be treated as subper- sons but because this objection does not give sufficient weight to the current reality that they often *are* treated as such. To consider the body in this car- diological study as a non-raced, general body is to operate with something like ideal theory, when what is needed instead is nonideal theory. As Charles Mills explains, in the realm of political philosophy "ideal theory asks what justice demands in a perfectly just society while nonideal theory asks what

---

[82] David R. Williams, Yan Yu, James S. Jackson, and Norman B. Anderson, "Racial Differences in Physical and Mental Health," *Journal of Health Psychology*, 1997, 2(3): 325–351; Michael C. Lu and Neal Halfon, "Racial and Ethnic Disparities in Birth Outcomes: A Life-Course Perspective," *Maternal and Child Health Journal*, 2003, 7(1): 14.

[83] See W. E. B. Du Bois's classic analysis of the social and psychological wages of whiteness for poor and working-class white people in *Black Reconstruction in America, 1860–1880* (New York: The Free Press, 1995), especially pages 700–701.

[84] For more on class, race, and the white middle-class use of "white trash" to perpetuate white domination of people of color, see Sullivan, *Good White People*, especially Chapter 1.

justice demands in a society with a history of injustice."[85] Both theories hold that justice is important, but ideal political theory explores its requirements and limitations in a society that has already achieved it. Nonideal political theory, in contrast, acknowledges that society is not (yet) just and then, from that starting point, analyzes what would be needed to bring about greater justice. The difference between the two theories is profound. By dismissing existing injustices as theoretically unimportant, ideal political theory tends to perpetuate them, undercutting its own (alleged) goal of understanding and promoting a more just world. While "nonideal theory is concerned with corrective measures, with remedial or rectificatory justice," the misnamed ideal theory "is in crucial respects obfuscatory, and can indeed be thought of as in part *ideological,* in the pejorative sense of a set of group ideas that reflect, and contribute to perpetuating, illicit group privilege."[86]

Likewise we could say that ideal medical theory asks what good health demands in a perfectly healthy society. Nonideal medical theory, in contrast, would ask what good health demands in a society with a history of systematically damaging the health of some of its members. Both theories have healthiness as their goal, but the difference in their starting points is tremendous. It is the difference between recognizing or ignoring that systematic health inequalities exist and often impede medical efforts to augment good health. The ignorance of ideal medical theory is not benign, nor is it accidental, even though it might not have been consciously constructed. It interferes with remedial or rectificatory health measures, and in that way it is ideological, perpetuating the ongoing health problems of people of color by neglecting corrective measures—racial justice—that would do the most to improve the health of people of color.

The upshot here is that just as racism often courses through the bodies of people of color, damaging their health, white privilege courses through the bodies of white people, benefiting them. To understand how it does so, we need to distinguish between two related, but different issues concerning whiteness. One is the way that whiteness often functions as a neutral baseline for human health and physiological functioning. The other is the way that, as sociologists Jesse Daniels and Amy J. Schulz have argued, "whiteness is protective of heath."[87] In both cases, whiteness tends to operate unmarked and unnoticed, furnishing a baseline of security and comfort for white people that subtends their relative good health.

---

[85] Charles Mills, "Racial Liberalism," *Proceedings of the Modern Language Association,* 2008, 1384–1385.

[86] Mills, "Racial Liberalism," 1385; Charles Mills, "'Ideal Theory' as Ideology," *Hypatia,* 2005, 20(3): 166.

[87] Jessie Daniels and Amy J. Schulz, "Constructing Whiteness in Health Disparities Research," in *Gender, Race, Class and Health: Intersectional Approaches,* eds. Amy J. Schulz and Leath Mullings (San Francisco: Jossey Bass, 2006) 102.

Let me begin with the first issue. The allegedly neutral baseline of white physiology contributes to a false universalization of white health as human health, as if white people's psychophysiological experience in the (white) world were neutral and available to all people. Their lower rates of cardiovascular disease, for example, tend to be seen as normal, and the higher rates of cardiovascular disease for African Americans as deviations from the norm. Even more striking, as Daniels and Schulz have documented, is the way that whiteness invisibly structures our knowledge about the human genome.[88] Declared officially completed in 2003, the Human Genome Project analyzed the structure of human DNA and approximately 25,000 genes associated with various diseases. In addition to providing potential information for diagnosing, preventing, and treating disease and inheritable disorders, the Human Genome Project also "helped to inform us about how remarkably similar all human beings are—99.9% at the DNA level," as the director of the National Human Genome Research Institute has claimed.[89] Race thus allegedly has no place in human population genetics. At the level of DNA, human beings are virtually identical to each other.

It turns out, however, that this claim of shared humanity is based largely on the DNA samples taken from white people. On the academic side, scientists working on the Human Genome Project claimed to sample the chromosomal structures of a diverse range of human beings. On the privately funded side (led by the biotech firm Celera), scientists supposedly used DNA samples from five subjects drawn from a wide pool: one African American, one Asian Chinese, one Hispanic Mexican, and two Caucasians. But in fact, as Daniels and Schulz reveal, "the chromosomal reference samples for the academic HGP were taken from 'sixty-seven northern American and northern European men' with a large portion oversampled from Utah"; even more shocking is the fact that Celera's CEO, a white man, disclosed at the end of the project that "the mapping his firm had done had not been on the diverse chromosomal sample of donated DNA but rather on *his. . .* own DNA."[90] The universal humanity studied in the Human Genome Project turns out to be the genetic humanity of a predominantly Caucasian group of people.

If human DNA really is 99.9% similar across the human population, then it shouldn't matter whom the samples for mapping DNA were drawn from. The problem here, of course, is the circular reasoning involved in this reassurance. The result of the Human Genome Project was allegedly to demonstrate that in the wide diversity of human beings, our DNA is 99.9% similar. We can't assume such similarity in order to justify limiting the samples to

---

[88] The information on the Human Genome Project in the next three paragraphs comes from Daniels and Schulz, "Constructing Whitness in Health Disparities Research," 104–110.

[89] Quoted in Daniels and Schulz, "Constructing Whitness in Health Disparities Research," 106.

[90] Daniels and Schulz, "Constructing Whitness in Health Disparities Research," 108.

only white people without begging the initial question. What apparently has allowed this question to be begged without much comment is the normative force of whiteness. Whiteness supposedly is neutral, not race specific, and thus it can function as universal and representing humanity as such. Even if the mapping of human DNA is based on the chromosomal sample of one single person—such as the Celera CEO—the information we glean from that mapping can apply to everyone as long as the single person was white. A black, Hispanic, or Asian person could not play this role. (Just imagine the likely reaction of white people if it were revealed that Celera's entire Human Genome Project had been based on one person of color.) And yet the role of whiteness in the Human Genome Project tends to be invisible. "In a very real sense," as Daniels and Schulz explain, "the mapping of the human genome is both a universal appeal to humankind and based on the DNA of a putatively white genome. Yet this is rarely explicitly stated or called into question."[91]

If we reject the false universalization of whiteness, then we should be very wary of using the physiological data or states of white people as a neutral baseline for human health against which other races are compared, even if that comparison is made in the name of improving the health of people of color. In the attempt to improve African Americans' heart health, for example, white people's lower rates of cardiovascular disease tend to be seen as normal, and the higher rates of cardiovascular disease for African Americans as deviations from the norm. This allows a white privileged norm to remain in place, unmarked and unquestioned. I would argue, in contrast, that neither rate of cardiovascular disease is normal or neutral. This entails not just the relatively easy acknowledgment that African American heart health is the specific product of racism—as perhaps, slowly, the medical sciences are beginning to admit—but also, as I will turn to next, the more difficult acknowledgment (at least for white people) that white heart health is the specific product of white domination. Perhaps a new norm for health will be needed and created, and the health of all people can be measured against it. I'm not sure if that would be necessary or desirable. But in any case, white people's racial-existential experience should no longer be able to establish the physiological, medical standard for others.[92] As Daniels and Schulz claim, "the often invisible—or at least underinterrogated—concept of whiteness within the context of the literature on racial disparities in health" must be made visible and challenged if those disparities are to be eliminated.[93]

The second issue, to which I've just alluded, is that eliminating racism and white domination would impact not just the health of people of color, but

---

[91] Daniels and Schulz, "Constructing Whiteness in Health Disparities Research," 109.

[92] As, of course, it long has. See Stephen Jay Gould, *The Mismeasure of Man* (New York: W. W. Norton, 1996).

[93] Daniels and Schulz, "Constructing Whiteness in Health Disparities Research," 90.

also that of white people. In certain respects, this admittedly could mean an improvement in white people's health. Recalling Brittney, we could say that if relaxed and engaged interaction with people of color is foreclosed for many white people, then those white people already are sclerotic and their physiological functioning would benefit from the elimination of their racist anxieties.[94] But I think there also is a significant chance that white health would deteriorate in comparison to its current state. While this claim might sound alarming (to white people), one must remember that the current state of white health is the product of unjust privilege. In other words, the term "deteriorate" is accurate here only when measuring the change against the norm of white domination. When that norm is removed—that is, when white people cannot use white privilege to bolster their health—then the nature of any comparison necessarily will change.

Recall the example of telomere length that I briefly mentioned in Chapter 3. Telomeres are the ends of chromosomes, and they shorten over time as the body becomes weathered. They thus are a measurement of physiological age, which may or may not match a person's chronological age. Based on telomere length, African American women between the ages of 49 and 55 on average are physiologically seven and a half years older than their white counterparts.[95] This difference appears to be due to a lifetime of racial microaggressions, which do not immediately threaten one's life or obviously cause physical harm but which are physiologically damaging through the high allostatic load to which they contribute. (The insults and slights that are characteristic of racial microaggressions thus are misunderstood when they are considered narrowly psychological and not biological.) As Chapter 3 explained and as ample empirical research demonstrates, racial microaggressions harm the health of people of color.

What is missing in the empirical literature, however, is acknowledgment and discussion of the flip-side of racial microaggressions: how the health of white people correspondingly *benefits* from the small gestures of respect and

---

[94] Thanks to an anonymous reviewer for this point. I acknowledge that with something like a transvaluation of values in the United States and the Western world more generally (Nietzschean overtones intended), it's possible that the end of white domination of people of color would improve white psychosomatic health. "Improvement" and "health" here would mean something very different than they do given our current system of valuation, of course, something that can only be gestured at from a present-day, white-saturated perspective. The point here, however, is that something as significant as transvaluation is needed before the changes in white health could be improvements. Until then, the changes I am discussing are likely both to be and to be experienced by white people as deteriorations. Thanks to Leah McClimans and other members of University of South Carolina's philosophy department for discussing this issue with me.

[95] Arline T. Geronimus, Margaret T. Hicken, Jay A. Pearson, Sarah J. Seashols, Kelly L. Brown, and Tracey Dawson Cruz, "Do US Black Women Experience Stress-Related Accelerated Biological Aging? A Novel Theory and First Population-Based Test of Black-White Differences in Telomere Length," *Human Nature*, 2010, 21(1): 19–38.

consideration that they receive because they are white. I will call these incidents "racial microkindnesses." These are the little things that help smooth life along: instead of being tailed in a department store, a pleasant clerk asks if she can take the blouse in your arms and put it in the dressing room for you. Instead of charging you the full daily rate for the lost parking ticket as per the parking garage's policy, the attendant believes your explanation that you only pulled in one hour ago and lets you pay the hourly fee to exit the garage. Instead of merely shrugging when you ask the location of a (nonexistent, it turns out) pay phone because your cell phone has died, the clerk at the convenience store offers to let you use her phone to make your pressing call. Small kindnesses such as these help make the frustrations and hassles of everyday life a little easier to handle.

There are two related points connected to these examples that are important to note. First, these are not neutral acts, located somewhere between kindness and aggression. They are acts of kindness. One might object that while the garage attendant and the convenience store clerk perhaps were being kind, the department store clerk wasn't. Her job is to help sell clothes by encouraging people to try them on, and we shouldn't mistake her helpfulness for kindness. By extension, so the objection goes, a lot of the little things that smooth life along, especially in a consumer-driven economy, aren't kindnesses. They are job requirements. But I think this objection is mistaken: even in the case of the department store, kindness is written into the clerk's job description. He or she is expected to be (or at least to pretend to be) helpful and friendly to customers to help sell the store's merchandise. Racial (and other types of) microkindnesses can be generated structurally, in other words. They aren't necessarily driven by individual good will. (The same perhaps is true of racial microaggressions.) The central question thus remains: Who tends to be the beneficiary of microkindnesses, even if they are somewhat manufactured, rather than genuinely felt?

Small acts of kindness don't often seem like kindnesses, at least not to middle-class white people. They just seem like generic acts of kindnesses, or perhaps not as kindnesses but "normal" interpersonal interactions, as in the case of the department store clerk. This leads to the second point, which is that these are *racial* microkindnesses. They often tend to be class-based as well. In the United States and other white-dominated societies, white people tend to benefit from these types of acts more than people of color do, and this benefit is largely invisible to white people. Of course, a white person can't be certain that it was because of her whiteness that she benefited from a microkindness. (Likewise, a person of color often isn't certain that it was because of her race that she was the target of a microaggression.) It also is true that white people don't always receive the benefit of the doubt, as in the case of the parking garage example; class differences between white people can make a significant difference in how often one benefits or not from racial microkindnesses.

Finally, it's true that in an ideal world, everyone would benefit from small acts of kindness no matter what his or her race. But we do not live in that world. Our world generally is one where whiteness typically connotes innocence and goodness, rather than criminality and guilt, and so it is white people, especially middle-to-upper class ones, who tend to be treated as honest, upstanding people who deserve generosity rather than suspicion. The bottom line is that racial patterns exist concerning who is slighted and who is respected in various micro encounters, and this fact does not describe only the lives of people of color. It also describes the lives of white people.

Given that racial microaggressions contribute to the weathering of African American women's physiology and thus to the shortening of their telomeres, it makes sense to posit in turn that racial microkindnesses contribute to the preservation of white women's physiology and thus to the maintenance of their telomere length. It is not just that the African American women's telomeres were shorter than they would be if they didn't suffer from the stress of racism. It also is that the white women's telomeres were longer than they would be if they didn't benefit from the relatively stress-less ease of a world contoured with "invisible" white privilege. There is no "normal" telomere length against which to measure both the white women's and the African American women's telomere length. Why is telomere length X rather than telomere length Y the "proper" telomere length for a 50-year-old woman to have, for example? How was that measuring stick developed? There is no neutral, race-free answer to those questions because there is no neutral, race-free physiological body against which to measure a person's chronological age. I suspect that telomere length of the white women is being used as the "normal" telomere length for 47–55-year-old women, and then African American women's telomere length is being measured against it. In that case, the white body would be silently functioning as a universal physiological norm for people of all races. A better scenario would be if the white body were not being used as a universal norm by which to gauge physiological versus chronological age. In that case, the particularity of white people's experiences and lives, as well as those of people of color, would be openly acknowledged. In either case, however, we need to abandon a medical model in which white health rates are the human norm that medical science tries to help people of color attain.

It is likely that in a world without white privilege smoothing out many of the stresses of daily life, white health would not be as robust as it is today. Telomere lengths likely would be a bit shorter for white people, just as they likely would be a bit longer for African Americans and other people of color. Would they end up the same? I think there is no way to know the answer to that question at this moment in history. The larger point about changes in white physiology and health still stands, however. White privilege is like playing a video game on "easy" mode while people of color have to play it on "difficult" (and we could complicate the analogy with different difficulty levels for different groups of color).[96] Both groups have obstacles to overcome, enemies to combat, quests to accomplish, and so on, but the obstacles generally are a bit easier, the enemies not as fierce, and the quests more rewarding when one is white. When white people aren't allowed to play on easy mode and benefit from racial microkindnesses, the game (of life, we could say) is likely to become more stressful. Given the documented physiological effects of chronic stress, this means that white health likely would deteriorate.

The whiteness of medical standards tends to be invisible to white people, and thus it contributes to white people's ignorance of the very world that they built. White people often are incapable of recognizing the injustice that lies at the heart of their physiology (pun intended), and this ignorance is crucial to the ongoing operation of white domination. White people can believe that they are good people and take for granted their relative good health, all the while enjoying the unjust physiological and other benefits of their racial privilege. When they have difficulty giving up these assumptions and habits—which they almost always do—we need to query not just their cognitive beliefs but also their hearts and guts (pun intended once again). Because white ignorance operates courtesy of the hormones, tissues, and fibers of white people's bodies, eliminating white domination necessarily will alter their physiological functioning.

As José Medina rightly argues, white ignorance is not just a cognitive, but also an affective and emotional failure. White people tend to be deliberately ignorant of their own and other people's social positionality, and "this ignorance contains crucial *affective* elements."[97] The particular form of white ignorance on which Medina focuses is color-blindness, which involves what he calls affective numbness ("emotional numbness" on my terms): not being able to feel with people of color or achieve particular emotional relationships with them as a result of a cultivated lack in interest in them.[98] Given the identity of emotions and bodily states, we might say that white people who are color-blind are physiologically incapable of moving in the same ways that racially knowledgeable people do. They are numb—oblivious—to certain aspects of their world, and their numbness manifests itself physiologically, as well as interpersonally. The result of their emotional failure is a knowledge

---

[96] Thanks to Russell Ford for providing this analogy, which comes from John Skalzi's blog entry, "Straight White Male: The Lowest Difficulty Setting There Is," http://kotaku.com/5910857/straight-white-male-the-lowest-difficulty-setting-there-is, accessed May 23, 2014. As Skalzi remarks, "the player who plays on the 'Gay Minority Female' setting? *Hardcore.*"

[97] José Medina, "Color Blindness, Meta-Ignorance, and the Racial Imagination," *Critical Philosophy of Race*, 2013 1(1): 49.

[98] Medina, "Color Blindness, Meta-Ignorance, and the Racial Imagination," 49.

that is "blind," that cannot understand ("see") the racial hierarchies in which white people and people of color are embedded.

Affective numbness is not the only form that the emotional aspects of white ignorance can take. White ignorance also can manifest itself through strong emotions, as Brittney's stomach demonstrated. Brittney's knowledge about the world—for example, when and where the world supposedly is dangerous—is racially delineated by her intense fear of black men. It also is emotionally supported by her anger at other people's "politically correct" refusal to admit how the world "really" is. We might say that Brittney's stomach muscles and acidic fluids are overactive in the presence of a black man, unsettled by a race-fueled anxiety. She does not have a cultivated lack of interest in black men, as the affectively numb person does. On the contrary: she is extremely attuned to them, hypersensitive to their presence and their (presumed) intentions, needs, and desires. Even though they bypass or eliminate affective numbness, strong affects vis-à-vis race are not necessarily an antidote for white ignorance.

What then, finally, to say to Brittney? While I am critical of her physiological reactions to black men, I also think feminists and critical philosophers of race can learn something important from her. Medina poses an important question about affective numbness to consider in this context. Is affective numbness a pretend numbness in which a person denies what she feels, or a genuine numbness resulting from having been trained not to feel?[99] Brittney effectively accused our class of the first option, of lying about what we (mainly white women) physiologically and emotionally feel in the presence of black men. (She might also accuse the handful of white men and women of color in the classroom of the same thing, given the objective threat that black men allegedly present.) In that case, racial justice movements would be better served by Brittney's honesty than by white deception and denial.

But it also is possible that the second option is more accurate, that white habits have been so carefully cultivated in a society without de jure Jim Crow that white people are thoroughly physiologically obtuse and truly do not know what they are physically feeling regarding matters of race. This would be a different way of understanding the human "ability [or lack thereof] to feel the body as the place where the psyche lives," transmuting it beyond victims of trauma to trauma's perpetrators.[100] If white people generally are physiologically obtuse about race and racism, then the prognosis for them is even grimmer than one might have thought. White ignorance is so deep in their

---

[99] I take this question from Medina, "Color Blindness, Meta-Ignorance, and the Racial Imagination," 43, where he asks whether color-blind white people deny seeing race or they genuinely don't see it.

[100] Donald Winnicott, quoted in Bessel Van der Kolk, *The Body Keeps the Score: Brain, Mind and Body in the Healing of Trauma* (New York: Viking, 2014) 113.

bones that it will be extremely difficult to uproot. Here, too, I think from a racial justice perspective, Brittney's emotional liveliness—racist though it was—is preferable to white affective numbness. At least in Brittney's case, the racial fears that white people (especially women) often have of black men are out on the table and can be addressed.

I also think that Brittney's form of white ignorance is no worse than, and in fact is probably preferable to, the type represented by "Tiffany, Friend of People of Color."[101] Tiffany is an example of a contemporary white person who typically is considered to have the appropriate stance on matters of race and racism, and for that reason we should be wary of her. Tiffany is the Good White Person who tries hard to be and to appear intensely anti-racist, in contrast with the Bad White People who are racists. The teaching assistant in Brittney's class could be considered an example of Tiffany, in my view. In turn, Tiffany would consider Brittney to be one of the Bad White People, as my teaching assistant clearly did. Tiffany's anti-racism, which highly prizes friendships and other close relationships with people of color, focuses on securing her moral goodness as a white person, even if she doesn't consciously recognize this motivation. Not all white people who are friends with people of color are Tiffanys, of course. Genuine friendships between white people and people of color do exist. But Tiffany is more common than white people probably like to think, and she does not necessarily represent an advance in racial progress in comparison to Brittany, as one might assume.

Like Brittney, Tiffany is extremely attuned to people of color and the ongoing oppression and discrimination that they face. Unlike Brittney, however, Tiffany is avowedly anti-racist, and so both her affective attunement and her white ignorance take a different form than Brittney's. Tiffany deliberately loves, rather than fears, people of color, but her "love" functions primarily to boost her own moral goodness rather than to eliminate racial injustice. She has sought out people of color with whom to work and volunteer and to befriend, and she "has always been connected to people of color and has had any number of near-color experiences—perhaps a former African American boyfriend, a Korean-American school friend in first grade, or a memorable teaching experience involving foreigners."[102] Through those cross-racial emotional relationships, Tiffany has established her Good White Person credentials.

I won't repeat the problems for racial justice movements caused by Good White People, which I have elaborated elsewhere.[103] What I wish to point out

---

[101] Audrey Thompson, "Tiffany, Friend of People of Color: White Investments in Anti-Racism," *International Journal of Qualitative Studies in Education*, 2003, 16(1): 7–29. See also the blog entry in *Diverse Issues in Higher Education* about "Christie, Colored Friend of Tiffany," who problematically protects Tiffany's racial ignorance (http://diverseeducation.com/article/31297/#, accessed May 13, 2013).

[102] Thompson, "Tiffany, Friend of People of Color," 9.

[103] See Sullivan, *Good White People*.

here is that Tiffany would *never* stand up in front of one hundred other students and announce that she experiences a tense stomach at the sight of a black man. In fact, Tiffany would never admit such things to anyone, not even herself. They are not what a Friend of People of Color feels. That's what made Brittney's remarks so startling. White people who wish to fight racial injustice do not have stomachs that seize up with fear at the sight of a black man in an isolated area, Tiffany would exclaim emphatically. And she would be right in a way, but she would use that insight as a self-righteous stick with which to beat other white people, rather than a possible moment for psychosomatic self-examination and transformation. I am not claiming that all the Tiffanys of the world actually have, but deny having, experiences of gut reactions to black men that are similar to Brittney's. I have no way of knowing for sure. I suspect, however, that many white women, including the Tiffanys among us, are more similar to Brittney than we like to admit and that we don't acknowledge our physiological reactions to the presence of black people (especially men) because it would be too psychologically painful to do so. White women often are not consciously aware of what their stomachs (or shoulders or jaws) are feeling as they tense up in the presence of black men, and their lack of awareness is not always accidental.[104] It is an effect of biologically unconscious habits that function to keep them ignorant of their role in systems of white domination. Like an allegedly color-blind person, then, the Good White Person who sees race can be affectively obtuse regarding racism. Her white ignorance can function through the warm, intimate connections that she feels she has—and insists on having—with people of color. Brittney's skepticism of both types of white people is well placed, even if it also is a vehicle for her own specific form of white ignorance.

White ignorance is widespread and multifaceted. At this moment in history, there probably is no way for a white person not to be racially ignorant and for that ignorance not to manifest itself physiologically. A great deal of bodily, biological change must take place if and when the world is rid of white domination. Those changes will be difficult to make, but they are not impossible. No person, white or non-white, is locked into a static condition because of his or her physiology. This is why we can respond to Brittney with a kind of affirmation, rather than hostile attack. Yes, your frightened gut response to the black man on the street is real, you really felt that, but your stomach's reaction is the beginning of the story, not the end. It is the psychophysiological symptom of a sociopolitical problem, not irrefutable evidence of a racially hierarchical reality. Likewise, white people's relatively low rates of stress-related diseases are also a sign of white domination, not a neutral medical condition to which all people should aspire. This doesn't mean that we shouldn't try to

---

[104] For more on these claims, see Shannon Sullivan, *Revealing Whiteness: The Unconscious Habits of Racial Privilege* (Bloomington: Indiana University Press, 2006).

improve the health of people of color or, alternatively, that we should neglect the health of white people. It also doesn't mean that white people will happily or easily give up their gut belief in white superiority. Even when care is taken not to trigger white people's racialized defense mechanisms, their grip on white privilege tends to be tenacious. What it means is recognizing that our current understanding of what constitutes good health is fundamentally shaped by white supremacy and white privilege. As a white-dominated society, we haven't yet thought through the former apart from the latter.

To undertake that process, we need to explore further: How did a white woman's physiology come to be in a state such that her stomach seized up when she saw a black man, and how might her reaction to this and similar situations be changed? More broadly, how can our ideas about optimal human health be rethought critically, free of the dictates of white domination? The answer to these questions cannot be one that reductively appeals to physiology. There is no anti-racism pill being suggested here as a solution, nor is the solution to try to isolate the medical and biological sciences from sociopolitical matters. But the answer also should not ignore physiology. It must challenge the biopsychosocial complexities of white supremacy and white privilege, and feminist philosophy and critical philosophy of race must be up to the task.

Conclusion

SOCIAL-POLITICAL CHANGE AND
PHYSIOLOGICAL TRANSFORMATION

This book has examined how sexist and racist oppression can be incorporated in the literal cells, fibers, muscles, and chemicals of the human body. The effects of sexism and racism can go all the way down to the bone, as the saying goes, and also down to the tissues, hormones, and genetic markers that constitute human beings. The effects of sexism and racism are not only social, political, and economic, but also physiological—which is to say psychological, affective, and often emotional. Their physiological dimensions help explain why their effects often are so intimately personal, in addition to being institutional and global, even if they are not always or often consciously felt. Because sexism and racism help shape human physiology, they influence our affective investments in and emotional relationships with the world as we transact with it. This is true whether one is the beneficiary or the victim of sexist and racist oppression. Sexism and racism physiologically affect us all, though of course their effects tend to be radically different depending on whether one is harmed or privileged by them.

The reach of sexist and racist oppression thus is more pervasive than feminists and critical philosophers of race perhaps have thought. Let me repeat, however, that a turn to physiology and biology does not entail fatalism. Sometimes it is assumed that human culture and habits are easy to change, while human biology and physiology are not. I think that both aspects of this assumption are significantly mistaken. In addition to implying that culture and biology are entirely separate domains, this assumption is far too sanguine about the prospects for cultural change. On the one hand, both individual and institutional habits, whether raced and gendered or not, can be extremely durable, stubborn, and difficult to alter. On the other hand, it is not the case that human beings of any race or gender are determined by their physiology, for example, due to the "programming" provided by their genes. Human beings' bodily states and conditions, including their psychophysiological health, are somewhat malleable and plastic, rather than fixed. Human physiology might be as difficult to transform and improve as human culture, but neither aspect of human existence is completely rigid or frozen.

How then might the harmful physiological effects of sexism and racism be fought? How might human bodies be transformed in ways that challenge sexist and racist oppression? In Chapter 4, I briefly criticized acontextual appeals to stress-management techniques for addressing only the symptoms, and not the root causes of many of black people's cardio maladies. As I have argued, the primary root cause is white people's institutional and (inter)personal habits of racial supremacy and privilege. Likewise, the root cause of many women's gastrointestinal health problems is not a malfunctioning gut or pelvic floor considered in an isolated fashion.[1] It is a sexist and male-privileged world that generally licenses the domination and abuse of women, girls, and other feminized people. For these reasons, the first answer to the question of how to fight the physiological effects of sexism and racism must focus on institutional transformations. We need social and political change to eliminate geographical, economic, educational, legal, and other institutional practices that have sexist and racist effects.

To begin, equitable health policies would do a great deal to reduce raced, sexed, and gendered health disparities. For example, in 2005 black women in Chicago were (and are) twice as likely as white women to die of breast cancer, even though white women are slightly more likely to get the disease.[2] Their mortality rates were identical in 1985, but the gap emerged when hospitals that predominantly served white women benefited from advances in mammography, radiation, and other breast cancer treatments. The hospitals located in or near black neighborhoods in Chicago have fewer facilities for breast cancer screening, and they are financially forced to rely on older equipment that provides less accurate diagnoses than newer digital machines. To make matters worse, many hospitals in Chicago won't accept Medicaid for mammography screenings since Medicaid covers only half of the cost. So even if a black woman on Medicaid can find the time to get across town to a hospital in a predominantly white neighborhood for her mammography appointment, she has to wait longer for and then is likely to be denied service—unless she can manage to pay the entire, substantial cost by herself. Political changes that addressed the inequities of racial geographical segregation in Chicago and that adequately funded all its hospitals, including those

---

[1] The point about considering women's GI disturbances in complex sociopolitical contexts rather than in abstract isolation from the world helps explain why I don't consider Brittney's case to be of the same type as that of, e.g., Ginette. While each could be described broadly as having a GI disturbance, the nature and context of their gut reactions to the world are very different.

[2] The following information on breast cancer rates in Chicago is taken from Dorothy Roberts, *Fatal Invention: How Science, Politics, and Big Business Re-create Race in the Twenty-First Century* (New York: The New Press, 2012) 123–127.

in poor neighborhoods which tend to be black, would go a long way to eliminating some of the physiological effects of racism on black women in the city.

Likewise, empirical research on racial gaps in infant mortality and death in the United States has demonstrated the significant impact of economic priorities and civil rights on black health.[3] Between 1966 and 1980, the black-white mortality gap for infants diminished, and social epidemiologists have argued that this temporary improvement can be credited to social policies and laws such as the War on Poverty, the Civil Rights Act of 1964, the construction of community health centers, and the creation of Medicaid and Medicare. Reductions of many of these programs, including ones that affected the acceptance of Medicaid for mammography in Chicago area hospitals, began in the 1980s under the Reagan administration. The result was that the deathly chasm between black and white children's mortality rates returned. Renewed political and financial support for those programs would help reduce morbidity and mortality rates for African American children.

So, too, would the life-course approach promoted by physician Michael Lu and other obstetricians, gynecologists, and pediatricians. Lu's life-course perspective attempts to shrink the black-white gap in premature birth rates by "conceptualiz[ing] birth outcomes as the end product of not only the nine months of pregnancy but the entire life course of the mother before the pregnancy."[4] As such, Lu developed a twelve-point plan that, in addition to increasing African American women's access to and quality of prenatal health care, seeks to expand health care access across a person's life course; invest in community building, urban renewal, and family support services; close the education gap and create social capital in African American communities; support working mothers and families; and fight both poverty and racism.[5] This is a tall list, and to my knowledge Lu doesn't control any federal purse strings to make funding for such programs happen. He is a doctor promoting a life-course approach in medical journals, writing for an audience of other physicians and health specialists. But that is precisely the point. Doctors and other health specialists need to see "non-medical" institutional, social, and political changes that would counteract racism as crucial to the medical, physiological care of their African American patients and other patients of color.

If something like Lu's twelve-point plan were put into place in the United States, the result probably would be significant changes not just to black and other non-white bodies, but also to many white bodies. As discussed in Chapter 4, this probably will be a difficult idea for many white people to

---

[3] Roberts, *Fatal Invention*, 144–145.

[4] Michael C. Lu, Milton Kotelchuck, Vijaya Hogan, Loretta Jones, Kynna Wright, and Neal Halfon, "Closing the Black-White Gap in Birth Outcomes: A Life-Course Approach," *Ethnicity and Disease*, 2010, 20: S2–62.

[5] Lu et al., "Closing the Black-White Gap in Birth Outcomes," S2–63.

accept, but I think it needs to be confronted outright. If medical, economic, educational, and other institutional changes were made that improved the quality of African American and other non-white people's lives, the current quality of many white people's lives—their medical, educational, economic, and other opportunities—probably would fall, both relatively and absolutely. At least in comparison, the quality of white health would diminish relative to black health, for example, if black health improved. Many white people would perceive this as a loss for them, not just a gain for black people. It's not just the Other that can't be understood apart from the One, as Simone de Beauvoir has argued; the One also doesn't exist as the One without the Other.[6] In the context of race, this means that what counts as good (white) health would change if black people also possessed it.

Probably even more difficult for white people to accept, however, is that the absolute, or non-relative health of many white people likely would diminish if institutional changes were made to improve the health of people of color. I think this is true even though, for example, lowering infectious disease rates in one population can help lower the rates for others.[7] The blunt financial reality in the United States (and elsewhere) is that federal and other monies spent in one place are not available to spend in others. The economy might not always be a zero-sum game, but the nature of money is that it is a finite, limited resource. Decisions have to be made about where it will be dispersed. Money spent to benefit low-income neighborhoods by improving their hospitals and medical equipment, providing high-quality affordable housing, and so on, won't be available to distribute to medical and other institutions that primarily serve middle- to upper-class white people. I specifically say "middle- to upper-class" here since changes that benefit low-income neighborhoods also would help many poor and lower class white people. The larger point remains, however, that a group of people in the United States accustomed to a certain level of physiological well-being—mostly white people, even if not all of them—would find that level decrease if money were shifted away from them to institutions and communities that support people of color.

To take an oversimplified example, if the high-quality mammography equipment in Chicago were equally available to all women in the city—financially, geographically, and otherwise—then black women and poor white women not only would be screened faster and thus their breast cancer would be caught earlier than it currently is, but middle- to upper-class white women also would have to wait longer for their turn and thus their breast cancer would be caught later than it currently is. (To complicate the example, one might object that more high-quality mammography equipment

---

[6] Simone de Beauvoir, *The Second Sex,* trans. Constance Borde and Shelia Malovany-Chevallier (New York: Vintage Books, 2011) 6.

[7] Thanks to an anonymous reviewer for this point.

should be procured so that all women could have short waiting times, but this only backs up the original question a step. Where/who would the money for the additional, upgraded equipment be taken from?) The waiting period for each group of women would be the same on this simple scenario and thus it also would be more just than it currently is, but white women's overall rates of breast cancer probably would increase (even as the rates for poor white women likely would improve). If the overall current rate of breast cancer for white women is possible only because of racial injustice, then its recalibration in a racially just world should not be upsetting to them or anyone else. That rate wouldn't have to be passively accepted; medical research and care could and should still work to decrease it. But efforts to lower rates of breast cancer would benefit all women on this scenario. They wouldn't be achieved for one group by denying high-quality equipment and care to another.

The problem with this rosy-lensed picture, of course, is that middle- to upper-class white Americans are accustomed to the health benefits of a racially unjust world, even if they tend to be whitely ignorant of those benefits. And it is those same white people who economically and politically control much of the money in the United States. Probably nothing would make them dig in their white privileged heels against institutional change more than rising death rates for white people. This fact highlights the importance of structural change that puts more people of color in charge of economic, political, educational, and other institutions. It also points to the importance of psychosomatic change for white people so that their non-conscious and unconscious affective investments in the world no longer are fueled by racism. This latter form of change probably will need a great deal of time to be accomplished. While it is not the goal of racial justice movements—that, of course, is eliminating the racial oppression of people of color—changing the psychosomatic constitution of white people could be seen as one sign of its ultimate success.

The two kinds of change are related, but the first one has greater weight in their relation and thus should be prioritized by racial justice movements. Whether or not white people psychosomatically change, institutional changes can bring about a more racially just world. In a cyclical fashion, however, institutional changes could have the effect of helping white people accomplish some psychosomatic soul work that could cure them of their racism. (I will return to this issue later.) White people then might be more likely to support institutional changes that further racial justice. Without that kind of affective and emotional work, the simmering racial resentment primarily associated with so-called angry white men but also experienced by white women is likely to increase and interfere with racial justice movements.[8] (We shouldn't be

---

[8] On angry white men in particular, see Jeffrey T. Nealon, "Performing Resentment: White Male Anger; or, 'Lack' and Nietzschean Political Theory," in *Why Nietzsche Still: Reflections on Drama, Culture, and Politics*, ed. Alan D. Schrift (Berkeley: University of California Press, 2000).

fooled by white women's lack of apparent anger in this context. It can be just another instance of their not being allowed or knowing how to openly feel it.) Defusing the volatile cocktail of white resentment would help end the reign of racism more quickly.

I will say more below about individual change in the context of psychosomatic healing for women and people of color who have been harmed by sexism and racism. Returning to the topic of institutional change for now, we can find a second answer suggested by Lu's life-course approach to the question of how to combat the physiological effects of sexism and racism. As surgeon Ghislain Devroede has urged, the ontology often assumed by the institution of Western medicine needs to be transformed. Just as Western medicine needs to tear down the wall between the medical and the social-political, medical practitioners need to stop functioning as if they are in physical and temporal silos, treating a section of the body as if it is unrelated both to other body "parts" and to the ancestral past. Thinking cloacally, to use Devroede's term, would help medical practitioners recognize how one area of the human body might sympathize with another, and thus how symptoms in the intestines and anus, for example, might be related to a traumatic experience that took place in the vagina or with the breasts. It would help them recognize how this sympathetic relationship can extend interpersonally, even generationally, connecting the bodies and symptoms of one person to another. It also would help medical practitioners combat lingering mind-body dualisms in their profession and appreciate how human physiology is always already psychological and affectively engaged, as its symptoms often reveal.

Thinking cloacally might help medical practitioners to better grapple with functional and autoimmune diseases that disproportionately afflict women and that currently are very poorly understood. In addition to disorders such as IBS and Crohn's disease, one such illness is reflex sympathetic dystrophy (RSD), also referred to as algodystrophy complex regional pain syndrome and/or chronic regional pain syndrome.[9] "The syndrome is as complicated as its nomenclature," one health specialist admits.[10] As of this writing, doctors have virtually no understanding of the etiology of RSD, which affects women over twice as often as men, at a rate of seven to three.[11] (There currently is no race known to have a particular predilection for the illness.[12]) It is described as "a chronic pain condition" that involves "irritation and

---

[9] Thanks to Stephanie Jenkins for bringing RSD to my attention.

[10] Carol Eustice, "What Is Reflex Sympathetic Dystrophy Syndrome (RSD)?" 2012, http://arthritis.about.com/od/rsd/a/rsd.htm, accessed May 17, 2013.

[11] Satishchandra Kale, "Reflex Sympathetic Dystrophy Surgery," 2012, http://emedicine.medscape.com/article/1269453-overview#a0199, accessed May 17, 2013.

[12] Kale, "Reflex Sympathetic Dystrophy Surgery," http://emedicine.medscape.com/article/1269453-overview#a0199, accessed May 17, 2013.

abnormal excitation of nervous tissue, leading to abnormal impulses along nerves that affect blood vessels and skin."[13] More concretely, RSD is characterized by severe, burning pain that begins at a localized spot on a limb of the body and then tends to spread. Sometimes the spot is the site of a slight injury, such as a bruise or a hard knock on the arm if one bumps into a piece of furniture. But in one-third of patients with RSD there is no event or trauma that triggered the onset of the illness, and when an injury is involved, it is "very frequently trivial."[14] It's significant that with RSD, no nerves were damaged, and there are no lesions, chronic illnesses, or other central nervous system disturbances that would explain the spreading pain.[15] Absent an explanatory injury, a person's arm or perhaps leg—onset of the illness on upper extremities is twice as common as on lower extremities[16]—begins to be extra sensitive, then excruciatingly painful, and the pain is accompanied by striking changes in skin temperature, texture, and color. While the illness doesn't have a high mortality rate, it is extremely debilitating and is accompanied by very high morbidity rates.[17]

I don't purport to know why or how RSD develops, but I bet that a form of cloacal thinking that appreciates biologically unconscious habits would help make headway toward better understanding the illness. Even though RSD clearly involves the nerves because of the pain it produces, a narrow medical focus on the nervous system is unlikely to bear fruit. In RSD, parts of the body develop an unusual sympathy with each other, which is possible because their original relationship already was sympathetic. Indeed, as one medical source describes the illness, it is best thought of as an "excessive *sympathetic* reaction of joints and periarticular soft tissues to any insult, traumatic or unknown."[18] Although the pain of RSD often spreads to surrounding tissues, the sympathy manifest in the illness is not restricted by physical proximity. Pain not only can spread from finger to arm, but also can travel from one arm

---

[13] Eustice, "What is Reflex Sympathetic Dystrophy Syndrome (RSD)?" http://arthritis.about. com/od/rsd/a/rsd.htm, accessed May 17, 2013.

[14] Kale, "Reflex Sympathetic Dystrophy Surgery," http://emedicine.medscape.com/article/ 1269453-overview, accessed May 17, 2013; Angela Mailis and Judith Wade, "Profile of Caucasion Women with Possible Genetic Predisposition to Reflex Sympathetic Dystrophy: A Pilot Study," *The Clinical Journal of Pain*, 1994, 10(3): 210. It is worth noting that the incidence of RSD is high in wartime injuries (Satishchandra Kale, "Reflex Sympathetic Dystrophy Surgery Clinical Presentation," 2012, http://emedicine.medscape.com/article/1269453-clinical#a0218, accessed May 17, 2013).

[15] Mailis and Wade, "Profile of Caucasion Women," 210.

[16] Kale, "Reflex Sympathetic Dystrophy Surgery," http://emedicine.medscape.com/article/1269453- overview#a0199, accessed May 17, 2013.

[17] See Tzipi's autobiographical account of her battle with RSD at fightrsd.blogspot.fr. Tzipi was twenty-two years old when her thigh was mildly injured by a car accident and she subsequently developed a severe form of RSD.

[18] Kale, "Reflex Sympathetic Dystrophy Surgery," http://emedicine.medscape.com/article/ 1269453-overview, emphasis added, accessed May 17, 2013.

to the other, for example, without apparently involving the intervening tissues of the chest, neck, or shoulders.[19]

The physical pain of RSD tends to worsen when a person undergoes emotional stress, which isn't too surprising when we appreciate pain as a homeostatic emotion.[20] We can surmise that through its pain, the body with RSD is trying to say something that it is unable to say or to be heard saying in another way. The right arm, for example, to which the pain spreads is like a sounding board, amplifying the left arm's screams, which in turn have amplified the left hand's initial whispers. What was the biopsychosocial situation that evidently was ignored or dismissed and thus led to the hand's whispers and subsequent screaming? Why is it women's bodies in particular that are screaming in this way? What are they saying that cannot be said or heard in another way? To solve the mystery of RSD, the education and training of medical practitioners needs to be not just biological but also psychosocial. It needs to grapple with the sympathetic body and to blur the boundaries between various medical specialties, including the ones that sharply separate psychiatry (which treats the mind) from the rest of medical science (which treats the body).

The answers to the question of physiological transformation that I have considered to this point primarily address medically related changes that are needed at institutional levels. Geographical racial segregation and economic discrimination must be combated socially and politically, for example, so that people of color have access to high-quality health care. Women with IBS, Crohn's disease, RSD, anismus, and other functional illnesses would be better served if the formal training of surgeons, nurses, and biofeedback technicians has prepared them for the psychosomatic complexities and affective sympathies of physiological dysfunctions. These and other institutional transformations are important changes that would make a significant difference to the health of many women and men. Human physiology can be reconstituted, at least to a certain extent, by means of social and political changes made at an institutional level.

It also can be meaningfully reconstituted by means of bodily changes made at an individual, personal level. This is the level of what has been called somaesthetics, which, as Richard Shusterman explains, combines theory and practice "to enrich not only our abstract, discursive knowledge of the body but also our lived somatic experience and performance."[21] Individual bodily practices cannot address all the ways that racism and sexism affect human

---

[19] Eustice, "What Is Reflex Sympathetic Dystrophy Syndrome (RSD)?,"http://arthritis.about.com/od/rsd/a/rsd.htm, accessed May 17, 2013.

[20] Eustice, "What Is Reflex Sympathetic Dystrophy Syndrome (RSD)?" http://arthritis.about.com/od/rsd/a/rsd.htm, accessed May 17, 2013.

[21] Richard Shusterman, *Thinking Through the Body: Essays in Somaesthetics* (New York: Cambridge University Press, 2012) 27.

physiology. They are not likely, for example, to change a person's epigenetic markers (though they could change her future grandchildren's epigenome by changing their ancestral environment). Institutional, rather than personal, changes are what are needed to eliminate the epigenomic likelihood of premature birth for African American women discussed in Chapter 3. The personal level of somaesthetics should not be viewed as in competition with the institutional, however. Since personal and institutional habits coexist in a transactional fashion, their relationship is like that of a spiral, in which each can reinforce and build upon the other. This also means that changes on one level can bring about changes on the other. Both the institutional and the personal are relevant to efforts to counter the unjust and harmful physiological effects of sexism and racism, even if the degree of their relevance will vary depending on the situation or context in question.

Many methods of transforming physiology at the individual level focus on bringing bodily states to conscious attention. The biofeedback therapy that Ginette used to cure her anismus, discussed in Chapter 2, would be an example of such a method. But there also exist methods of encouraging physiological change that don't involve conscious awareness at all, and a great number of methods operate with a mixture of conscious, non-conscious, and unconscious engagement. A continuum of transformative bodily practices exists at the individual level involving different degrees of conscious attention. As Shusterman develops it, the continuum of somaesthetic practices ranges from the "rationalist" Alexander Technique on one end, to the "irrational" practice of bioenergetics on the other, with the Feldenkrais method falling between but closer to the Alexander Technique.[22] While I am most interested here in developing the unconscious pole of this continuum, let me briefly contrast it with the conscious pole to bring out their different attitudes toward the creative capabilities and epistemological value of the body.

Developed by F. M. Alexander in the early twentieth century, the Alexander Technique helps a person better align his or her skeletal structure, particularly the bones of the neck since they support the significant weight of the head (eight to twelve pounds for the average adult). Via the guidance of an Alexander technician, a person learns not to pull her head down in misalignment with her neck, but to bring it forward and up. The result should be relief from physical discomfort as well as improved mental capabilities. This result might well be achieved, but what nevertheless is significant about the Alexander Technique for my purposes is its mistrust of the body. Even as the technique emphasizes the importance of physiological structures for the quality of human life, it does not place much faith in the body's ability to transform itself. As Shusterman explains, for Alexander a method for somatic

---

[22] Richard Shusterman, *Performing Live: Aesthetic Alternatives for the Ends of Art* (Ithaca, NY: Cornell University Press, 2000) 169.

transformation "cannot be mere physical training; it requires primarily the 'mental' mastery of conscious control of the body. . . . Unable to trust our unconscious and instinctive body mechanisms that were slowly acquired over millions of years of evolutionary adaptation, we must use our evolutionary gift of consciousness to reform and govern our bodily behavior more deliberately, forwarding it in the direction of the evolution of civilization—toward greater consciousness, rationality, and control."[23] On Alexander's account, the body itself is not much of a source of knowledge, creativity, or possible solutions to societal problems.

The Feldenkrais method fares slightly better. Developed by Moshe Feldenkrais in the 1970s, the Feldenkrais Method aims to improve human life by improving the quality of bodily movement.[24] Through gentle movements and manipulations of a student's body, Feldenkrais practitioners help their students discern the somatic causes of their bodily discomforts and tensions so that they can rectify them.[25] Even though the Feldenkrais method was influenced by the Alexander Technique and emphasizes the importance of "heightened mental awareness" of one's bodily condition to produce greater somatic harmony and functioning, it appreciates that bodily improvement also can take place on a non-conscious level.[26] It is significant, however, that the Feldenkrais Method works on an educational, rather than a therapeutic model, ultimately prioritizing conscious knowledge. "Self-knowledge through awareness is the goal of reeducation," as Feldkenkrais explains.[27] Bodily re-education cannot take place by means of unconscious habits alone. Feldenkrais practitioners give lessons, not therapy sessions, to their students, who are not patients—terminology which underscores that for Feldenkrais physiological re-education primarily occurs through cognitive awareness of bodily states and positions.

Lying on the extreme end from the Alexander Technique and to a lesser degree the Feldenkrais Method, bioenergetics emphasizes the flow of energy and feeling rather than conscious control of the body.[28] Rooted in the theory and practice of psychoanalyst and sexologist Wilhelm Reich and founded by Reich's patient Alexander Lowen in the mid-twentieth century, bioenergetics emphasizes emotion and the heart rather than reason and the mind.[29] It valorizes turbulent (e)motions and experiences to shock the body out of its inhibition and numbness, which are thought to be produced by a civilization that represses human beings, especially sexually. Orgasm thus is particularly

[23] Shusterman, *Performing Live*, 164.
[24] Shusterman, *Performing Live*, 169.
[25] Shusterman, *Thinking Through the Body*, 44.
[26] Shusterman, *Thinking Through the Body*, 43.
[27] Quoted in Shusterman, *Performing Live*, 168.
[28] Shusterman, *Performing Live*, 174.
[29] Shusterman, *Performing Live*, 175.

important to Lowen's and Reich's conception of bioenergetics because it releases tension and blocked energy. It also gives a person a powerful experience of losing control and succumbing to involuntary, irrational forces. According to Lowen and Reich, far from being the answer to our physiological woes, increased rationality is precisely the problem. Bioenergetic therapists thus enable and provoke bodily experiences that surpass conscious control and promote greater physiological spontaneity.[30]

Although its emphasis on the unconscious is valuable, especially in contrast to the tight conscious control valorized by the Alexander Technique, bioenergetics is problematic because it fails to adequately challenge the dualism between reason and the irrational. For all their differences, both the Alexander Technique and Lowen's bioenergetics implicitly hold that conscious techniques for bodily transformation that emphasize the mind are rational, while techniques that downplay or bypass conscious control are irrational. The difference between the two practices is that bioenergetics tends to malign reason and glorify the irrational, but this position robs the body of any reason of its own, casting it as something dumb and unthinking. On Lowen and Reich's account, for all its value, the body itself, including its unconscious habits, does not provide insight or knowledge about anything—either itself or the world—with which one could engage societal problems. It is merely an escape from the constrictions of the world.

While bioenergetics warrants Shusterman's description of "irrational," I want to reject this label for the unconscious end of the somaesthetics continuum as such. I think there are some thoughtful bodily practices—that is, full of thought—that can transform a person's biologically unconscious habits without relying on conscious awareness but that nonetheless are not irrational. Without dismissing the power of conscious reflection to make change in one's life, I want in the remainder of this conclusion to explore how psychophysiological healing might take place directly through unconscious physiological means, without being brokered by conscious thinking. Conscious reflection can be an important means toward the end of psychophysiological healing, but it is a means only, not an end in itself. Sometimes other means can be just as, if not more, effective for improving a person's psychosomatic health.

To explore one of those means, I provide a final vignette concerning a woman named Wendy. Her case illustrates the power of what I will call physiological therapy, which uses various forms of bodily movement to directly address and transform unconscious bodily habits. Physiological therapy contrasts with traditional forms of therapy that target the mind-stuff of the brain and/or that include bodily changes only insofar as they primarily can

---

[30] Shusterman, *Performing Live*, 177.

be controlled by conscious thought. Physiological therapy can be, and perhaps even works best when combined with traditional talk therapies, but the two forms of therapy are not identical. They can be teased apart functionally, at least in theory and probably also in practice. Significant therapeutic work countering the harmful physiological effects of sexism and racism can be done on the body *by* the body itself.

In the 1990s, Wendy was a successful social worker and therapist in her early forties longing for a long-term love relationship after divorcing her possessive and controlling husband.[31] Despite medication and several years of psychotherapy, her chronic depression persisted, and so she began taking yoga classes in hopes that they would help. In the beginning, Wendy often cried "for no good reason" when she was kneeling with her head forward on the ground, in a position known as child pose.[32] After two years of practicing yoga, Wendy's depression was gone and she was off medication, but she still had only short-term love relationships that she was the one to break off. It was around this time that Wendy began sobbing "like a baby" when she was in plough pose, an advanced posture based in a shoulder stand with the legs stretched out and over the head, touching the floor, and the rear-end sticking up exposed.[33] This experience happened each day when Wendy did plough pose, and although it frightened her at first, she began to welcome the experience because of how good she felt afterward. There were no memories associated with the emotional event, at least not initially. "At first, the release was purely physical," as Wendy's yoga instructor explained.[34]

We should read "purely physical" here as meaning merely that Wendy had no conscious awareness of the connection that her emotional release had to her past. It does not mean that the release was non-psychological. In fact, we could just as accurately say that Wendy's release while in plough pose initially was purely unconscious, rather than purely physical, since it exercised and reconfigured psychobiological habits of which Wendy had no conscious understanding. This became clear, as Wendy's yoga instructor elaborates, when "Wendy began to associate plough pose with the position in which she must have been in as an infant on the diaper-changing table when the enemas began."[35] Wendy's mother regularly administered enemas to her infant daughter, "not [because] of conscious sexual abuse on her mother's part" but because of her mother's desire that her first-born "be the perfect reflection of her ability to mother, ... [which] meant daily bowel movements and an

---

[31] Amy Weintraub, *Yoga for Depression: A Compassionate Guide to Relieve Suffering Through Yoga* (New York: Broadway Books, 2004) 204–205.

[32] Quoted in Weintraub, *Yoga for Depression*, 206.

[33] Quoted in Weintraub, *Yoga for Depression*, 211.

[34] Weintraub, *Yoga for Depression*, 215.

[35] Weintraub, *Yoga for Depression*, 216.

extremely early toilet training."[36] With her therapist's agreement, Wendy began bringing her yoga mat to her therapy sessions to explore the trauma bond she felt she had with her mother. In the emotionally safe setting of her therapist's office, Wendy began to feel additional unexpected physical sensations while in plough pose: not just the expected pressure and constriction in the neck, shoulders, and chest, but also a tight squeeze on her ankles and lower calves, "as though [her] mother's hands were pinning me down."[37] Working through this experience on the mat and with the support of her therapist, Wendy began to express her anger at her mother for the enema abuse, vigorously kicking away the felt restraints on her ankles while in plough pose and demanding that she be let go.[38]

Wendy's biologically unconscious habits included ones of rage at her experiences of childhood abuse. We might say that her rage was repressed—we are told that Wendy's perfect mother did not allow Wendy to express anger and other negative emotions[39]—but only if this doesn't mean that she first felt conscious anger that later was converted into an unconscious form. Wendy's rage didn't turn into physiological habits. It was physiological from the beginning. Those habits were simultaneously psychological and emotional, interfering with Wendy's ability to open herself up to others in loving relationships. Physically invaded by her mother's "loving" control of her pelvic floor, "Wendy became so protective of her boundaries, she was unable to achieve that essential dissolution of self so necessary in love."[40] While I disagree with the description of genuine love as an experience of dissolution—it resembles too closely the metaphysical cannibalism of women by men[41]—boundaries between self and other are particularly permeable and fluid in loving relationships, and it was this type of permeability that Wendy could not tolerate. Five years of psychotherapy alone had done little to nothing to revive or address Wendy's memories of her childhood abuse.[42] But her body had not forgotten. Her psychosomatic habits of angry boundary protection, manifested in her depression and failed relationships, "re-membered" the traumatic experience. When her bodily movements and habits were exercised in ways that repeated the physical position Wendy was in when she was abused, then she was able to work through the trauma. Sometime after Wendy's cathartic plough pose experience, she was able to talk about her childhood enema experiences with her mother, softening their stiff relationship, and she also

---

[36] Weintraub, *Yoga for Depression*, 209.

[37] Weintraub, *Yoga for Depression*, 217.

[38] Weintraub, *Yoga for Depression*, 217.

[39] Weintraub, *Yoga for Depression*, 210.

[40] Weintraub, *Yoga for Depression*, 210.

[41] On metaphysical cannibalism, see Marilyn Frye, *The Politics of Reality: Essays in Feminist Theory* (Freedom, CA: Crossing Press, 1983) 75.

[42] Weintraub, *Yoga for Depression*, 210.

fell in love with a new partner "in a new, less wary way," enabling a fulfilling long-term relationship.[43]

It's helpful for us—we outsiders reading about Wendy's experience—that Wendy eventually consciously remembered her childhood abuse (memories that later were confirmed by her mother, moreover). Her conscious awareness of the enemas and her resulting anger fills in the story and helps us to understand the particular source and nature of Wendy's unconscious biological habits. And it probably helped Wendy to understand the particular source and nature of her sobbing plough pose experiences as well. But strictly speaking, conscious awareness of her unconscious biological habits was not necessary to bring about Wendy's healing. Psychosomatic recovery from past trauma can take place purely at the level of unconscious biological habits themselves. As Wendy's yoga instructor explains her own experience with emotional release during yoga practice, "Sometimes there's a story that goes along with the release, and sometimes it's simply a deep and profound letting go without any sort of knowing why.... [We should] question the need to always know the story behind the release."[44] Psychotherapist and yoga instructor Sylvia Boorstein also argues that conscious awareness is not always necessary for the transformation of biologically unconscious habits. As Boorstein asks, "How do I know that these things didn't release themselves quite apart from my ever knowing what they were? Maybe they don't always have to come through the cognitive processes. Maybe I don't have to know that there was a time that my mother did 'this' or my father did 'that.' Maybe we get healed in other ways."[45]

When Wendy's yoga instructor said that Wendy began to associate plough pose with the position in which she received childhood enemas, we can think of Freud's psychoanalytic method of free association. In free association, a person talks without either censoring herself or trying to make logical connections between the (seemingly) nonsensical things that might pop into her mind.[46] The goal of the process is to gain access to ideas and beliefs hidden from consciousness, and for that reason "the logic of association" has been described as "a form of unconscious thinking."[47] Along these lines, we can consider yoga and similar bodily practices, such as dance/movement therapy (which I will discuss below), as a kind of physiological free association in

---

[43] Weintraub, *Yoga for Depression*, 218.

[44] Weintraub, *Yoga for Depression*, 214.

[45] Quoted in Weintraub, *Yoga for Depression*, 214. Boorstein is the author of several books on Buddhist meditation, including most recently *It's Easier Than You Think: The Buddhist Way to Happiness* (New York: HarperCollins Publishers, 2011).

[46] Sigmund Freud, *Introductory Lectures on Psycho-Analysis*, in volume XVI of *The Standard Edition of the Complete Psychological Works of Sigmund Freud*, ed. James Strachey (London: The Hogarth Press and the Institute of Psycho-analysis, 1950) 328.

[47] Christopher Bollas, *The Evocative Object World* (New York: Routledge, 2008) 21.

which various postures engage different unconscious bodily habits. In verbal free association, one doesn't know or try to control how one thought might link to another and trigger an unconscious memory or feeling. In a similar manner, one doesn't know and can't typically control when a particular yoga posture, such as plough pose or triangle pose, which moved Michael Lee's hips in Chapter 1, might tap into unconscious biological habits.

Understanding the two forms of free association in parallel fashion could be misleading, however, if it suggests that a parallel exists between the psyche and the body. Psyche and body are not in a parallel relationship because they are not separated or separable. It is not the case that verbal free association taps into the unconscious mind while physiological free association taps into the unconscious body. They take up the same thing: unconscious habits, which are thoroughly physiological, however they might be engaged. In that respect, then, verbal free association and physiological free association are more than just similar. They are the same in that they work with the same body stuff. But in another important respect, they should be recognized as different. To get at body stuff, verbal free association tends to work more closely with conscious thought than physiological free association does. (And the fact that both can work reminds us of the transactional, non-dualistic relationship between the linguistic and the physiological.) In contrast, physiological free association does its work at the level of biologically unconscious habits themselves.

This kind of work is not unique to yoga. It can take place in and through other bodily practices, such as dancing. Recognizing this, the profession of dance/movement therapy was developed in the United States in the 1960s. As its name indicates, dance/movement therapy, also known as dance/movement psychotherapy in the United Kingdom, therapeutically reworks unconscious habits through dance and related bodily movements.[48] The goal of dance/movement therapy is not to turn its practitioners into skilled dancers, but to expand their movement repertoire.[49] Reminiscent of Reich's and Lowen's "*Lebensphilosophie* that sees life as movement of feeling," dance/movement therapy holds that increased movement and different kinds of movement can make possible different and improved relationships with the world.[50] It puts into therapeutic practice the Jamesian claim that moving one's muscles allows a person to better understand the emotional world around her and that lack of movement tends to emotionally isolate a person from others. In

---

[48] Susan T. Loman, "Dance/Movement Therapy," in *Expressive Therapies*, ed. Cathy A. Malchiodi (New York: Guilford Press, 2006) 68–89; http://www.adta.org/, accessed June 17, 2013; and http://www.admt.org.uk/, accessed June 17, 2013.

[49] Loman, "Dance/Movement Therapy," 76.

[50] Shusterman, *Performing Live*, 175. See also Bessel Van der Kolk's "bottom up" approach to healing trauma, which emphasizes the importance of physical movement to create new visceral experiences that counter the psychosomatic effects of traumatic events (Van der Kolk, *The Body Keeps the Score: Brain, Mind, and Body in the Healing of Trauma* [New York: Viking, 2014]).

particular, dance/movement therapy has been effective for women suffering from eating disorders, who often have been victims of sexual abuse, helping them reconstitute their relationship with their body and their sexuality. (It also has been effective for children with autism and other people who cannot verbalize their emotions well.[51]) "Since many memories of abuse . . . are often held in unconscious somatic schemata," as dance/movement therapist Penny Lewis argues, they "can only be recalled [and/or healed] by kinesthetic and movement reconstruction."[52]

The practice of dancing to counter the harmful effects of trauma dates well before the 1960s, however. "Rooted in the use of dance throughout early human history for healing," dance/movement therapy recalls the importance of African slave dancing for surviving and resisting enslavement in the United States and elsewhere.[53] Sufficiently similar across ethnic lines, West African dance enabled communication and the creation of solidarity between slaves better than verbal language initially did. The bodily movements of African dance were complex, sophisticated, and wide-ranging:

> Brought to the Americas in the motor-muscle memory of the various West African ethnic groups, the dance was characterized by segmentation and delineation of various body parts, including hips, torso, head, arms, hands, and legs; the use of multiple meter as polyrhythmic sensitivity; angularity; multiple centers of movement; asymmetry as balance, percussive performance; mimetic performance; improvisation; and derision.[54]

Through these physical movements, which initially were inseparably religious and secular, African slaves fought the trauma of their uprooting and formed life-sustaining communities and connections with each other. As Frederick Douglass asserts, "but for those [dances, frolics, holidays] the rigors of bondage would have become too severe for endurance."[55] The bodily movement of dance helped slaves withstand the terrors of their enslavement.

As Douglass also attests, however, slave dancing could be a double-edged sword. Slave masters used it as a way of staving off insurrection, of appeasing their slaves' desire for merriment (as slaveholders narrowly saw it) and thus dampening their slaves' desire to rebel.[56] Slave ship captains also used forced "dancing"—jumping in irons as crewmembers swatted whips or

---

[51] Loman, "Dance/Movement Therapy," 68.

[52] Quoted in Loman, "Dance/Movement Therapy," 69. See Penny Lewis, "Depth Psychotherapy in Dance/Movement Therapy," *American Journal of Dance Therapy*, Fall/Winter 1996, 18(2): 95–114.

[53] Loman, "Dance/Movement Therapy," 69.

[54] Katrina Hazzard-Gordon, *Jookin': The Rise of Social Dance Formations in African-American Culture* (Philadelphia: Temple University Press, 1990) 18. Thanks to Lindsey Stewart for bringing this material to my attention.

[55] Quoted in Hazzard-Gordon, *Jookin'*, 31. The bracketed addition is Hazzard-Gordon's.

[56] Hazzard-Gordon, *Jookin'*, 31, 22.

cat-o-nine-tails at their bloody ankles—to exercise slaves during the Middle Passage.[57] Nonetheless, white people's overall wary attitude toward slave dancing was and is one of the greatest testimonies to the subversively therapeutic power of dance. White slaveholders knew that "because it was a means of solidifying the slave community, dance could threaten white dominance."[58] If oppressive "trauma results in a breakdown of attuned physical synchrony" with others, than re-establishing that synchrony can be an important way to resist oppression.[59] Many slaveholders thus forbade slave dancing or allowed it only under the watchful eye of white people. It is not merely that the noisy activity of slave dances provided an opportunity for them to consciously plot insurrection, but also that (e)motion of dancing could unconsciously rouse and strengthen a rebellious spirit.[60] Too much dancing could psychosomatically and affectively transform black slaves from being submissive and weak to being defiant and strong, to the point of challenging white authority.

As we think about the psychosomatic work involved in yoga, contemporary and historical dance therapies, and other bodily practices as forms of physiological free association, we can understand them by means of Freud's concept of working-through. Freud explains the importance of working through unconscious resistances once they have been unearthed during psychotherapy. One cannot assume, as Freud worries that beginner therapists sometimes do, that merely bringing a resistance to conscious attention will dissolve it.[61] Unconscious habits are far too sturdy and durable to be willed away that quickly. As in the case of all habits, unconscious or non-conscious, habits do not just disappear. They must be transformed into different habits, and that takes time. As Freud explains, "One must allow the patient time to become more conversant with this resistance with which he has now become acquainted, to *work through* it, to overcome it, by continuing, in defiance of it, the analytic work according to the fundamental rule of analysis."[62] It takes ongoing work for a person to become familiar with and overcome her habits of resistance and thus to recover memories of the past that could help ease her suffering.[63]

The work of remembering that characterizes psychoanalysis also characterizes, in a different way, the physiological work of engaging unconscious biological habits.[64] Rather than consciously remembering the past,

---

[57] Hazzard-Gordon, *Jookin'*, 6–9.

[58] Hazzard-Gordon, *Jookin'*, 22.

[59] Van der Kolk, *The Body Keeps the Score*, 213.

[60] Hazzard-Gordon, *Jookin'*, 34.

[61] Sigmund Freud, "Remembering, Repeating, and Working-Through," in volume XII of *The Standard Edition of the Complete Psychological Works of Sigmund Freud*, ed. James Strachey (London: The Hogarth Press and the Institute of Psycho-analysis, 1950) 155.

[62] Freud, "Remembering, Repeating, and Working-Through," 155.

[63] Freud, "Remembering, Repeating, and Working-Through," 155–156, 148.

[64] Freud, "Remembering, Repeating, and Working-Through," 153.

physiological working-through can unconsciously "re-member" it. It can exercise and reorganize bodily tissues and fibers, helping produce different emotions and affects by means of physiological change. This will take time. One yoga class or dance session will not fully overcome physiological resistances and transform unconscious biological habits, even if a person experiences unexpected sobbing while dancing or holding a pose. The work of dis-membering and re-membering must including working-through physiological resistances—knotted muscles, tight tendons and ligaments, tense postures, and the like—which are simultaneously psychological and emotional resistances to the transformation of one's habits. Ongoing practice in defiance of the resistances thrown up by the body might be called the fundamental rule of physiological work on unconscious habits.

The physiological work of re-membering also tends to be interpersonal, and in this way it closely resembles the working-through of traditional psychotherapy. It is not a coincidence that Wendy first began to physiologically process her past trauma in the company of a sympathetic yoga instructor and then a psychotherapist open to non-traditional methods. Likewise, Michael Lee credits a friend's supportive presence with enabling Lee to undergo, rather than abort, his hips' re-membering while on the yoga mat. As Lee explains,

> One of my friends was using a wall to support me in the triangle pose on my right side when my body began to quiver uncontrollably. . . . Placing his hand gently against my chest, my friend embraced my growing resistance by encouraging me to stay in the pose a while longer. His affirming presence made me feel safe and I surrendered again and again into what was happening in the moment, deepening my breath and simply witnessing the strange noises emanating from my mouth and my throat.[65]

The double meaning of "support" is significant here. Lee's friend's support was inseparably physical and emotional. By helping Lee physically maintain the stretch of triangle pose, the friend enabled Lee's unconscious psychosomatic habits to associate themselves differently. Not just any person could have done this. A stranger or person hostile to Lee would not have had the same psychosomatic effect, even if that person understood how to help someone assume triangle pose. The sympathies between Lee and his friend allowed Lee's body to reorganize itself, just as Wendy's feelings of safety in the presence of her therapist allowed her body to overcome unconscious resistances to re-membering her past abuse.

Physiological free association and re-membering also can be communal and take place in psychosomatic experiences that involve more than two people. African slave dancing, for example, was a powerful communal experience,

---

[65] Quoted in Weintraub, *Yoga for Depression*, 213.

tying an individual to the larger group, as well as the larger human group to the spiritual world.[66] Slave dancing tended to take place in groups, rather than via individual or partner dancing, and the bodily pleasure of dancing often was simultaneously a spiritual method of praising and supplicating the gods.[67] The call-and-response pattern of dancing and singing that developed in African American communities, for example, weaves together dancers and musicians into a multifaceted whole. Coordinating the bodily movements of the dancers, "the caller, invoking the dancers to ever-greater feats of endurance and virtuosity, recalls the African drummer who challenged and was challenged by ceremonial dancers."[68] This dynamic, communal experience also occurs in twentieth century and contemporary jazz, an African American musical form that can be considered a kind of bodily conversation necessarily taking place between multiple people (including even one's ancestors, human and/or spiritual).[69] Along with the improvisation of African dance, the improvisation of jazz can be seen as a "vibrant for[m] of human sociality" that involves "surrendering one's conscious control to spontaneous promptings" and that operates as a physiological method of free association.[70]

If the work of physiological free association and re-membering happens outside the domain of conscious control and memory, however, how can one know for sure whether that work has impacted one's unconscious habits? The invisibility of biologically unconscious habits might make it seem impossible to try to change them without bringing them to conscious awareness. Physical practices alone wouldn't seem to be enough. How could something like a little bit of stretching do anything as grand as transform unconscious habits, one might skeptically ask. And even if yoga, dance, or similar physical activities actually do the work of re-membering, how can we know with certainty whether their effects on biologically unconscious habits are helpful? Doesn't such knowledge demand conscious thought? Aren't therapeutic methods that prioritize conscious awareness essential for any kind of healing that is truly psychosomatic and not narrowly physiological?

To the epistemological question posed here, an important answer is found in the affective body itself. We know, for example, some of the beneficial physiological results of ongoing yoga practice: cortisol levels tend to drop and the

---

[66] Hazzard-Gordon, *Jookin'*, 3.

[67] Hazzard-Gordon, *Jookin'*, 16, 81. Likewise, Zora Neale Hurston argues that "Negro spirituals are not solo or quartette material. . . . *Negro songs to be heard truly must be sung by a group*" (Zora Neale Hurston, "Spirituals and Neo-Spirituals," in *Voices from the Harlem Renaissance*, second edition, ed. Nathan Irvin Huggins [New York: Oxford University Press, 1995] 344–345, emphasis in original). Thanks to Lindsey Stewart for bringing this essay to my attention.

[68] Hazzard-Gordon, *Jookin'*, 45.

[69] Vincent Colapietro, "Psychoanalysis and Jazz: Familiar Bedfellows in a Strange Setting," in *Semiotics 2008: Proceedings of the 33rd Annual Meeting of the Semiotic Society of America*, eds. John Deely and Leonard Sbrocchi (Ottawa, Canada: Legas Publishing, 2008) 784–796.

[70] Colapietro, "Psychoanalysis and Jazz," 792.

peripheral glandular system produces adrenaline and norepenephrin-type compounds (stimulants).[71] Likewise, dancing and other moderately aerobic activities can release endorphins, which are similar to morphine in their ability to alleviate pain and provide relaxation.[72] More generally, we also would know if the re-membering of physiological therapy helped heal a person if her affective relationship with herself and the world was changed in ways that helped her flourish, both psychologically and physically. We admittedly would not be able to know with conscious certainty that, for example, a person's increased interest and joy in living was a result of a loosened hip tendon or that the tendon had tightened years ago as a result of psychosomatically bracing against repeated sexual assaults. But if her relationship with other people became less braced, less wary, as a result of her physiological practices, then we could conclude well enough that these practices were beneficial. Likewise, we cannot know with absolute certainty that dancing increased and increases black people's spiritual strength and psychosomatic capacities for resisting enslavement and white domination. But the bodily experience of many black people, as well as the importance of dance in black culture, testifies to the powerful re-membering that dance can produce in the face of racist trauma and oppression.

To the question of whether something as "insignificant" as bodily movement can do the work of reaching and transforming unconscious habits, the answer is simple and easy in many respects. Yes, it can. What is not easy about this answer, however, is that it requires relinquishing skepticism of the body and its capabilities. Like the effects of sexism and racism, skepticism of the body goes down to the bone in the Western world. But if we really are going to shed the mind-body dualisms that have plagued Western philosophy and culture, we need to transform our habitual mistrust of the body even as we appreciate the body's capacities critically. We especially need to appreciate the psychological complexity of the body's physiological abilities. As Michael Gershon has argued (somewhat competitively) in praise of the gut's abilities to think without involving the central nervous system, "the ugly gut is more intellectual than the heart and may have a greater capacity for 'feeling.'. . . [I]t must be considered possible that the brain in the bowel may also have its own psychoneuroses."[73] Gershon's scare quotes around the word "feeling" appropriately indicate that this capacity takes place via affects and emotions without necessarily being consciously felt. We can extend Gershon's admiration of the gut to the entire body, including the heart that he downplays. Speaking of the body as a whole, "the scope of the [psychosomatic] behaviors

---

[71] Weintraub, *Yoga for Depression*, 59.

[72] http://www.webmd.com/depression/guide/exercise-depression, accessed June 26, 2013.

[73] Michael D. Gershon, *The Second Brain: A Groundbreaking New Understanding of Nervous Disorders of the Stomach and Intestines* (New York: Harper Paperbacks, 1999) xiii, xiv.

it controls remains unknown. . . . Therein lies the marvel of this system. It is an uncharted frontier."[74] The physiological body possesses an amazing socio-psychological sophistication that we are only beginning to understand.

Could something like physiological therapy also be relevant to members of dominant groups, such as white people? Could it work against white privilege and white supremacy, for example, by re-membering the bodies of white people so that their "racialized expressions of biology" are diminished and perhaps even eliminated?[75] I'll wager that the answer to these questions is yes. This is because the transactional account of physiology, affect, and emotion, and social oppression that this book provides applies to all people, not just to members of subordinated groups. All human bodies are sociopsychologically sophisticated in ways that we are only beginning to understand.[76] How physiological therapy would work in the case of white people is a much more difficult question to answer, however. With regard to this question, it's important to realize that physiological therapy for white people probably would not look like physiological therapy for members of oppressed groups. To be clear, I am not suggesting that if white people took up yoga or began to dance more often, for example, then they would rid themselves of their habits of white domination. Instead, I am proposing that feminists and critical philosophers of race explore not just conscious but also non-conscious and unconscious means by which white people's physiological habits of whiteness might be changed.

Fully exploring that proposal will require more work than I am able to do here. For now, my hunch is that one significant way to think of physiological therapy for white people is as a form of white soul work.[77] The soul in question here isn't something opposed to the body; it instead is another way of speaking of embodiment. It isn't necessarily tied to religion and it doesn't concern anything like an afterlife. It is the type of soul that W. E. B. DuBois describes when he peers into the souls of white folks and sees "great billows . . . of human hatred," along with seething jealousy and greed.[78] The soul on this usage is what motivates, animates, and interests a person. It is, in other words, another name for the body's affective ties and emotional relationships with itself, others, and the world at large.

Given the affective nature of the body and the bodily basis of emotion, it's not just that bodily changes can produce emotions, but also that changing a person's affects and emotions can change her physiology. Meaningful changes

---

[74] Gershon, *The Second Brain*, xv.

[75] Nancy Krieger, "Discrimination and Health," in *Social Epidemiology*, eds. Lisa F. Berkman and Ichiro Kawachi (New York: Oxford University Press, 2000) 62.

[76] Perhaps non-human bodies are, too, but that important topic is beyond the scope of this book.

[77] On soul work, see Shannon Sullivan, *Good White People: The Problem of Middle Class White Anti-Racism* (Albany,: State University of New York Press, 2014). Thanks to Lucius Outlaw for suggesting this term.

[78] W. E. B. Du Bois, *Darkwater: Voices from Within the Veil* (New York: Harcourt Brace, 1999) 19.

to white people's physiology thus might be brought about through transformations to their racialized affects and emotions. Rather than directly aiming to change a white person's physiological habits of whiteness—a strategy that too easily could lead to ontologically expansive "solutions" that merely mimic physiological therapy for oppressed groups[79]—I think that a tactic that approaches them at an angle is likely to be more successful. Working on physiological habits of whiteness via transformations to white people's affects and emotions would be one such tactic. It would operate on both personal and interpersonal/communal levels, much in the way that physiological therapy for people of color would do. Like physiological therapy for people of color, moreover, the effects of physiological therapy for white people wouldn't be instantaneous. Working through the resistances of white bodies and souls will take time.

In particular, middle-class white people need to be engaged in a type of soul work that develops a critical form of self-love, instead of the oft-recommended emotions of white guilt, shame, and betrayal. I won't repeat here my arguments for this claim.[80] Instead I want to close with the point that changing middle-class white people's affective relationships to themselves and to other white people could transform their unconscious physiological habits in beneficial ways. Given that "spiritually positive emotions are an effect—as well as a cause, in an ongoing transactional spiral—of an affective-ontological reconfiguration of a being's relations with other beings in which the active thriving of one is intimately linked to the active thriving of others," white people's physiological transformations could be a cause, as well as an effect, of personal and institutional changes that would help reduce white privilege and white supremacy.[81]

Whatever a body's race, the remarkable level of its biopsychosocial capabilities means that the body could be considered a site of transcendence. Rather than flatten or eliminate the transcendental and spiritual aspects of human life, an account of emotional and affective habits as thoroughly physiological can refresh our sense of what the transcendental and the spiritual might mean. Rather than look outside human situations and contexts, we can find "the transcendentals of experience" in human physiology.[82] As Victor Kestenbaum has eloquently argued, the transcendence provided by human habits need not indicate something supernatural or formally religious. Understood as a kind of hermeneutic horizon, transcendence more broadly can be considered "the source of what comes into view and . . . the limiting

---

[79] For more on ontological expansiveness, see Shannon Sullivan, *Revealing Whiteness: The Unconscious Habits of Racial Privilege* (Bloomington: Indiana University Press, 2006).

[80] See Sullivan, *Good White People*, especially Chapter 4 and the conclusion.

[81] Sullivan, *Good White People*, 148.

[82] Victor Kestenbaum, The *Grace and Severity of the Ideal: John Dewey and the Transcencent* (Chicago: University of Chicago Press, 2002) 2.

condition of what is viewable, that is, of what transcends my view."[83] A person's "view" involves much more than what she can literally see. It is that of which she is consciously aware, conditioned by an immeasurable number of things of which she is not. Our physiological habits are part of that horizon, one of primary sources and limiting conditions of what transcends conscious life. In and through her physiological, affective life, a person transcends him- or herself. There is always more to his or her life, "an existing *beyond*" as William James poetically put it, and that "more" can be found in the physiological functions and character of the body.[84] Far from being reductive, physiological habits can be a site of transcendence that is thoroughly engaged with one's social and political environments.

This is why they also can be an important site of social and political change. Turning to physiology could make a meaningful and positive difference to feminist philosophy and critical philosophy of race's approach to pressing social problems such as sexism and racism. Biology does not have to be the enemy of an ethics of social justice. It can be an ally. It can help us understand that human physiology, not just conscious beliefs, needs to be changed in order for oppression and domination to be eliminated. It can help us better hear when bodies are crying out in pain from oppressive situations, as in the case of gastrointestinal dysfunction and the sexual abuse of women. And as in the case of the dry-mouthed, nauseous white woman in the elevator, it can help us perceive ongoing, subterranean white privilege in a post–Jim Crow era when most good white people would never openly endorse racism and often claim not to even see race at all. Biology certainly will not and cannot solve every problem having to do with sexism and racism. Given the past and present uses of biology to support oppression and domination, biology and all other sciences of human life need to be approached not just sympathetically, but also critically. Rather than disregard what biology and other hard sciences tell us about human embodiment, however, feminist philosophers and critical philosophers of race can use biological knowledge to work for social justice. Doing so would be to the benefit of all.

---

[83] Kestenbaum, The *Grace and Severity of the Ideal*, 3.
[84] Quoted in Jeremy Carrette, *William James's Hidden Religious Imagination: A Universe of Relations* (New York: Routledge, 2013) 46, emphasis in original.

{ BIBLIOGRAPHY }

Aagaard, Kjersti, Jun Ma, Kathleen M. Antony, Radhiku Ganu, Joseph Petrosino, and James Versalovic. 2014. "The Placenta Harbors a Unique Microbiome." *Science Translation Medicine* 6(237): 237ra65.

Ahmed, Sara. 2004. *The Cultural Politics of Emotion*. New York: Routledge.

Alaimo, Stacy, and Susan Hekman, eds. 2008. *Material Feminisms*. Bloomington: Indiana University Press.

Alcoff, Linda Martín. 1998. "Toward a Phenomenology of Racial Embodiment." *Radical Philosophy* 95: 15–26.

Alcoff, Linda Martín. 2006. *Visible Identities: Race, Gender, and the Self*. New York: Oxford University Press.

Alexander, Michelle. 2012. *The New Jim Crow: Mass Incarceration in the Age of Colorblindness*. Revised edition. New York: The New Press.

Aristotle. 1985. *Nicomachean Ethics*. Trans. Terence Irwin. Indianapolis: Hackett Publishing.

Aristotle. 1989. *The Metaphysics*. Trans. Hugh Tredennick. Cambridge, MA: Harvard University Press.

Barad, Karen. 1997. "Meeting the Universe Halfway: Realism and Social Constructivism Without Contradiction." In *Feminism, Science, and the Philosophy of Science*. Eds. Lynn Hankinson Nelson and Jack Nelson. Norwell, MA: Kluwer Academic Publishers, 161–194.

Barad, Karen. 2003. "Posthumanist Performativity: Toward an Understanding of how Matter Comes to Matter." *Signs: Journal of Women in Culture and Society* 23(3): 801–831.

Baylin, S., and K. Schuebel. 2007. "The Epigenomic Era Opens." *Nature* 448: 548–549.

Beauvoir, Simone de. 1972. *The Coming of Age*. Trans. Patrick O'Brian. New York: G. P. Putnam's Sons.

Beauvoir, Simone de. 2011. *The Second Sex*. Trans. Constance Borde and Shelia Malovany-Chevallier. New York: Vintage Books.

Bell, Derrick. 1993. *Faces at the Bottom of the Well: The Permanence of Racism*. New York: Basic Books.

Berkman, Lisa F., and Ichiro Kawachi. 2000. "A Historical Framework for Social Epidemiology." In *Social Epidemiology*. Eds. Lisa F. Berkman and Ichiro Kawachi. New York: Oxford University Press, 3–12.

Blencowe, Claire. 2011. "Biology, Contingency, and the Problem of Racism in Feminist Discourse." *Theory, Culture, and Society* 28(3): 3–27.

Blitstein, Ryan. 2009. "Racism's Hidden Toll." *Miller-McCune*. http://www.psmag.com/health/racisms-hidden-toll-3643/, accessed December 3, 2012.

Bollas, Christopher. 2008. *The Evocative Object World*. New York: Routledge.

Boorstein, Sylvia. 2011. *It's Easier Than You Think: The Buddhist Way to Happiness.* New York: HarperCollins Publishers.

Brennan, Teresa. 2004. *The Transmission of Affect.* Ithaca, NY: Cornell University Press.

Brunner, Eric J. 2000. "Toward a New Social Biology." In *Social Epidemiology.* Eds. Lisa F. Berkman and Ichiro Kawachi. New York: Oxford University Press, 306–331.

California Newsreel. 2008. "Unnatural Causes: When the Bough Breaks." http://www. unnaturalcauses.org/assets/uploads/file/UC_Transcript_2.pdf, accessed December 2, 2012, pp. 1–9.

Carrette, Jeremy. 2013. *William James's Hidden Religious Imagination: A Universe of Relations.* New York: Routledge.

Centers for Disease Control. 2012. "Premature Birth." http://www.cdc.gov/features/prematurebirth/, accessed December 3, 2012.

Choi, Sang-Woon, and Simonetta Friso. 2010. "Epigenetics: A New Bridge Between Nutrition and Health." *Advances in Nutrition* 1: 8–16.

Christakis, Nicholas, and James Fowler. 2009. *Connected: The Surprising Power of our Social Networks and How They Shape Our Lives.* New York: Little, Brown.

"Christie, Colored Friend of Tiffany." 2010. *Diverse Issues in Higher Education* (blog entry). http://diverseeducation.com/article/31297/#, accessed June 15, 2013.

Clavier, Bruno. 2013. *Les fantômes familiaux: Psychanalyse transgénérationnelle.* Paris: Payot & Rivages.

Cloud, John. 2010. "Why Your DNA Isn't Your Destiny." *Time.* http://www.time.com/ time/magazine/article/0,9171,1952313,00.html, accessed November 30, 2012.

Colapietro, Vincent. 2009. "Psychoanalysis and Jazz: Familiar Bedfellows in a Strange Setting." In *Semiotics 2008: Proceedings of the 33rd Annual Meeting of the Semiotic Society of America.* Eds. John Deely and Leonard Sbrocchi. Ottawa, Canada: Legas Publishing, 784–796.

Crisinel, Annie-Sylvie, Stefan Cosser, Scott King, Russ Jones, James Petrie, and Charles Spence. 2012. "A Bittersweet Symphony: Systematically Modulating the Taste of Food by Changing the Sonic Properties of the Soundtrack Playing in the Background." *Food Quality and Preference* 24(1): 201–204.

Cytowic, Richard E. 1993. *The Man Who Tasted Shapes: A Bizarre Medical Mystery Offers Revolutionary Insights into Emotions, Reasoning, and Consciousness.* New York: G. P. Putnams Sons.

Damasio, Antonio. 1999. *The Feeling of What Happens: Body and Emotion in the Making of Consciousness.* New York: Harcourt.

Daniels, Jessie, and Amy J. Schulz. 2006. "Constructing Whiteness in Health Disparities Research." In *Gender, Race, Class and Health: Intersectional Approaches.* Eds. Amy J. Schulz and Leith Mullings. San Francisco: Jossey-Bass, 89–127.

David, R. J., and J. W. Collins, Jr. 1991. "Bad Outcomes in Black Babies: Race or Racism?" *Ethnicity and Disease* 1(3): 236–244.

David, Richard, and James Collins, Jr. 2007. "Disparities in Infant Mortality: What's Genetics Got to Do with It?" *American Journal of Public Health* 97(7): 1191–1197.

Deigh, John. 2001. "Emotions: The Legacy of James and Freud." *International Journal of Psychoanalysis* 82: 1247–1256.

Deleuze, Gilles. 2001. *Spinoza: Practical Philosophy.* Trans. Robert Hurley. San Francisco: City Lights Publishers.

Delphy, Christine. 1980. "A Materialist Feminism Is Possible." *Feminist Review* 4: 79–105. http://www.palgrave-journals.com/fr/journal/v4/n1/full/fr19808a.html, accessed June 24, 2013.

Devroede, Ghislain. N.d. "La pensée cloacale." http://www.crifip.com/articles/la-pensee-cloacale.html, accessed May 21, 2013.

Devroede, Ghislain. 1999. "Front and Rear: The Pelvic Floor is an Integrated Structure." *Medical Hypotheses* 52(2): 147–153.

Devroede, Ghislain. 2000. "Early Life Abuses in the Past History of Patients with Gastrointestinal Tract and Pelvic Floor Dysfunctions." In Volume 122 of *Progress in Brain Research*. Eds. E. A. Mayer and C. B. Saper. New York: Elsevier Science, 131–155.

Devroede, Ghislain. 2002. *Ce que les maux de ventre dissent de notre passé.* Paris: Payot & Rivages.

Dewey, John. 1988. *Human Nature and Conduct.* Volume 14 of *The Middle Works: 1899–1924.* Ed. Jo Ann Boydston. Carbondale: Southern Illinois University Press.

Dewey, John. 1988. *Experience and Nature.* Volume 1 of *The Later Works: 1825–1953.* Ed. Jo Ann Boydston. Carbondale: Southern Illinois University Press.

Doyle, Bertram Wilbur. 1937. *The Etiquette of Race Relations in the South: A Study in Social Control.* Chicago: University of Chicago Press.

Drexler, Madeline. 2007. "How Racism Hurts—Literally." *The Boston Globe.* http://www.boston.com/news/globe/ideas/articles/2007/07/15/how_racism_hurts____literally/?page=full, accessed November 30, 2012.

Drossman, Douglas A., ed. 1994. *The Functional Gastrointestinal Disorders: Diagnosis, Pathophysiology, and Treatment—A Multinational Consensus.* New York: Little, Brown.

Drossman, D. A., J. Leserman, G. Nachman, et al. 1990. "Sexual and Physical Abuse in Women with Functional or Organic Gastrointestinal Disorders." *Annals of Internal Medicine* 133(11): 828–833.

Drossman, D. A., N. J. Talley, J. Lesserman, et al. 1995. "Sexual and Physical Abuse and Gastrointestinal Illness—Review and Recommendations." *Annals of Internal Medicine* 123(10): 782–794.

Dryden-Edwards, Roxann, and William C. Shiel, Jr. 2010. "Women and Depression." http://www.medicinenet.com/script/main/art.asp?articlekey=18987, accessed June 15, 2013.

Du Bois, W. E. B. 1984. *Dusk of Dawn: An Essay Toward an Autobiography of a Race Concept.* New York: Schocken Books.

Du Bois, W. E. B. 1995. *Black Reconstruction in America, 1860–1880.* New York: The Free Press.

Du Bois, W. E. B. 1999. *Darkwater: Voices from Within the Veil.* New York: Harcourt Brace.

Dubow, Saul, 2010. "South Africa: Paradoxes in the Place of Race." In *The Oxford Handbook of the History of Eugenics.* Eds. Alison Bashford and Philippa Levine. New York: Oxford University Press, 274–288.

Duster, Troy. 2003. "Buried Alive: The Concept of Race in Science." In *Genetic Nature/Culture: Anthropology and Science beyond the Two-Culture Divide.* Eds. Alan H. Goodman, Deborah Heath, and M. Susan Lindee. Berkeley: University of California Press, 258–277.

Duster, Troy. 2006. "Lessons from History: Why Race and Ethnicity Have Played a Major Role in Biomedical Research." *Journal of Law, Medicine & Ethics,* 34(3): 1–11.

Dworkin, Andrea. 1986. "Women in the Public Domain." In *Women and Values: Readings in Recent Feminist Philosophy*. Ed. Marilyn Pearsall. Belmont, CA: Wadsworth Publishing, 221–229.

Eustice, Carol. 2012. "What Is Reflex Sympathetic Dystrophy Syndrome (RSD)?" http://arthritis.about.com/od/rsd/a/rsd.htm, accessed June 15, 2013.

Faulkner, William. 1951. *Requiem for a Nun*. New York: Random House.

Fausto-Sterling, Anne. 2003. "The Problem with Sex/Gender and Nature/Nurture." In *Debating Biology: Sociological Reflections on Health, Medicine and Society*. Eds. S. J. Williams, L. Birke, and G. A. Bendelow. London: Routledge, 123–132.

Fausto-Sterling, Anne. 2005. "The Bare Bones of Sex: Part 1—Sex and Gender." *Signs* 30(2): 1491–1527.

Fausto-Sterling, Anne. 2008. "The Bare Bones of Race." *Social Science & Medicine* 38(5): 657–694.

Fausto-Sterling, Anne. 2012. *Sex/Gender: Biology in a Social World*. New York: Routledge.

Fehr, Carla. 2011. "Feminist Philosophy of Biology." *Stanford Encyclopedia of Philosophy*. http://plato.stanford.edu/entries/feminist-philosophy-biology/, accessed February 21, 2013.

Felitti, V. J. 1991. "Long-Term Medical Consequences of Incest, Rape, and Molestation." *Southern Medical Journal* 84(3): 328–331.

Fredrickson, Barbara L. 2008. "Promoting Positive Affect." In *The Science of Subjective Well-Being*. Eds. Michael Eid and Randy J. Larson. New York: The Guilford Press, 449–468.

Freud, Sigmund. 1950a. *Introductory Lectures on Psycho-Analysis*. In volume XVI of *The Standard Edition of the Complete Psychological Works of Sigmund Freud*. Ed. and trans. James Strachey. London: The Hogarth Press and the Institute of Psycho-analysis.

Freud, Sigmund. 1950b. "Remembering, Repeating, and Working-Through." In volume XII of *The Standard Edition of the Complete Psychological Works of Sigmund Freud*. Ed. and trans. James Strachey. London: The Hogarth Press and the Institute of Psycho-analysis.

Freud, Sigmund. 1959. *Group Psychology and the Analysis of the Ego*. Ed. and trans. James Strachey. New York: W. W. Norton.

Freud, Sigmund. 1960. "Three Essays on Sexuality." In Volume VII of *The Standard Edition of the Complete Psychological Works of Sigmund Freud*. Ed. and trans. James Strachey. New York: W. W. Norton.

Francis, Richard C. 2011. *Epigenetics: The Ultimate Mystery of Inheritance*. New York: W. W. Norton.

Friedman, Asia. 2006. "Unintended Consequences of the Feminist Sex/Gender Distinction." *Genders* 43. http://www.genders.org/g43/g43_friedman.html, accessed June 12, 2013.

Frye, Marilyn. 1983. *The Politics of Reality: Essays in Feminist Theory*. Freedom, CA: Crossing Press.

Furness, John B., and Nadine Clerc. 2000. "Responses of Afferent Neurons to the Contents of the Digestive Tract, and Their Relation to Endocrine and Immune Responses." In Volume 122 of *Progress in Brain Research*. Eds. E. A. Mayer and C. B. Saper. New York: Elsevier Science, 159–171.

Gapp, Katharina, Ali Jawaid, Peter Sarkies, Johannes Bohacek, Pawel Pelczar, Julien Prados, Laurent Farinelli, Eric Miska, and Isabelle M. Mansuy. 2014. "Implication of Sperm RNAs in Transgenerational Inheritance of the Effects of Early Trauma in Mice." *Nature Neuroscience* 17(5): 667–671.

Geronimus, Arlene T., Margaret Hicken, Danya Keene, and John Bound. 2006. " 'Weathering' and Age Patterns of Allostatic Load Scores Amount Blacks and Whites in the United States." *American Journal of Public Health* 96(5): 826–833.

Geronimus, Arlene T., Margaret T. Hicken, Jay A. Pearson, Sarah J. Seashols, Kelly L. Brown, and Tracey Dawson Cruz. 2010. "Do US Black Women Experience Stress-Related Accelerated Biological Aging? A Novel Theory and First Population-Based Test of Black-White Differences in Telomere Length." *Human Nature* 21(1): 19–38.

Gershon, Michael D. 1999. *The Second Brain: A Groundbreaking New Understanding of Nervous Disorders of the Stomach and Intestines*. New York: Harper Paperbacks.

Gould, Stephen Jay. 1981. *The Mismeasure of Man*. New York: W.W. Norton.

Gravlee, Clarence C. 2009. "How Race Becomes Biology: Embodiment of Social Inequality." *American Journal of Physical Anthropology* 139: 47–57.

Gray, John. 2004. *Men Are from Mars, Women Are from Venus: The Classic Guide to Understanding the Opposite Sex*. New York: Harper Publishers.

Griffiths, Paul. 2008. "Philosophy of Biology." *Stanford Encyclopedia of Philosophy*. http://plato.stanford.edu/entries/biology-philosophy/, accessed February 19, 2013.

Grosz, Elizabeth. 2011. *Becoming Undone: Darwinian Reflections on Life, Politics, and Art*. Durham, NC: Duke University Press.

Guerry, John D., and Paul D. Hastings. 2011. "In Search of HPA Axis Dysregulation in Child and Adolescent Depression." *Clinical Child and Family Psychology Review* 14(2): 135–160.

Guyll, Max, Karen A. Matthews, and Joyce T. Bromberger. 2001. "Discrimination and Unfair Treatment: Relationship to Cardiovascular Reactivity Among African American and European American Women." *Health Psychology* 20(5): 315–325.

Haraway, Donna. 1991. *Simians, Cyborgs and Women: The Reinvention of Nature*. New York: Routledge.

Harding, Sandra. 2001. *Whose Science? Whose Knowledge? Thinking from Women's Lives*. Ithaca, NY: Cornell University Press.

Hatemi, Peter K., and Rose McDermott. 2011. "The Normative Implications of Biological Research." *PS: Political Science and Politics* 44: 325–329.

Hazzard-Gordon, Katrina. 1990. *Jookin': The Rise of Social Dance Formations in African-American Culture*. Philadelphia: Temple University Press.

Hennessy, Rosemary, and Chrys Ingraham, eds. 1997. *Materialist Feminism: A Reader in Class, Difference, and Women's Lives*. New York: Routledge.

Herrnstein, Richard J., and Charles Murray. 1996. *The Bell Curve: Intelligence and Class Structure in American Life*. New York: Free Press.

Heyes, Cressida J. 2007. *Self Transformations: Foucault, Ethics, and Normalized Bodies*. New York: Oxford University Press.

Hillman, David, and Carla Mazzio. 1997. *The Body in Parts: Fantasies of Corporeality in Early Modern Europe*. New York: Routledge.

Hobson, Fred. 1999. *But Now I See: The White Southern Racial Conversion Narrative*. Baton Rouge: Louisiana State University Press.

hooks, bell. 1995. *Killing Rage: Ending Racism*. New York: Henry Holt.

hooks, bell. 1999a. *Black Looks: Race and Representation*. Boston: South End Press.

hooks, bell. 1999b. *Yearning: Race, Gender, and Cultural Politics*. Boston: South End Press.

hooks, bell. 2000. *All About Love: New Visions*. New York: HarperCollins Publishers.

hooks, bell. 2001. *Salvation: Black People and Love*. New York: HarperCollins Publishers.

Hurston, Zora Neale. 1995. "Spirituals and Neo-Spirituals." In *Voices from the Harlem Renaissance*. Second edition. Ed. Nathan Irvin Huggins. New York: Oxford University Press, 344–347.

Jackson, Pamela Braboy, and David R. Williams. 2004. "The Intersections of Race, Gender, and SES: Health Paradoxes." In *Gender, Race, Class and Health: Intersectional Approaches*. Eds. Amy J. Schulz and Leith Mullings. San Francisco: Jossey-Bass, 131–162.

James, William. 1950. *The Principles of Psychology*, Volume Two. New York: Dover Publications.

Jordan-Young, Rebecca M. 2010. *Brainstorm: The Flaws in the Science of Sex Differences*. Cambridge, MA: Harvard University Press.

Judy. 2013. "The Attic of the Body: A Workshop to Open and Release the Hips." http://www.yogawithjudy.com/, accessed February 12, 2015.

Kahn, Jonathan. 2012. *Race in a Bottle: The Story of BiDil and Racialized Medicine in a Post-Genomic Age*. New York: Columbia University Press.

Kaiser, Anelis, Sven Haller, Sigrid Schmitz, and Cordula Nitsch. 2009. "On Sex/Gender Related Similarities and Differences in fMRI Language Research." *Brain Research Reviews* 61(2): 49–59.

Kam, Katherine. 2010. "Why Are African Americans at Greater Risk for Heart Disease?" http://www.webmd.com/heart-disease/features/why-african-americans-greater-risk-heart-disease, accessed November 30, 2012.

Kaplan, Jonathan Michael. 2010. "When Socially Determined Categories Make Biological Realities: Understanding Black/White Health Disparities in the U.S." *The Monist* 93(2): 281–297.

Katz, Jackson. 2006. *The Macho Paradox: Why Some Men Hurt Women and How All Men Can Help*. Naperville, IL: Sourcebooks.

Keller, Evelyn Fox. 2010. *The Mirage of a Space Between Nature and Nurture*. Durham, NC: Duke University Press.

Kennedy, D. 2002. "Breakthrough of the Year." *Science* 298: 2283.

Kestenbaum, Victor. 2002. The *Grace and Severity of the Ideal: John Dewey and the Transcencent*. Chicago: University of Chicago Press.

Khoury, Miun J., and Sholom Wacholder. 2008. "Invited Commentary: From Genome-Wide Association Studies to Gene-Environment-Wide Interaction Studies—Challenges and Opportunities." *American Journal of Epidemiology* 169(2): 227–230.

Kim, K., A. Doi, B. Wen, K. Ng, R. Zhao, P. Cahan, J. Kim, M. J. Arvee, H. Ji, L. I. R. Erhlich, A. Yabuuchi, A. Takeuchi, K. C. Cunnif, H. Hongguang, S. Mckinney-Freeman, O. Naveiras, T. J. Yoon, R. A. Irizarry, N. Jung, J. Seita, J. Hanna, P. Murakami, R. Jaenisch, R. Weissleder, S.H. Orkin, I. L. Weissman, A. P. Feinberg, and G. Q. Daley. 2010. "Epigenetic Memory in Induced Pluripotent Stem Cells." *Nature* 467: 285–290.

Knöferle, Klemens, and Charles Spence. 2012. "Crossmodal Correspondences Between Sounds and Tastes." *Psychonomic Bulletin and Review*. http://www.academia.

edu/1932968/Crossmodal_correspondences_between_sounds_and_tastes, accessed June 17, 2013.

Krieger, Nancy. 2000. "Discrimination and Health." In *Social Epidemiology*. Eds. Lisa F. Berkman and Ichiro Kawachi. New York: Oxford University Press, 36–75.

Krieger, Nancy. 2005a. "Embodiment: A Conceptual Glossary for Epidemiology." *Journal of Epidemiology & Community Health* 59: 350–355.

Krieger, Nancy. 2005b. "Stormy Weather: Race, Gene Expression, and the Science of Health Disparities." *American Journal of Public Health* 95(12): 2155–2180.

Krieger, Nancy. 2008. "Does Racism Harm Health? Did Child Abuse Exist before 1962? On Explicit Questions, Critical Science, and Current Controversies: An Ecosocial Perspective." *American Journal of Public Health* 98(Supplement 1): S20–S25.

Krieger, Nancy, and George Davey Smith. 2004. "'Bodies Count,' and Body Counts: Social Epidemiology and Embodying Inequality." *Epidemiologic Reviews* 26(1): 92–103.

Kubzansky, Laura D., and Ichiro Kawachi. 2000. "Affective States and Health." In *Social Epidemiology*. Eds. Lisa F. Berkman and Ichiro Kawachi. New York: Oxford University Press, 213–241.

Kuzawa, Christopher W., and Elizabeth Sweet. 2009. "Epigenetics and the Embodiment of Race: Developmental Origins of U.S. Racial Disparities in Cardiovascular Health." *American Journal of Human Biology* 21(1): 2–15.

Kuzawa, Christopher W., and Zaneta M. Thayer. 2011. "Timescales of Human Adaptation: The Role of Epigenetic Processes." *Epigenomics* 3(2): 221–234.

Lauren. 2012. "Open Hips, Out Come the Emotions." http://bluelotusyogamaine.blogspot.fr/2012/08/open-hips-out-come-emotions.html, accessed June 20, 2013.

Lee, Sandra S., Barbara A. Koenig, and Sarah S. Richardson, eds. 2008. *Revisiting Race in a Genomic Age*. Piscataway, NJ: Rutgers University Press.

Lewis, Penny. 1996. "Depth Psychotherapy in Dance/Movement Therapy." *American Journal of Dance Therapy* 18(2): 95–114.

Loman, Susan T. 2006. "Dance/Movement Therapy." In *Expressive Therapies*. Ed. Cathy A. Malchiodi. New York: Guilford Press, 68–89.

Lu, Michael C., and Belinda Chen. 2004. "Racial and Ethnic Disparities in Preterm Birth: The Role of Stressful Life Events." *American Journal of Obstetrics and Gynecology* 191: 691–699.

Lu, Michael C., and Neal Halfon. 2003. "Racial and Ethnic Disparities in Birth Outcomes: A Life-Course Perspective." *Maternal and Child Health Journal* 7(1): 13–30.

Lu, Michael C., Milton Kotelchuck, Vijaya Hogan, Loretta Jones, Kynna Wright, and Neal Halfon. 2010. "Closing the Black-White Gap in Birth Outcomes: A Life-Course Approach." *Ethnicity and Disease* 20: 62–76.

Luhby, Tami. 2012. "Worsening Wealth Inequality by Race." *CNNMoney*. http://money.cnn.com/2012/06/21/news/economy/wealth-gap-race/index.htm, accessed December 10, 2012.

Mailis, Angela, and Judith Wade. 1994. "Profile of Caucasion Women with Possible Genetic Predisposition to Reflex Sympathetic Dystrophy: A Pilot Study." *The Clinical Journal of Pain* 10(3): 210–217.

Malabou, Catherine. 2008. *What Should We Do with Our Brain?* Trans. Sebastian Rand. Bronx, NY: Fordham University Press.

Malabou, Catherine. 2012. *The New Wounded: From Neurosis to Brain Damage*. Trans. Steven Miller. Bronx, NY: Fordham University Press.

Malpas, Simon C. 2010. "Sympathetic Nervous System Overactivity and Its Role in the Development of Cardiovascular Disease." *Physiological Reviews* 90(2): 513–557.

Mayer, Emeran A., Bruce Naliboff, and Julie Munakata. 2000. "The Evolving Neurobiology of Gut Feelings." In Volume 122 of *Progress in Brain Research*. Eds. E. A. Mayer and C. B. Saper. New York: Elsevier Science, 195–205.

Mayo Clinic. 2011. "Complications." http://www.mayoclinic.com/health/premature-birth/DS00137/DSECTION=complications, accessed December 3, 2012.

McClintock, Martha K. 1971. "Menstrual Synchrony and Suppression." *Nature* 229: 244–245.

McCraty, Rollin, and Doc Childre. 2004. "The Grateful Heart: The Psychophysiology of Appreciation." In *The Psychology of Gratitude*. Eds. Robert A Emmons and Michael E. McCullough. New York: Oxford University Press, 230–256.

McWhorter, Ladelle. 2009. *Racism and Sexual Oppression in Anglo-America: A Genealogy*. Bloomington: Indiana University Press.

Medina, José. 2013. "Color Blindness, Meta-Ignorance, and the Racial Imagination." *Critical Philosophy of Race* 1(1): 38–67.

Merleau-Ponty, Maurice. 1962. *Phenomenology of Perception*. Trans. Colin Smith. London: The Humanities Press.

Mills, Charles. 1997. *The Racial Contract*. Ithaca, NY: Cornell University Press.

Mills, Charles. 1998. *Blackness Visible: Essays on Philosophy and Race*. Ithaca, NY: Cornell University Press.

Mills, Charles. 2005. "'Ideal Theory' as Ideology." *Hypatia* 20(3): 165–183.

Mills, Charles. 2008. "Racial Liberalism." *Proceedings of the Modern Language Association* 123(5): 1380–1397.

Mills, Richard. 2011. "Epigenetics and Hypertension." *Current Hypertension Reports* 13(1): 21–28.

Moynihan, Daniel Patrick. 1965. "The Negro Family: A Case for National Action." US Department of Labor. http://www.dol.gov/oasam/programs/history/webid-meynihan.htm#.UMXrOKXjfpA, accessed December 10, 2012.

Mullings, Leith. 2004. "Resistance and Resilience: The Sojourner Syndrome and the Social Context of Reproduction in Central Harlem." In *Gender, Race, Class and Health: Intersectional Approaches*. Eds. Amy J. Schulz and Leith Mullings. San Francisco: Jossey-Bass, 345–370.

Murray, Charles. 2014. "Book Review: 'A Troublesome Inheritance' by Nicholas Wade." *The Wall Street Journal*. May 2, http://online.wsj.com/news/articles/SB10001424052702303380004579521482247869 87, accessed May 14, 2014.

Naliboff, Bruce B., Lin Change, Julie Munakata, and Emeran A. Mayer. 2000. "Towards an Integrative Model of Irritable Bowel Syndrome." In Volume 122 of *Progress in Brain Research*. Eds. E. A. Mayer and C. B. Saper. New York: Elsevier Science, 413–423.

National Cancer Institute at the National Institute of Health. 2013. "Metastatic Cancer." http://www.cancer.gov/cancertopics/factsheet/Sites-Types/metastatic, accessed May 16, 2013.

Nealon, Jeffrey T. 2000. "Performing Resentment: White Male Anger; or, 'Lack' and Nietzschean Political Theory." In *Why Nietzsche Still: Reflections on Drama, Culture, and Politics.* Ed. Alan D. Schrift. Berkeley: University of California Press, 274–292.

O'Mara, Cameron. 2013. *Feminist Reflections on the Nature/Culture Distinction in Merleau-Pontyan Philosophy.* University Park: Penn State University (dissertation).

Ossario, Pilar, and Troy Duster. 2005. "Race and Genetics: Controversies in Biomedical, Behavioral, and Forensic Sciences." *American Psychologist* 60(1): 115–128.

Palencik, Joseph T. 2007. "William James and the Psychology of Emotion: From 1884 to the Present." *Transactions of the Charles S. Peirce Society* 43(4): 769–786.

Pile, Steve. 2009. "Emotions and Affect in Recent Human Geography." *Transactions of the Institute of British Geography* 35: 5–20.

"Pollakiuria: Definition, Symptoms, Causes, Tests and Preventive Measure." 2012. http://www.rayur.com/pollakiuria-definition-symptoms-causes-tests-and-preventive-measure.html, accessed June 17, 2013.

Pollan, Michael. 2013. "Say Hello to the 100 Trillion Bacteria That Make Up Your Microbiome." *New York Times.* http://www.nytimes.com/2013/05/19/magazine/say-hello-to-the-100-trillion-bacteria-that-make-up-your-microbiome.html?hp&pagewanted=all&_r=0, accessed June 10, 2013.

Pollock, Anne. 2012. *Medicating Race: Heart Disease and Durable Preoccupations with Difference.* Durham, NC: Duke University Press.

"Prenatal Exposure to Famine May Lead to Persistent Epigenetic Changes." 2008. http://www.sciencedaily.com/releases/2008/10/081030110959.htm, accessed June 20, 2013.

Prinz, Jesse. 2004. *Gut Reactions: A Perceptual Theory of Emotion.* New York: Oxford University Press.

Purnis, Jan. 2010. "The Stomach and Early Modern Emotion." *University of Toronto Quarterly* 79(2): 800–818.

Rabb, Chris. 2010. *Invisible Capital: How Unseen Forces Shape Entrepreneurial Opportunity.* San Francisco: Berrett-Koehler Publishers.

Rape, Abuse, and Incest National Network (RAINN), http://www.rainn.org/get-information/statistics/sexual-assault-victims, accessed June 11, 2013.

Raskin, Donna. N.d. "Emotions in Motion." http://www.yogajournal.com/practice/1215, accessed June 20, 2013.

Read, N. W. 2000. "Bridging the Gap Between Mind and Body: Do Cultural and Psychoanalytic Concepts of Visceral Disease Have an Explanation in Contemporary Neuroscience?" In Volume 122 of *Progress in Brain Research.* Eds. E. A. Mayer and C. B. Saper. New York: Elsevier Science, 427–443.

Reid, Bryan J., Douglas S. Levine, Gary Longton, Patricia L. Blount, and Peter S. Rabinovitch. 2000. "Predictors of Progression to Cancer in Barrett's Esophagus: Baseline Histology and Flow Cytometry Identify Low- and High-Risk Patient Subsets." *American Journal of Gastroenterology* 95(7): 1669–1676.

Richardson, Sarah S. 2013. *Sex Itself: The Search for Male and Female in the Human Genome.* Chicago: The University of Chicago Press.

Richeson, Jennifer A., and Sophie Trawalter. 2005. "Why Do Interracial Interactions Impair Executive Function? A Resource Depletion Account." In *Journal of Personality and Social Psychology* 88(6): 934–947.

Ritterhouse, Jennifer. 2006. *Growing Up Jim Crow: How Black and White Southern Children Learned Race.* Chapel Hill: University of North Carolina Press.

Roberts, Dorothy. 2012. *Fatal Invention: How Science, Politics, and Big Business Re-create Race in the Twenty-First Century.* New York: The New Press.

Ruse, Michael, ed. 2007. *Philosophy of Biology,* second edition. Amherst, NY: Prometheus Books.

Ryff, Carol D., and Burton H. Singer. 2003. "The Role of Emotion on Pathways to Positive Health." In *The Handbook of Affective Sciences.* Eds. Richard J. Davidson, Klaus R. Scherer, and H. Hill Goldsmith. New York: Oxford University Press, 1083–1104.

Santillano, Vicki. N.d. "How Yoga Unlocks Emotions: Camel Pose, Then Crying?" http://www.divinecaroline.com/beauty/how-yoga-unlocks-emotions-camel-pose-then-crying, accessed June 20, 2013.

ScienceDaily. 2008. "Prenatal Exposure to Famine May Lead to Persistent Epigenetic Changes." http://www.sciencedaily.com/releases/2008/10/081030110959.htm, accessed November 30, 2012.

Shapiro, Thomas, Tatjana Meschede, and Sam Osoro. 2013. "The Roots of the Widening Racial Wealth Gap: Explaining the Black-White Economic Divide." Institute on Assets and Social Policy Research and Policy Brief: 1–8. http://iasp.brandeis.edu/pdfs/Author/shapiro-thomas-m/racialwealthgapbrief.pdf, accessed June 25, 2013.

Sharp, Joanne. 2009. "Geography and Gender: What Belongs to Feminist Geography? Emotion, Power, and Change." *Progress in Human Geography* 33(1): 74–80.

Shusterman, Richard. 2000. *Performing Live: Aesthetic Alternatives for the Ends of Art.* Ithaca, NY: Cornell University Press.

Shusterman, Richard. 2012. *Thinking Through the Body: Essays in Somaesthetics.* New York: Cambridge University Press.

Smedley, Brian, Michael Jeffries, Larry Adelman, and Jean Cheng. N.d. "Briefing Paper: Race, Racial Inequality, and Health Inequalities: Separating Myth from Fact." http://www.emfp.org/MainMenuCategory/Library/ResearchResourceLinks/RaceRacialInequalityandHealthInequitiespdf.aspx, accessed November 30, 2012, pp. 1–15.

Solms, Mark, and Oliver H. Turnbull. 2011. "What Is Neuropsychoanalysis?" *Neuropsychoanalysis* 13(2): 133–145.

Solomon, Andrew. 2002. *The Noonday Demon: An Atlas of Depression.* New York: Scribner.

Sparrow, Tom, and Adam Hutchinson, eds. 2013. *A History of Habit: From Aristotle to Bourdieu.* Lanham, MD: Lexington Press.

Spelman, Elizabeth. 1992. "Anger and Insubordination." In *Women, Knowledge, and Reality: Explorations in Feminist Philosophy,* eds. Ann Garry and Marilyn Pearsall. New York: Routledge, 263–274.

Sperberg, E. D., and S. D. Stabb. 1998. "Depression in Women as Related to Anger and Mutuality in Relationships." *Psychology of Women Quarterly* 22: 223–238.

Springer, Kristen W., Jeanne Mager Stellman, and Rebecca M. Jordan-Young. 2012. "Beyond a Catalogue of Differences: A Theoretical Frame and Good Practice Guidelines for Researching Sex/Gender in Human Health." *Social Science & Medicine* 74(11): 1817–1824.

Staples, Brent. 1986. "Just Walk on By: A Black Man Ponders His Power to Alter Public Space." *Ms.,* September, 54, 88.

Stern, Kathleen, and Martha K. McClintock. 1998. "Regulation of Ovulation by Human Pheromones." *Nature* 392: 177–179.

Stern, R. M. 2002. "The Psychophysiology of Nausea." *Acta Biologica Hungaria* 53(4): 589–599.

Sternthal, Michelle J., Natalie Slopen, and David R. Williams. 2011. "Racial Disparities in Health—How Much Does Stress Matter?" *Du Bois Review: Social Science Research on Race* 8(1): 95–113.

Sullivan, Shannon. 2001. *Living Across and Through Skins: Transactional Bodies, Pragmatism, and Feminism*. Bloomington: Indiana University Press.

Sullivan, Shannon. 2006. *Revealing Whiteness: The Unconscious Habits of Racial Privilege*. Bloomington: Indiana University Press.

Sullivan, Shannon. 2014. *Good White People: The Problem with Middle-Class White Anti-Racism*. Albany: State University of New York Press.

Sullivan, Shannon, and Nancy Tuana, eds., 2007. *Race and the Epistemologies of Ignorance*. Albany: State University of New York Press.

Tate, Greg. 2003. *Everything but the Burden: What White People Are Taking from Black Culture*. New York: Harlem Moon.

Tavernise, Sabrina. 2013. "The Health Toll of Immigration." *New York Times*. http://www.nytimes.com/2013/05/19/health/the-health-toll-of-immigration.html, accessed June 10, 2013.

Thandeka. 2007. *Learning to Be White: Money, Race, and God in America*. New York: Continuum.

Thayer, Zaneta M., and Christopher W. Kuzawa. 2011. "Biological Memories of Past Environments: Epigenetic Pathways to Health Disparities." *Epigenetics* 6(7): 1–6.

Thien, Deborah. 2005. "After or Beyond Feeling? A Consideration of Affect and Emotion in Geography." *Area* 37(4): 450–456.

Thompson, Audrey. 2003. "Tiffany, Friend of People of Color: White Investments in Antiracism." *Qualitative Studies in Education* 16(1): 7–29.

Thrift, Nigel. 2008. *Non-representational Theory: Space Politics Affect*. New York: Routledge.

US Department of Justice. 2002. "Acquaintance Rape of College Students." www.cops.usdoj.gov/pdf/e03021472.pdf, accessed June 15, 2013.

Vaglio, Stefano. 2009. "Chemical Communication and Mother-Infant Recognition." *Communicative and Integrative Biology* 2(3): 279–281, http://www.ncbi.nlm.nih.gov/pmc/articles/PMC2717541/, accessed June 17, 2013.

Van der Kolk, Bessel. 2014. *The Body Keeps the Score: Brain, Mind, and Body in the Healing of Trauma*. New York: Viking.

Varendi, H., R. H. Porter, and J. Winberg. 1996. "Attractiveness of Amniotic Fluid Odor: Evidence of Prenatal Olfactory Learning?" *Acta Paediatricia* 85(10): 1223–1227.

Vignemont, F. de, M. Tsakiris, and P. Haggard. 2005. "Body Mereology." In *Human Perception from Inside Out*. Eds. G. Knoblich, I.M. Thorton, M. Grosjean, and M. Shiffrar. New York: Oxford University Press, 147–170.

Weintraub, Amy. 2004. *Yoga for Depression: A Compassionate Guide to Relieve Suffering Through Yoga*. New York: Broadway Books.

West, Cornel. 1993. *Race Matters*. Boston: Beacon Press.

Whiteman, Honor. 2014. "Placenta 'Not a Sterile Environment,' Study Suggests." *Medical News Today*, http://www.medicalnewstoday.com/articles/277206.php, accessed May 29, 2014.

Williams, David R. 1999. "Race, Socioeconomic Status, and Health: The Added Effects of Racism and Discrimination." *Annals of the New York Academy of Sciences* 896: 173–188.

Williams, David R., Yan Yu, James S. Jackson, and Norman B. Anderson. 1997. "Racial Differences in Physical and Mental Health." *Journal of Health Psychology* 2(3): 325–351.

Wilshire, Bruce. 1968. *William James and Phenomenology: A Study of the Principles of Psychology*. Bloomington: Indiana University Press.

Wilson, Elizabeth A. 2004a. "Gut Feminism." *Differences: A Journal of Feminist Cultural Studies* 15(3): 66–94.

Wilson, Elizabeth A. 2004b. *Psychosomatic: Feminism and the Neurological Body*. Durham, NC: Duke University Press.

Wise, Tim. 2005. *White Like Me: Reflections on Race from a Privileged Son*. Brooklyn, NY: Soft Skull Press.

Wittig, Monique. 1992. *The Straight Mind and Other Essays*. Boston: Beacon Press.

Woods-Giscombé, Cheryl L. 2010. "Superwoman Schema: African American Women's Views on Stress, Strength, and Health." *Qualitative Health Research* 20: 668–683.

Yancy, George. 2008. *Black Bodies, White Gazes: The Continuing Significance of Race*. Lanham, MD: Rowman and Littlefield.

Yancy, George. 2012. *Look, a White! Philosophical Essays on Whiteness*. Philadelphia: Temple University Press.

Yancy, George, ed. 2004. *What White Looks Like: African-American Philosophers on the Whiteness Question*. New York: Routledge.

Young, Iris Marion. 2005. *On Female Bodily Experience: "Throwing Like a Girl" and Other Essays*. New York: Oxford University Press.

Zimmer, Carl. 2013. "DNA Double Take." *New York Times*, http://www.nytimes.com/2013/09/17/science/dna-double-take.html?adxnnl=1&adxnnlx=1416103288-FJVr/Y/5HF1PI1XFhlih6w, accessed November 15, 2014.

{ INDEX }

Made in the USA
Las Vegas, NV
22 October 2022

57891317R00127